# THE TIGER VANQUISHED

CW00552225

# THE TIGER VANQUISHED

## LTTE's Story

**M R Narayan Swamy**

Ⓢ SAGE  www.sagepublications.com
Los Angeles ● London ● New Delhi ● Singapore ● Washington DC

*Copyright © M R Narayan Swamy, 2010*

All rights reserved. No part of this book may be reproduced or utilized in any form or by any means, electronic or mechanical, including photocopying, recording or by any information storage or retrieval system, without permission in writing from the publisher.

*First published in 2010 by*

**SAGE Publications India Pvt Ltd**
B1/I-1 Mohan Cooperative Industrial Area
Mathura Road, New Delhi 110 044, India
*www.sagepub.in*

**SAGE Publications Inc**
2455 Teller Road
Thousand Oaks, California 91320, USA

**SAGE Publications Ltd**
1 Oliver's Yard, 55 City Road
London EC1Y 1SP, United Kingdom

**SAGE Publications Asia-Pacific Pte Ltd**
33 Pekin Street
#02-01 Far East Square
Singapore 048763

Published by Vivek Mehra for SAGE Publications India Pvt Ltd, typeset in 10/13pt AGaramond by Star Compugraphics Private Limited, Delhi and printed at Chaman Enterprises, New Delhi.

**Library of Congress Cataloging-in-Publication Data**

Narayan Swamy, M. R.
   The tiger vanquished : LTTE's story/M. R. Narayan Swamy.
      p.   cm.
   1. Tami_li_la Vitutalaippulikal (Association) 2. Sri Lanka—History—Civil War, 1983–2009.
3. Sri Lanka—Politics and government—21st century. 4. Tamil (Indic people)—Sri Lanka—Politics and government. 5. Ethnic conflict—Sri Lanka. I. Title.

DS489.84.N37            954.9303'2—dc22            2010            2010011344

**ISBN:** 978-81-321-0459-9 (PB)

**The SAGE Team:** Rekha Natarajan, Sushmita Banerjee, Sanjeev Kumar Sharma
                        and Trinankur Banerjee

*Cover photo: Courtesy AFP*

*In memory of*
*M.A. Raman and T.S.L.V. Sarma*
*I miss them enormously*

# Contents

## 2007

## 2008

# Acknowledgements

THE people who have helped me the most to write news stories and commentaries on Sri Lanka over the years—and this volume too—wish to remain anonymous. Some have gone out of their way and repeatedly too, to provide me a better understanding of Sri Lanka and the many complexities of its brutal conflict. They include Sri Lankans, Indians and people of other nationalities. My interactions with them helped me to shed many cobwebs and to place perplexing events in their perspective. For understandable reasons, some of my sources did not want to be named; others, I know, also would prefer it that way. I am beholden to them all.

I would like to particularly thank newsmakers in Sri Lanka and Norway, who freely spoke to me, often at length, whenever I sought their views. Some of them held—and still hold—influential positions. They need not have taken my telephone calls or responded to me, but they did. I am grateful to them.

Many others in Sri Lanka have helped me in many ways. These include rights activists, a breed whose commitment to human values is often misunderstood; journalists, who have faced extreme adversity in recent times; as well as ordinary civilians from the north and east, the war theatre for over a quarter century.

Sreeram Chaulia, a voracious reader and a prolific writer, deserves my gratitude for more reasons than one. I thank Vipin Das for poring over the first draft. I owe special thanks to Rajani, my wife and Vidya, our daughter. Rajani's admirable command over English is a source of strength to me. Vidya provides inspiration for what we do.

This is a collection of some of the stories and analytical articles I wrote from 2003, when the LTTE suddenly walked out of the international peace process, to 2009, when the Tamil Tigers were finally defeated. They also include interviews. Most of the writing was done for IANS, the news agency I have worked for since returning to India from Singapore in 2001.

I also wrote, on request, for *Mainstream, The Week, The Hindustan Times, The Telegraph, Asian Affairs, Journal of International Peace Operations,* Institute of Peace and Conflict Studies, *Hard News* and *World Focus*. I thank all these organizations for permitting to reproduce, for this book, what I had written for them.

I have always maintained that there are no experts on the LTTE—outside of the group. The one man who fathered the outfit and was enormously suited to narrate its full story (I doubt he would have done that) was killed in May 2009. Those of us who are students of this conflict can only, hopefully, contribute to a larger and better understanding of the LTTE, the causes that gave birth to it, the reasons it grew into such a formidable entity and the factors that led to its destruction.

The idea for this book was born from this limited agenda. I hope it serves the purpose.

As a nation Sri Lanka has suffered enormously because of the conflict. The terrible agony the war unleashed cannot be adequately gauged even if one is numbed by the voluminous statistics of death, destruction and displacement. Most unfortunately, even the devastating 2004 tsunami failed to bring peace. I do hope, at least now, all communities in Sri Lanka will get their act together for a better future for themselves and their country.

# Key years in LTTE history

| | |
|---|---|
| 1954 | Velupillai Prabhakaran is born. |
| 1975 | Prabhakaran assassinates Jaffna Mayor. |
| 1976 | LTTE is formed. |
| 1978 | LTTE issues first press statement. |
| 1982 | Prabhakaran arrested in India, bailed. |
| 1983 | Prabhakaran shifts to India after anti-Tamil violence. |
| | Eelam War I is on. |
| | India arms, trains Tamil militants. |
| 1984 | LTTE starts buying weapons from abroad. |
| 1985 | LTTE massacres Buddhists at Anuradhapura. |
| 1986 | LTTE crushes rival group TELO. |
| | LTTE 'bans' rival group PLOT. |
| 1987 | Prabhakaran quits India. |
| | Indian troops deployed in Sri Lanka. |
| | LTTE goes to war against India. |
| 1988 | Ranasinghe Premadasa elected president. |
| 1989 | Premadasa asks Indian troops to go home. |
| | Premadasa, LTTE in peace talks. |
| | LTTE assassinates Tamil leader Amirthalingam. |
| 1990 | Indian troops quit Sri Lanka; LTTE controls Jaffna. |
| | LTTE ignites Eelam War II. |
| | LTTE massacres leaders of rival group EPRLF. |
| 1991 | LTTE assassinates Rajiv Gandhi. |
| 1992 | India outlaws LTTE. |
| 1993 | LTTE leader Kittu commits suicide. |
| | LTTE assassinates Premadasa. |
| 1994 | Chandrika Kumaratunga elected president, offers peace. |
| | LTTE executes former no. 2 Mahattaya. |

| | |
|---|---|
| 1995 | LTTE starts Eelam War III. |
| 1996–99 | Military stalemate. |
| 1999 | Kumaratunga survives assassination attempt. |
| 2001 | Norway's Erik Solheim meets Prabhakaran. |
| 2002 | LTTE, Sri Lanka sign Ceasefire Agreement. |
| | Prabhakaran addresses press conference. |
| 2003 | LTTE pulls out of peace talks. |
| 2004 | LTTE splits, Karuna walks away. |
| 2005 | LTTE assassinates Foreign Minister Lakshman Kadirgamar. |
| | Mahinda Rajapaksa elected president. |
| 2006 | Army chief survives suicide attack. |
| | Eelam War IV starts. |
| | President's brother Gotabaya survives suicide bomber. |
| | LTTE's Anton Balasingham dies of cancer. |
| 2007 | Sri Lanka drives out LTTE from east. |
| | LTTE leader Tamilchelvan killed in air strike. |
| 2008 | Sri Lanka scraps ceasefire agreement with LTTE. |
| | Cornered Prabhakaran says India is "superpower". |
| 2009 | Military captures LTTE hub Kilinochchi. |
| | Velupillai Prabhakaran killed, LTTE defeated. |

# The final conversation: May 2009

THE telephone rings in a humble Sri Lankan Tamil home in a European country. It is a call its inmates have been eagerly awaiting.

The man at the other end, in LTTE territory, sounds dejected and tired. He says he can only speak briefly because he is using a satellite telephone.

In broken sentences, the man says that it is all over.

His family realizes the import of what he is muttering. The LTTE is about to become history.

How are you, he is asked. It is a silly question given the boom of gunfire and exploding shells they can hear in the background.

I am surviving, he says. It is a callous answer.

The family is worried about others it knows.

How is Francis, the man is asked. He is dead, he replies, sounding casual to the point of being disinterested. How is Selva? He too is dead.

There is a brief silence.

At the Tamil home, a woman now grabs the phone. She is desperate to know the man's well-being.

Speaking slowly, he repeats what he has already said. It is all over.

After another brief silence, the man speaks again. Although his voice is still feeble, his words now sound like an exploding volcano.

"I will not be around for long," he mumbles.

The woman shrieks. "Don't say that, please don't say that, everything will be all right, please don't say that!" She is now crying.

The man goes on: "This is my last call."

"No! No! Don't say that, please don't say that," the woman is now screaming at the top of her voice.

The man is sounding philosophical. He knows the war is ending. There is no escape. He will be dead soon.

In choking voice, he tells the family: "Please take care."

The conversation ends.

The telephone line goes dead.

# Introduction

Prabhakaran and other such tinpot heroes ... are leading the Tamils towards a long-term political and moral disaster... Despite the struggle, I now think that there will neither be Eelam, nor "true" federalism, nor genuine devolution, nor anything else which is just and fair to the Tamils this century, if ever.[1]

**I**

THE surreal end of Velupillai Prabhakaran and almost all his senior lieutenants at one go marked the most dramatic and unexpected decimation of the seemingly indestructible Tamil Tigers, bringing down the curtains on one of the world's longest running insurgencies that had torn apart Sri Lanka for over a quarter century.

Year after year, it had looked as if Tamil militancy would never end in the once idyllic Indian Ocean island nation and the Liberation Tigers of Tamil Eelam (LTTE) would never breathe its last. Successive governments in Sri Lanka, of course, tried to crush the Tigers, only to get badly bruised, at times to the point of humiliation. In the process, the LTTE's image, as an outfit that cannot be defeated by anyone, only got reinforced, making it the most feared, fanatic and ruthless outlaw, its ability to destroy, next only to Al Qaeda's.

Yet, in the scorching month of May 2009, what for long had seemed impossible, was made possible by a barely four-year-old regime in Sri Lanka sworn to stamp out the LTTE. When he took over the presidency in November 2005, Mahinda Rajapaksa, a Sinhalese Buddhist politician from the country's deep south, confided to an Asian diplomat[2] he counted as a friend that one of his priorities was to decimate the awesome LTTE. As the war progressed, Rajapaksa went public with that claim. In the light of Sri Lanka's past quarter century when the LTTE had only grown from strength to strength, few took him seriously.

But Rajapaksa was deadly serious. In an earlier decade, the man had passionately battled human rights abuses by security forces when thousands of youths were butchered in the wake of an insurrection launched by the Sinhalese-Marxist group,

Janatha Vimukti Peramuna (JVP).[3] The times were now different. He was presiding over a conflict-torn country whose fortunes seemed wedded to the whims and fancies of a Tamil man called Prabhakaran. Like the newly elected president, Prabhakaran too was a determined man. But his aim was different. He had pledged to break up Sri Lanka.

A school dropout with low intellect but with a passion and precision for violence, Prabhakaran had been calling the shots in Sri Lanka both during phases of war and ceasefire since giving birth to the LTTE in 1976.[4] Rajapaksa knew this and was determined to chart a path different from his predecessors—one that Prabhakaran would not be able to influence. Fortunately for him, the LTTE chief ignited the spark that led to the final of Eelam wars[5] that finished off the Tigers, lock, stock, and barrel, near a lagoon in Mullaitivu district, which until then had been Prabhakaran's seemingly impregnable hideout.

After declaring in his annual speech of November 2005 that he would give Rajapaksa a year to prove his sincerity vis-à-vis the Tamils, Prabhakaran did not wait even for a month before beginning to militarily provoke the new president. It was a foolish move. It helped to convince Rajapaksa that the assessment of the LTTE provided by his aides was right. Prabhakaran's publicly stated loyalty to peace was a sham. Further negotiations with the Tigers would not lead Sri Lanka anywhere. The external peace facilitator, Norway's, passion for negotiations was based on wrong surmises. The time had come for the president to make history. The single-minded Rajapaksa did just that.

I was one of the journalists who covered that blood-soaked story, albeit from a distance.[6]


## II

RAJAPAKSA was not only a determined and calculating politician but also a lucky one. One of his predecessors, Ranasinghe Premadasa, had been blown up by the LTTE in 1993 after trying to make peace with the group. Another head of state who had been a long-standing sympathizer of Tamil grievances, Chandrika Kumaratunga, lost an eye during a suicide bombing aimed at killing her. Yet another, Junius Jayewardene, otherwise considered a wily fox, had earlier gone politically bankrupt fighting the Tigers. Fortunately for Rajapaksa, even before he took over the reins of Sri Lanka, luck had slowly begun to desert Prabhakaran, after being on his side for an unusually long, long time.

When Rajapaksa became the head of state in 2005, Prabhakaran remained arrogantly confident of success in the long run, notwithstanding an unexpected and crippling split in the LTTE the previous year. The Tigers were an unusual cocktail of classical insurgency and sheer terror. Besides being the only insurgent outfit to own a shipping fleet (after the PLO—Palestine Liberation Organization—and IRA—Irish Republican Army), the LTTE had its own army, a small but lethal naval wing, a nascent air force, artillery units, a feared intelligence wing, a police force, a clandestine radio, and an efficient logistics division to buy and ferry war material from around the world in the most secretive and sophisticated manner. The group's tentacles reached almost every country. And the LTTE had proved its mettle by repeatedly harassing the Sri Lankan military—and for over two years the much bigger Indian Army too.

More importantly, the LTTE had an elite corps of suicide bombers known as Black Tigers. Whenever Prabhakaran wished, he could dispatch one or more of them to extinguish a foe of Tamil Eelam, real or perceived, Sinhalese or Tamil, Sri Lankan or Indian. The LTTE's ability to kill any key person, in the military or the government, inevitably dented the state's counter-insurgency, making Prabhakaran look exactly like his childhood comic hero—the Phantom, the masked jungle hero who could never be vanquished.

More often that not, the suicide bombers succeeded in their grotesque missions, blowing up themselves as well as their intended victims. Married to the belief that aggression pays, Prabhakaran picked Sarath Fonseka, the Sri Lankan army chief and a man close to Rajapaksa, as his first VVIP victim in the new Rajapaksa government. If Fonseka were to get killed, it would deal a huge blow to Colombo and surely derail the war machine that was taking shape.

The chosen killer was a young woman who managed to gain entry into the otherwise impregnable army headquarters in Colombo by pretending to be pregnant. She attended prenatal maternity classes at a hospital within the army complex. The subsequent arrest of a senior LTTE operative revealed that the entire plan was drawn up after detailed and meticulous study of the area and the intended victim's routine. The LTTE intelligence had also befriended a Tamil-speaking Muslim cook in the army to gain access to the complex. Prabhakaran gave the final green signal. The attack took place in April 2006 or just five months after Rajapaksa had assumed office.

The woman's audacious attempt to kill Fonseka by detonating explosives strapped to her body—a methodology first tried successfully in May 1991 on Rajiv Gandhi, the former prime minister of India—however failed. An alert guard riding a motorcycle kicked away the suicide bomber as she tried to get close to the army chief's car. But nothing could prevent the human bomb from exploding. She died instantly—along with eight bodyguards of the army commander.

The huge fireball triggered by the deafening blast, seriously injured Fonseka. Unfortunately for Prabhakaran, the veteran soldier was not destined to die. Fonseka, who had always held the LTTE in contempt, miraculously survived. He returned to his job following months of medical care in the country and abroad. Fonseka was now a wounded lion, determined to avenge his humiliation.

For Rajapaksa, the attempted assassination was a personal affront.

By then the LTTE had gone berserk. It killed soldiers and targeted high value military personnel, including those from the intelligence—the eyes and ears of Colombo. The armed forces, sick of a Norwegian-brokered ceasefire agreement they felt was loaded in favour of the LTTE and spoiling for a fight, retaliated without mercy. As in the past, the Tigers were in a hurry to influence events as they wished.

As ill luck would have it, the LTTE failed to accurately read the mindset of the enemy and went on to commit a blunder that was to push it to its gory end.

The Tigers closed down a sluice gate in an area they held in the eastern province, depriving irrigation water to thousands of farmers, mostly from the majority Sinhalese community living in the adjoining government zone. It quickly became a highly emotive issue. Conveniently, the Tigers denied responsibility; the Tamil people, the LTTE argued with an air of sarcasm, were acting on their own. Anyone who had even an inkling of the rebels knew that nothing could happen behind the Tigers' iron curtain without their nod.

The LTTE's refusal to back down despite international appeals formally triggered what came to be known as "Eelam War IV"—the final of the wars for a Tamil state that ended in May 2009 with the Tigers' ignominious defeat. Sporadic incidents that international actors overseeing the tottering peace process had assumed, could be tamed spiralled out of control. The military concluded, after four long years of uneasy ceasefire, that enough was enough and that the LTTE needed to be taught a lesson it would not forget.

The LTTE probably realized, somewhat late, that it had made a mistake. It was too late though. As the two antagonists took on one another in the east of Sri Lanka, a region where Tamils, Sinhalese and Muslims lived in almost equal numbers, the intensity of their fighting betrayed their unmasked hatred for one another. It was clear that the war this time would be different.

It was. The LTTE had carefully prepared for a showdown during the Norway-sponsored and internationally backed peace process that began formally in February 2002. One will not be too far off the mark to say in retrospect that if the devastating tsunami had not hit Sri Lanka in December 2004, the Tigers may have gone on the offensive around that time. War was very much in the air then.

Once large-scale fighting broke out in 2006, it dawned on Prabhakaran that Colombo too had psychologically prepared itself for war. Rajapaksa was ready to pay back in a fitting manner, whatever the consequences. Half-hearted peace talks held in Norway and Switzerland that year collapsed as quickly as they started. They were perhaps not meant to succeed.

Like in earlier times, capital Colombo became a fortress. The LTTE meant business. Bombs went off in areas far removed from the conflict theatre, killing innocents. Sri Lanka unleashed its air force and artillery barrages on LTTE areas like never before. For once, the state decided that it needed to be an LTTE to defeat the LTTE. Anyone with the slightest of suspected links with the LTTE got picked up. Abductions in government areas became rampant as the government embraced unconventional methods to break the LTTE's very deadly sleeper network. Many victims simply disappeared. The bodies of others turned up in unlikely places, at times with their hands tied and with bullets in their head. The media was muzzled.

In the east, the LTTE found itself on the defensive, thanks considerably to the breakaway group led by its former regional commander Vinayagamurthy Muralitharan alias Karuna. Forcible recruitment of children soared. Sri Lanka's war had become as dirty as it could. The Ceasefire Agreement of 2002, brokered by Norway between the government and the LTTE after months of painstaking backroom diplomacy, began to come apart, much to the dismay of the international community.

After failing to kill the army chief, Prabhakaran now tried to do away with Gotabaya Rajapaksa, the man spearheading Sri Lanka's war and a younger brother of the President. This was in December 2006. From Prabhakaran's perspective, killing Gotabaya Rajapaksa would fetch far greater dividends. It would surely destabilize Sri Lanka's war machinery. Unfortunately for Prabhakaran, he too survived miraculously although the attempt shook him up. It was a momentous event that ultimately would prove very costly to Prabhakaran.

It can be said without an iota of doubt that the attempt to blow up the younger Rajapaksa, on a Colombo street, was the most decisive turning point in the war against the LTTE. As a retired Sri Lankan army officer, who was an American citizen, he had returned to Colombo ahead of the 2005 presidential elections. After Mahinda Rajapaksa won, he had asked Gotabaya to stay on. Having fought the LTTE when he was in the army, Gotabaya Rajapaksa had a clear vision as much as the insurgent outfit was concerned. A no-nonsense man, he had firmed up much earlier that the only language the LTTE understood and respected was that of force. And that is what Colombo would now employ.

The attempt to kill Gotabaya Rajapaksa only steeled his resolve—and that of President Mahinda Rajapaksa—to go for the kill. They were now more than convinced that Prabhakaran and the band of men and women who made up the LTTE could never be trusted. As the army chief Fonseka would say later, using the terminology of cricket, a game that united Sri Lanka like perhaps nothing else, the government concluded that it would play for certain victory, not for a draw.

From then on, Sri Lanka would contemptuously reject the parrot-like suggestions that there could only be a negotiated end to the conflict. In the process, for the first time, Colombo took on not only Western countries but also international institutions, at times accusing them of bias towards the LTTE. Human rights activists were treated with contempt. The pontification from the Indian government about political and constitutional reforms was tolerated. But Sri Lanka was far less approving of the pro-LTTE noises made in Tamil Nadu, the Indian state separated from the island nation by a narrow strip of sea. Sri Lanka's unprecedented aggression, in the battlefield and in the diplomatic arena, stunned the LTTE leadership, which had expected the Rajapaksa regime to capitulate.

President Rajapaksa had other ideas. He would do what no government in Colombo had done before. He went for Prabhakaran's jugular. It would be do or die.

From the day he survived, it took Gotabaya Rajapaksa and a resurgent Sri Lankan military that reported to him just two and a half years to finish off the LTTE, an octopus that had played havoc for over a quarter century. It was nothing short of a miracle. May 2009 witnessed the macabre end of a horribly bloody saga that had brutalized Sri Lanka since 1983 and divided it ethnically, fractured its soul, claimed more than 90,000 lives, wounded and maimed thousands, and created a huge Tamil refugee population within the country and all across the world.

### III

ON the run since the dawn of 2009, Prabhakaran ended up trapped close to the coast in Mullaitivu with his closest aides and family members as well as a core group of LTTE fighters, many of who were in no mood to give up. The LTTE boss had calculated that the West, where for years he had had a free run, would somehow be able to halt the war and provide him another lease of life. There were also fears that he could take to the sea and disappear, possibly with his close aides to fight for another day.

Interviews with those who escaped from the region, reveal that Prabhakaran had hoped the military would halt its offensive after seizing Kilinochchi, the LTTE's political and administrative hub in the country's north, at the start of January 2009. That was not to be. After capturing Kilinochchi, the military kept relentlessly advancing into the rapidly shrinking LTTE zone.[7] For one last time, LTTE guerrillas literally fled for their lives, withdrawing repeatedly in large numbers. In the unprecedented confusion, they often left behind a large quantity of war material and precious internal documents. Many young fighters deserted and escaped. The LTTE's Sea Tigers and the famed suicide squads (Black Tigers) were bruised beyond recognition. Panic had set in.

The final days were as gory as hell. As the body count mounted in LTTE ranks, the Tigers desperately recruited more and more sacrificial lambs in the age group of

15–22 years. The unwilling fighters were given hurried one-week training in the use of weapons. Soon this got reduced to three days of training. Towards the very end, the youngsters were pushed to the war front after merely being told how to hold the weapon and how to fire![8] Until then, the "martyrs' families"—whose members had died fighting for the LTTE and who enjoyed special privileges—had been spared the threat of forced recruitment; now the LTTE asked them to cough up at least one more member for the cause.

Prabhakaran had been given to understand by some of his senior aides that mass protests by the Tamil diaspora in Western cities would surely lead to Western intervention—and ceasefire. That flicker of a hope faded away once the British and French foreign ministers ended their visit to Colombo at the end of April 2009 without achieving anything. Suddenly, the Tigers ceased to be cocky.

The LTTE had also hoped that vocal protests in Tamil Nadu in support of a truce would force the central Indian government to do a U-turn in its Sri Lanka policy since the Congress party faced a tough parliamentary election. Colombo too was aware that the LTTE would try to drag the war until the middle of May in the hope that a Congress defeat in India could lead to policy changes. This too did not happen. If anything, Tamil Nadu political parties vocally supportive of the LTTE were wiped out.

Far away from the make-believe world of the Tamil diaspora, clashes erupted between ordinary, but furious, Tamil parents and Tiger guerrillas who had forcibly recruited their children. After one ugly spat, a Tamil mob thrashed a group of guerrillas and set ablaze their vehicles. Simultaneously, Tamil civilians—most of who lacked sleep, adequate nourishment, basic medicines, and money—looked for ways to get out of the LTTE territory despite the enormous risks involved. Furious Tigers shot many of them.

The situation turned so ugly that some distraught men and women risked their lives by openly abusing Prabhakaran for landing them in a bloody mess. It was crystal clear that the armed struggle had gone horribly wrong, depriving the Tamils of whatever they had when it all began. Some civilians pleaded with the LTTE to hurriedly make up with India.

But the LTTE was not bothered. The LTTE threatened death to those questioning its ability to fight. And helpless parents were warned that they would be taken into custody if their kids ran away from the battlefield. Its leaders kept insisting that the war had to be fought and they were confident of overcoming their military setbacks. As if to prove its point, it simultaneously pushed many of its war veterans into taking on the military to somehow reverse the tide—only to lose en masse Theepan, Adhavan, Vidusa, Durga and Manivannan (all of the rank of Brigadier) as well as Seralathan and Rakesh (both Colonels).

This was a shattering blow to the LTTE. It stunned Prabhakaran. And for the first time, it led to murmurs of surrender in the LTTE ranks.

By then, the army had learnt a valuable lesson. It would keep up sustained attacks at LTTE positions so as to draw maximum fire from the Tigers. The aim was to exhaust Tiger ammunition and deplete the existing stocks, knowing well that fresh supplies were becoming near impossible.

The tactic paid off handsomely. LTTE fighters became desperate for weapons and ammunition towards the end of the war—when it mattered most. Things eventually became so bad that the Tigers could not put up even a semblance of effective retaliation against the monstrous onslaught of Sri Lanka's artillery and Multi-barrel Rocket Launcher (MBRL) barrage that killed civilians and combatants alike. Civilians saw badly wounded LTTE female cadres begging for cyanide to kill themselves and end their agony. An elderly Tamil man lamented to me: "When we fled the military, the LTTE could not save us. How could they have when they were unable to protect themselves?"

Unmindful of what the world thought, the LTTE had forced a large number of Tamil civilians—who had always borne the brunt of the dragging war—to withdraw with them into the interior. This happened in Jaffna in 1995 and it happened again in 2009. Prabhakaran had schemed that this mass of semi-starving men, women, and children would somehow prove to be a guarantee for his safety by generating Western intervention.[9] When that too failed to halt the military push, Prabhakaran's loyalists spread an eleventh hour rumour that the LTTE chief had escaped to Myanmar.[10]

But possessing high quality human and electronic intelligence they had lacked years earlier, Sri Lankan troops pressed on, determined to finish off the LTTE. It was a golden opportunity and it might not recur. Some Tamils who survived the war feel that once the Tigers concluded that all was lost, they became resigned to their fate and ceased to care for a population in whose name they were fighting. Prabhakaran, a man who had become a legend, was finally killed in the same callous and brutal manner he had so often used to send so many thousands to their death.

The final images of the man who for decades had cast a dark shadow on Sri Lanka were terrifying.

Prabhakaran was in his battle fatigues and sprawled on a stretcher, staring blankly with eyes wide open, the back of his head blown off and covered by a blue handkerchief, his face seemingly frozen in terror. Young soldiers milled all around him, some shooing away flies and others using their mobile phones to take the last pictures of a man who for so long presided over a state within a state, determining who would live and who would die in Sri Lanka.

Luck had finally deserted Prabhakaran. The Tiger boss was history.

# IV

THIS book is an overview of the final and no-holds-barred war against the LTTE as I viewed and recorded it from New Delhi, a city where Sri Lanka mattered a lot, and how and why the Tigers perished. I have been a long-time student of the conflict whose early years are still etched in my memory as if they took place only recently. My unauthorized biography of LTTE chief Prabhakaran, *Inside an Elusive Mind*, created a minor stir when it came out in 2003 for more reasons than one.[11] I continued to write both news stories and commentaries as Sri Lanka's peace process slowly ruptured.

I was fortunate because years of pursuing the story had enriched me with contacts on all sides of the ethnic fence in Sri Lanka as well as in India and other countries. These included people high in the echelons of governance, diplomats from around the world, police and military officers, spies, rights activists, Tamil, Sinhalese, and Muslim politicians, the very articulate and informed Sri Lankan journalists and, of course, the most important of them all, the ordinary Tamil folks in whose name the LTTE waged war. Most of my writings were done for IANS, the Indian news agency where I worked. I also contributed to Indian and foreign publications on request.

This book is a collection of some of my writings of that eventful period when Sri Lanka witnessed change of governments, cracks in the Norway-built peace process, a paralysing split in the LTTE, growing international involvement in Sri Lanka, a death-raining tsunami, a surge in Sinhalese nationalism, massive rights abuses, India's overt and covert involvement, the flow of refugees to India,[12] the relentless crackdown on LTTE cells in Tamil Nadu, the return of the war and, finally, the comprehensive defeat of the Tamil Tigers amid large-scale civilian suffering.

Contacts provide information, not necessarily knowledge. In the process, journalists—like all human beings—make assumptions and predictions that tend to go wrong. I was no exception to this time-tested truth. Like most observers of Sri Lanka, I did not expect the war to end so dramatically,[13] although I always maintained that the LTTE would never be able to carve out a Tamil Eelam and that it would never be amenable to peace.

After seeing the LTTE repeatedly wriggle out of tightest corners, I was among those who came to believe firmly that the conflict would never end without Prabhakaran's involvement. The Rajapaksa brothers turned the idea upside down—by killing him! Also, by taking the war to Prabhakaran's lair, Sri Lanka demolished another myth about the LTTE. While many Tigers did embrace death without fear, Sri Lanka's final military offensive proved that there were hypocrites in Tiger ranks who sent kids to fight and die but were eager to show the white flag when their own lives were at stake.

## V

ONE event that no one perhaps anticipated would play a crucial role in the unfolding Sri Lanka story was the unexpected change of guard in New Delhi in May 2004. This happened, coincidentally but significantly, just two months after the LTTE broke up and only a month after Mahinda Rajapaksa was catapulted as the prime minister following the defeat of Sri Lanka's ruling United National Party (UNP) in parliamentary elections.

I was in Colombo in April 2004 and was among the first journalists to meet Rajapaksa after the election results came out. I rushed to his residence for what turned out to be a brief and relaxed interview. Despite the trappings of newfound status, there was none of the choking security normally associated with South Asian VVIPs and which envelops him now. Immaculately dressed, the man was polite and amiable, choosing his words cautiously. His aides, with whom I chatted before talking to him, exuded confidence that Rajapaksa was destined to play a crucial innings. Looking back, I cannot say for sure if they said this out of a sense of loyalty to the man they served or because they knew him better or both.

But Rajapaksa was not in the good books of the politically weakened, yet, still charismatic President Chandrika Kumaratunga, the head of state. The lady would have probably preferred her suave and English-speaking Tamil foreign minister, Lakshman Kadirgamar, as prime minister. That was not to be for a variety of reasons. As for the Indian establishment, it quietly but firmly rooted for the Sinhalese Rajapaksa over the Tamil Kadirgamar in a cold-blooded reminder that strategic interests mattered more for New Delhi than ethnicity.

Why was the surprise victory of a Congress party-led coalition significant for Sri Lanka? Thereby hangs an extraordinary tale as far as India's Sri Lanka relations were concerned.

Once a coalition government led by the Bharatiya Janata Party (BJP) took office in 1998–99,[14] India quietly started to get pro-active in Sri Lanka (and in much of South Asia). This coincided with Colombo's search for international interlocutors, in a bid to bring the LTTE to the negotiating table. Devoid of the Sri Lanka baggage the Congress carried, the BJP wanted India to play a major role in the search for peace in the island nation. It would no more be a bystander to the conflict.

Overseen by National Security Advisor, Brajesh Mishra, a seasoned former diplomat, New Delhi decided to actively assist the Norway-brokered peace path, so as to help end a seemingly unending war. It was not too difficult a proposition for a country that had been an intimate part of the ethnic conflict since it began. India had lost nearly 1,200 soldiers to the LTTE during a failed attempt to bring peace over a decade earlier. Many hundreds of soldiers were also wounded and maimed.

India had pursued a largely hands-off approach, vis-à-vis the Sri Lankan conflict, ever since the LTTE assassinated Rajiv Gandhi. The policy continued both when the Congress party was in power from 1991 to 1996 and when the Congress propped up two short-lived coalition governments. But all along, besides the external affairs ministry, Indian intelligence agencies had kept a close tab on Sri Lanka, in particular the LTTE. But they stayed away from forging contacts with the Tigers because of the Indian government's ban on the group.[15] Once it was firmed up that India needed to change tracks on Sri Lanka, the Research and Analysis Wing (RAW), India's external intelligence agency, was asked to step in.

It was a bold move but none of this would come into public realm, either in India or Sri Lanka. An intelligence agency in India was entering a field normally reserved for the foreign policy establishment. The agency's penchant to work in secrecy was now linked to its lesser-known ability to perform in tandem with policymakers from distant countries.[16]

The Indian establishment decided early on that New Delhi would work behind the scenes in the light of its blood-soaked and controversial past in Sri Lanka. Barring a few in India, Sri Lanka and Norway, no one would know what Indian policymakers were up to. It was a radically new role for an intelligence agency, that had become notorious in Sri Lanka in the 1980s for training and arming Tamil militants, the LTTE included. Its mission now was to help bring peace to the very same country.

When I broke the story in February 2008 without naming RAW, many otherwise well informed people on the ethnic conflict, both in India and Sri Lanka, reacted in disbelief. I actually had the story from about the middle of 2007 but sat over it because of intense speculation that Sri Lanka might repudiate the ceasefire agreement any time. Even when Sri Lanka did that in January 2008, I waited for a month to pass, lest Colombo had a change of heart. I did not want my story to be seen as a calculated leak aimed at preventing the collapse of the truce.

One of the most honest and understandable reactions to my story came from Austin Fernando, who was Sri Lanka's Defence Secretary during the ceasefire period. In a hugely informative (but bulky) book, *My Belly is White*, Fernando referred to my revelation:

> The peacemaking process was a very sensitive political tool, maintaining the highest secrecy to which even I was sometimes not privy. For that matter I hear of Indian involvement in drafting the CFA only in February 2008, six years after the signing. Even now I am unaware whether this revelation is true or not.[17]

This was 100 per cent true.

Having burnt its fingers badly over the Tamil issue in an earlier decade, the Indian state wanted a different role. Sri Lankan sensibilities vis-à-vis New Delhi, right and wrong, had to be respected. It was felt that Norway could play the role of the facilitator for three reasons: it was physically far removed from South Asia; it had no territorial ambitions and it had a proven record in peace building.

A small group of RAW officials discussed the nuts and bolts of the peace process with an equally small group of veteran Norwegian diplomats in an exercise kept tightly under the wraps. (The Indian external affairs ministry came into the picture much later.) The drafts of the ceasefire documents submitted by the LTTE and Colombo were studied in New Delhi. In a bid to prevent the LTTE from derailing the process, the Indian state supported a Nordic umbrella to oversee a truce. It was the first time there would be an international body of peace monitors outside of the United Nations.

Only four senior Norwegian diplomats interacted with the Indian establishment, three of them intensely. Norway's main responsibility was to win over the LTTE to the idea of peace, which, it was assumed, would get cemented on the foundations of a ceasefire agreement.

New Delhi used all its influence, vis-à-vis Sri Lanka, to create the conditions for a peace accord. President Chandrika Kumaratunga, New Delhi felt, was incapable of making a bold leap towards peace. The need of the hour, so went the thinking, was a leader who could take bold and unconventional steps. In order to make it clear that it had no sympathy for the LTTE, India went on to offer training to the Sri Lankan Army's Special Forces, which would later play a critical role in the war, and to the Special Task Force (STF), which the Tigers always feared.[18]

All this is not to mean that Norway did not play the dominant role in the peace process and in knitting together the ceasefire agreement. What needs to be understood is that contrary to what has been known in India and abroad, New Delhi was in the thick of it all and was a key participant in the path-breaking peace process.

Vidar Helgesen, who was assistant foreign minister of Norway during the inception of the peace process, is probably the only Norwegian who has gone public about the critical and covert Indian role, albeit without revealing too much. After joining the Stockholm-based International Institute for Democracy and Electoral Assistance, he said:

> I may reasonably say that the Norwegian contribution in structuring the CFA (ceasefire agreement) ... was, indeed, crucial. However, we could not have achieved any success without the active role played by India at every step of the negotiations. Nothing could be attempted without Indian support at every step, including the CFA.

India's security establishment let the LTTE know through Norway that it was taking an active interest in the goings on. But the LTTE never learnt about the depth of RAW's involvement. At no point did the agency deal with the LTTE since it was outlawed in India after the assassination of Rajiv Gandhi. RAW's role in the peace process continued even after the Congress took power in May 2004, but in a diminished form. All along, the BJP-led Indian government made no concrete effort to dispel the popular impression that New Delhi had lost interest in Sri Lanka.

It is clear in hindsight that Prabhakaran had only a half-baked knowledge of what India was up to. This is why he claimed, very erroneously, at his April 2002 press conference at Kilinochchi that he expected New Delhi to lift the ban on the LTTE soon. But at no point did anyone in India even contemplate this. For the Indian security agencies, the Tigers were *persona non grata*. On this, India was in a very different league compared to the West.

## VI

INDIA was the first country to ban the LTTE as a terrorist organization. This happened in 1992, a year after a woman suicide bomber blew up Rajiv Gandhi at an election rally near Chennai. The ban was extended every two years—in 1994, 1996, 1998, and 2000 mainly on the strength of inputs from the Intelligence Bureau, India's low key but ruthlessly efficient domestic intelligence agency. Another extension was due in 2002 when Prabhakaran made his surprise statement. In what was clearly a rebuff to the LTTE chief (and a signal to Sri Lanka as well), India extended the ban for two more years. Then and later, despite requests from pro-LTTE quarters, New Delhi has refused to lift the ban, which remains in force even now.

The Indian assessment was that the LTTE, which, in 2002, held the upper hand militarily, needed to be securely tied to a peace process in order to de-fang it. At the same time, the legitimate political concerns of the Tamils in Sri Lanka needed to be recognized. It was vital to draw a line between the LTTE and the Tamil community (though the Tigers resented this) because otherwise it would become difficult for anyone in Colombo to give the Tamils the autonomy they longed for. This was also the understanding of the larger international community.

However, the LTTE and many others in Sri Lanka, although holding entirely different perspectives, felt that the peace process was legitimizing the Tamil Tigers. This was one of the unexpected and negative fallouts of the peace process. Ranil Wickremesinghe, the prime minister and one of the signatories to the 2002 ceasefire pact, likened the peace process to an international safety net.

That was the truth—as far as Sri Lanka was concerned.[19] It was Colombo's way of tackling the Tigers since it was unable, at that point of time, to subdue the LTTE militarily.[20] In other words, Wickremesinghe's calculated intention behind choosing the peace process was fundamentally no different from Rajapaksa's later decision to go to war. Both wanted to subdue the Tamil Tigers. Given the circumstances, their paths differed.

The Sri Lankan leader who invited Norway was no doubt President Chandrika Kumaratunga, but it is doubtful if she would have done this but for the LTTE's ascendancy and military supremacy. In short, she had no choice. She had taken charge of the government on a strong wicket in 1994, ending 17 long years of United National Party (UNP) rule, and offered peace to the LTTE. It was a widely hailed move. Her background and image as a liberal Sinhalese, one whose charismatic actor-husband had been assassinated by Sinhalese hardliners, cemented her popularity.

When the Tamil Tigers dramatically resumed the war in April 1995, she responded with a military offensive that led to the capture of Jaffna, the Tamil heartland the LTTE had controlled since 1990. After that, the military push surprisingly slackened. The Tigers went on to hit back with a ferocious blitzkrieg that stumped Sri Lanka. As Colombo tottered under the weight of the LTTE offensive, losing territory after territory, it sought out Norway to shake hands with the belligerent Tigers.[21]

Wickremesinghe, who headed the rival UNP, entered the picture after Kumaratunga's popularity got badly eroded because of repeated political and military setbacks. She led her Sri Lanka Freedom Party (SLFP) to a defeat in elections, towards the end of 2001, following political convulsions in the country.

What happened next was bizarre. While Prime Minister Wickremesinghe formed the government, Kumaratunga remained the powerful President. But they would not see eye-to-eye on vital issues. Wickremesinghe signed the February 2002 ceasefire agreement with LTTE chief Prabhakaran but without the full knowledge of the President, the commander-in-chief of the armed forces. The lady was predictably furious but fell in line reluctantly due to international pleadings. However, it was a bad start to an experiment that required pan-Sri Lanka support. It was the beginning of an uneasy co-habitation for the President and prime minister, a perfect recipe for disaster.

The ups and downs of the peace process only widened the gulf between the two leaders. Eventually, Kumaratunga sacked the Wickremesinghe government in November 2003 after the LTTE submitted a set of proposals for self-governance, widely seen in Sri Lanka as a stepping-stone to Tamil independence. Wickremesinghe came under widespread attack for virtually surrendering to the LTTE. Fresh parliamentary elections in April 2004 led to the defeat of his party, the UNP. Kumaratunga's SLFP was back in the saddle.

The March–April–May months of 2004 thus had a vital bearing on Sri Lanka because of three seemingly unrelated but critical developments: the split in the monolithic LTTE in March; the defeat of the UNP in Sri Lanka in April; and the defeat of the BJP and the return to power of the Congress in India in May. The last was to alter New Delhi's equations vis-à-vis the peace process.

A reading of LTTE and pro-LTTE literature of that period shows the Tigers were as stunned by the Congress victory as everyone else. The electoral verdict had made a woman widowed callously by Prabhakaran the most powerful person in India although she said "no" to the prime minister's office. Indeed, Sonia Gandhi may have been nowhere in politics if Prabhakaran had not ordered her husband's killing. There was no inkling to what she would now do.

The prime minister would be, Manmohan Singh, was a Gandhi family loyalist. The National Security Adviser (NSA) was J.N. Dixit, who even as India's envoy to Sri Lanka in the 1980s, never hid his dislike for the LTTE and its tactics. Indeed, he had contempt for the outfit. This dislike of the LTTE continued before and after India and Sri Lanka signed a pact in July 1987, to end Tamil separatism.

But Dixit was highly unpopular in Sri Lanka, among large sections of the Sinhalese majority, for what were seen as his overbearing ways.[22] He was no doubt hawkish. Few among the Sinhalese public cared to appreciate that Dixit thought like them on the LTTE. After his retirement, Dixit admitted candidly that he was in the wrong in his assessment of the LTTE's resilience and its ability to bounce back even in the most adverse circumstances.[23]

After his death as the National Security Advisor, the mantle fell on M.K. Narayanan, who had headed the Intelligence Bureau when the LTTE cold-bloodedly assassinated Rajiv Gandhi after pretending to befriend him. The Gandhi killing was a chapter the Intelligence Bureau would never forget—and never forgive the LTTE for.

Each of these individuals—Sonia Gandhi, Dixit, Narayanan, and even Manmohan Singh—had strong reasons to dislike, if not loathe, the LTTE and its leader Prabhakaran. In any case, by the time the Congress took over the reins of power in India, Sri Lanka's peace process was under severe strain.

It took some time for the new Congress regime to learn about India's covert involvement.[24] In the meantime, New Delhi continued its behind-the-scenes role. The truce held on but barely. In the long run, however, India's approach to Sri Lanka would undergo a slow but sure change. Once the war picked up, from 2006, New Delhi's tilt towards Colombo began to show. By the time the conflict approached its finale, India had publicly begun to denounce the LTTE as a terrorist group. The language had not been heard in New Delhi for a long time.

While India and Sri Lanka pursued their close interactions at the highest level, New Delhi was in contact, both collectively and individually, with the key global players: peace-broker Norway, the US, Japan, and the European Union. The four entities were together called the Co-Chairs and oversaw the peace process. But despite repeated private and public invitations, India firmly but politely declined to be an institutional part of the Co-Chairs per se, fearing it might then be forced to subjugate its strategic interests vis-à-vis Sri Lanka and the region to the whims of the largely Western players.

Again, New Delhi maintained an active interest in Sri Lanka even as the situation deteriorated from 2004–05, eventually resulting in full-scale war. There were occasions when Prime Minister Manmohan Singh and National Security Adviser M.K. Narayanan met exclusively to discuss Sri Lanka. At times one or more officials would join them.

These meetings never found their way to the media. Most of the Indian media was also unaware of Manmohan Singh's telephonic conversation with President Rajapaksa after communal violence directed at Tamil civilians erupted in Trincomalee in 2006. Several Tamils in Sri Lanka frantically telephoned the Indian High Commission in Colombo urging India to do something. The Trincomalee rioting was halted after Manmohan Singh's intervention.

The Congress regime in New Delhi assisted the Rajapaksa administration in several ways without much sound and fury—the quietly efficient style of governance preferred by Manmohan Singh and Sonia Gandhi. With one of its key coalition partners, the DMK, ruling Tamil Nadu (from May 2006), the Congress-led government played its cards carefully so as to ensure that Tamil sentiments in the state, vis-à-vis Colombo, never got out of hand. This was easy and difficult at the same time. It was easy because the LTTE, post Rajiv Gandhi, could never regain the popular sympathy it had once enjoyed in the sprawling state; it was difficult because many political parties and politicians in Tamil Nadu continued to speak vocally for the LTTE.[25]

Even as it provided select military support to Sri Lanka, overt and covert, New Delhi kept pressing Colombo not to deviate from its stated pledge to empower the minorities, the Tamils in particular. It continuously voiced concern over human rights abuses if and when civilians got hit in a major way. But it normally avoided going public with statements critical of Sri Lanka—in contrast to the mid-1980s.[26] Even as National Security Adviser Narayanan once publicly faulted Colombo for apparently not realizing that the Tamil man on the street was sullen, India trained the first batch of Tamil policemen for Sri Lanka. Not surprisingly, the Sri Lankan reaction to Narayanan's critical remarks were extremely mild—another contrast to the 1980s.

Simultaneously, the Indian government used its diplomatic clout, if and when there was too much Western heat on Sri Lanka. While dubbing the LTTE a terrorist organization, sections of the West were vocal about what they felt were the failings of

Sri Lanka on the war front. This was noticeably acute in the initial stages of the Rajapaksa administration, before it gained the upper hand militarily. European countries were more sharply critical of Sri Lanka than the US.

In 2006, as fighting escalated, some Western countries pressured Sri Lanka to disarm the breakaway LTTE led by Karuna who had split the organization two years earlier. This was also a key LTTE demand. Some of the countries that took this line probably felt that the Tigers could be persuaded to return to the negotiating table if only the Tigers were appeased on this front. There were indeed serious concerns about human rights abuses being committed by Karuna's men against Tamil and Muslim civilians in the east.

India, which understood the LTTE far better than many other countries, knew the crucial role Karuna was starting to play in the war for supremacy in the eastern province. Naturally, the LTTE, having failed to hunt down the former regional commander, decided to use the West to immobilize a man it saw as a "traitor"—a Tiger epithet to mean one who deserves to die. Precisely for the same reason, the Sri Lankan security establishment was firmly opposed to the fettering of Karuna and his men. India made it clear to the international interlocutors that it was against the peace process being held hostage over the Karuna issue.

The more India acted behind the scenes, influencing other players and at times events, the more frustrated the LTTE became. The LTTE suspected initially that Indians might have been linked to Karuna when he revolted with thousands of guerrillas in the eastern district of Batticaloa in March 2004. Karuna's public statements (after his rebellion) criticizing Prabhakaran for ordering the assassination of Rajiv Gandhi made the LTTE suspect a possible Indian connection. Adding to the LTTE's suspicions was the decision by the Eelam National Democratic Liberation Front (ENDLF), an India-based Sri Lankan Tamil group, to support Karuna.[27] It was the ENDLF link that fuelled intense speculation that Karuna had taken shelter in India for about six months after feeling seriously threatened in Sri Lanka.

As years rolled by after the 2002 ceasefire agreement, India remained firmly opposed to the LTTE, making it clear to everyone, Norway included, that New Delhi would never accept a "dictatorship" in the north and east of Sri Lanka. Over time, as it became pronounced that India's aloofness would be a permanent veto to the LTTE gaining political legitimacy, more and more Tiger operatives and high-profile supporters admitted, mostly off the record, that Rajiv Gandhi's killing was a first rate blunder by Prabhakaran.

Prabhakaran was, of course, too egoistic to admit that he had made a mistake. Such an admission could have dented the image of a man who claimed to act wisely on behalf of the Tamil community. But Indians visiting the LTTE territory returned with the impression that the feeling of remorse voiced by Tiger sympathizers could not have been possible without a nod from the Tiger boss. Anton Balasingham, the London-based colleague of Prabhakaran and the LTTE's political ideologue, came closest to anyone in the organization by offering a virtual public apology for Gandhi's murder.

In 2008, in what turned out to be his last annual 27 November speech, Prabhakaran shed his long-standing animosity, described India as a "superpower" and sought "a constructive relationship" with it. It was too little too late. New Delhi took notice of the speech but did not respond. India's security establishment had decreed a long time ago that the LTTE was untrustworthy. There was no question of lifting the ban on the LTTE. The grotesque Gandhi murder was not the only reason for this.

## VII

ONCE the LTTE gained control of Jaffna in early 1990 after the Indian troops sailed home, it quietly trained several insurgents from India. The Indians were in the dark initially. The LTTE had always had a strong anti-India streak although it carefully clouded this by friendly pronouncements. The Indian military intervention, however, made the LTTE change gears.[28]

Steeped in unforgiving tit-for-tat tactics, it concluded that if New Delhi could train outfits opposed to the Tigers, then it had the right to take revenge. And so it imparted training to the United Liberation Front of Asom (ULFA),[29] an insurgent group that sought to break away the tea- and oil-rich state of Assam from India. Interestingly, ULFA also had deep links with the intelligence agencies of both Pakistan and Bangladesh.

The ULFA training, which took place in Jaffna, ended in six months. One reason was that the ULFA members found the LTTE capsule too rough and tough. But the LTTE had other plans. Also from 1990, the LTTE helped train and set up a militant group in Tamil Nadu, suggestively called the Tamil National Retrieval Troops (TNRT). As its name revealed, it was to "retrieve" Tamil Nadu from India!

LTTE intelligence chief Shanmugalingam Sivashankar, alias Pottu Amman, personally passed on weapons, gold biscuits, and communication equipment to TNRT operatives. The apparent aim was to create mayhem in Tamil Nadu in the event there were attacks on innocent Tamils by non-Tamils in the wake of Gandhi's death—à la what happened to Sikhs in New Delhi after Indira Gandhi's assassination. The police crackdo̶w̶ following the Rajiv Gandhi killing smashed up the TNRT.

Tamil Nadu group, which the Indian authorities believed was trained by s Tamizhar Pasarai (Bastion of Tamils). The group planted a bomb at the secretariat in Chennai during a meeting of the National Integration Council in 1990. Fortunately, the bomb did not explode. (A key operative of the group, who is on the run, was last spotted in Bangalore.)

The LTTE also operated networks in Tamil Nadu to smuggle war material from the Indian state to Sri Lanka. While maintaining that it would never do anything to hurt Indian interests, LTTE men used Indian soil both to source goods needed to pursue the armed conflict and also as a transit point for sophisticated communication equipment bought in the West. The LTTE even attempted to build a 70 feet long vessel in Kerala for use by the Sea Tigers.

Naturally, there was much more behind the Indian decision to outlaw the LTTE than Gandhi's assassination.[30] True to its self, the LTTE never admitted training ULFA or other Indian insurgents. As the war in Sri Lanka escalated from 2006, the LTTE did a dramatic U-turn, emphasizing to its cadres that while sailing to Tamil Nadu they should not to get involved in any activity that could be deemed anti-India. LTTE guerrillas who fell into the police net said as much when they were interrogated.

Tamil Nadu was vital for the LTTE's larger scheme of things. It is where Prabhakaran had repeatedly fled to in the 1970s and early 1980s when the police hunt for him became intense in Sri Lanka. It is where the LTTE chief had been arrested—for the first and last time—way back in May 1982. (After securing bail, he lived in India for a while and then escaped to Sri Lanka.) It is also where he lived for over three productive years, until January 1987. The LTTE counted a large number of friends and sympathizers across the state. Not only was it an important place to whip up passions in support of its cause but it was also the nearest coastline to Sri Lanka's north, the main war theatre.

The LTTE routinely procured a wide variety of goods ranging from food and medicines to explosives in Tamil Nadu to be taken by speedboats to Sri Lanka. The coming to power of a DMK party government in Tamil Nadu in 2006 did not derail the crackdown on the Tiger smuggling cells even if the state police were not too enthusiastic about chasing the Tigers. Within a month of taking power, Tamil Nadu Chief Minister M. Karunanidhi made it abundantly clear that the Central government's Sri Lanka policy will be his policy too. This was one reason why one pro-LTTE website at one time ended up accusing Karunanidhi of betraying the Sri Lankan Tamils. It was a major development considering the sympathies Karunanidhi's DMK party had brazenly exhibited for the LTTE until Rajiv Gandhi was killed.

The main credit for the unending assaults on LTTE networks in Tamil Nadu and for denying the killers of Rajiv Gandhi a rear base in south India should go to the federal Intelligence Bureau. The Intelligence Bureau, born during the British colonial rule, was responsible for nearly 80 per cent of all seizures of war material in the sprawling coastal state during the last few years of the conflict in Sri Lanka. These included ball bearings used as shrapnel, aluminium bars, ordinary and electronic detonators, boat building equipment, walkie-talkies, batteries, petroleum products, chemicals, high-speed outboard engines for boats, cycle spares, tyres for cycles and motorcycles, power generators, surgical equipment and medicines, and even *beedis*, the poor man's cigarette.

None of this was in small quantity. Detonators were seized in thousands, while the quantity of chemicals ran into thousands of litres. It was a hugely creditable performance. The Q Branch of the Tamil Nadu Police, a unit meant to shadow and cripple insurgents, also played a key role in smashing up LTTE networks. It was the Q Branch's interrogation of arrested LTTE members that revealed that a boat seized from the Tigers and docked in the Chennai Port was packed with a huge quantity of concealed explosives.

From the time "Eelam War IV" resumed, the LTTE increasingly used former LTTE guerrillas settled in the West, particularly in Britain, to link up its units in Sri Lanka with the smuggling networks in Tamil Nadu so as to hoodwink the intelligence agencies. The last major coordinated attempt to smuggle sophisticated communication equipment (bought in the West) into Sri Lanka from Tamil Nadu took place in March 2009. And the last serious bid to send a large consignment of medicines, including insulin for Prabhakaran, from Tamil Nadu happened in May, just before the Tigers were crushed. The first operation was a failure, thanks mainly to the vigilance by Indian security agencies. The medicines managed to leave the Indian shore but they probably never reached the targeted audience because by then the LTTE was in complete disarray.

Notwithstanding statements from arrested LTTE members that the Tigers were in no mood to confront the Indian state, New Delhi never lowered its guard. Laxity had led to Rajiv Gandhi's killing. As if to prove that it indeed could not be expected to keep its word, the LTTE tried, in 2008, to assassinate an India-based senior Sri Lankan Tamil political activist it has always hated.

The intended victim was Annamali Varadaraja Perumal, who was chief minister of Sri Lanka's northeastern province when Indian troops were stationed there. He moved over to India with his wife and three daughters and lived under state protection from 1990. He belonged to the Eelam People's Revolutionary Liberation Front (EPRLF), whose top leader, K. Pathmanabha and many of his lieutenants were gunned down in Chennai in 1990.[31]

An LTTE intelligence sleeper who ran a taxi company in Tamil Nadu had befriended some relatives of Perumal. When one of Perumal's daughters got married in Ajmer in northern India, the LTTE agent told the relatives that he would be happy to drive them all the way to Ajmer. When he was arrested, the man confessed that the

LTTE had planned to abduct Perumal from India. It is another matter whether the daring scheme could have been executed successfully. But the episode proved one thing to the Indians: the Tigers would never, never change their stripes.

It was a lesson President Rajapaksa too learnt—and very quickly.

## VIII

IT will be no exaggeration to say that the LTTE's demise as a military machine began in March 2004 when it was rocked by a stunning and unprecedented rebellion by thousands of its cadres in the eastern province, made up of Trincomalee, Batticaloa, and Amparai districts. Unlike the predominantly Tamil north, the eastern wing was multi-racial where Tamils, Sinhalese and Muslims[32] lived in near equal numbers. Of the three eastern districts, Batticaloa, inclusive of its Muslims, was almost wholly Tamil speaking. This is where the LTTE broke up.

The development, which a few Sri Lankans had anticipated with remarkable foresight, shook the Tamil Tigers at their very roots. At the head of the epoch making event was 37-year-old Vinayagamurthy Muralitharan, widely known as Karuna Amman or Karuna, the LTTE's longest serving regional commander. He was in charge of Batticaloa and Amparai districts. The battle-hardened rebel had also been a former bodyguard of Prabhakaran—and for long his blue-eyed man.

Although an estimated 4,000–5,000 guerrillas had left the LTTE from the early 1980s and lived mostly in the West,[33] the group had never faced a mass revolt. In the LTTE, this was unthinkable. Only once before, had one man rebelled against Prabhakaran's authority—and paid with his life. That was Gopalasamy Mahendrarajah, alias Mahattaya, a former designated number two in the group. He was picked up by the LTTE intelligence in August 1993 on charges of being an Indian spy. He was executed along with his supporters in December next year after being tortured to confess.

Mahattaya's revolt became public knowledge only after he was taken into custody. Karuna was too cunning and too powerful for that. He played his cards well once he anticipated the impending danger from Prabhakaran because, as he told me in a July 2004 interview after going into hiding, "only a snake understands a snake".

Born into an agriculturist family in a place called Kiran in Batticaloa, Karuna was among the hundreds who flocked to Tamil militancy after anti-Tamil riots swept Sri Lanka in 1983. Karuna opted for the LTTE and was one of its many young soldiers. He underwent military training in Tamil Nadu when Prabhakaran lived in the safety of the Indian state. Karuna's commitment to the cause and ruthlessness helped him go up the ladder quickly. He was a leader of some standing in the LTTE by the time India deployed its army in Sri Lanka's north and east in 1987 to end Tamil separatism.

Karuna proved his skills against both the Indian and the Sri Lankan militaries. In no time, he became an object of reverence and terror—much like his mentor and boss, Prabhakaran.

Trouble followed. His military exploits and his standing among the LTTE cadres from the eastern province earned him a place in the Tiger delegations when peace talks opened with Colombo following the Norway-brokered 2002 ceasefire agreement. Karuna was with Balasingham in the Norwegian capital Oslo in December that year when the LTTE and Colombo signed a path-breaking document promising to find a federal solution to the dragging conflict—a revolutionary leap forward for the uncompromising Tigers. Prabhakaran, when he learnt about it, was livid. He had not been consulted.

The development led to an unprecedented chasm between Prabhakaran and Balasingham, otherwise best buddies in the LTTE leadership. Karuna did not escape censure. Even otherwise, Pottu Amman, the LTTE's cold-blooded intelligence chief, loathed Karuna. Karuna too hated Pottu Amman. Prabhakaran did always have a soft corner for Karuna, but the Tigers chief could not do without Pottu Amman, the LTTE's eyes and ears. In any case, Karuna was based far away in the east; Pottu Amman was almost constantly by Prabhakaran's side.[34]

Although Karuna's revolt took most people by surprise, some had seen it coming. At a December 2003 meeting of the Sri Lanka Monitoring Mission (SLMM), the five-nation Nordic body overseeing the truce, a former Tamil militant turned peace activist voiced apprehension that the LTTE might come apart in the eastern wing. To his small but startled audience, he went on to explain why.[35] The respected University Teachers for Human Rights (Jaffna), which enjoyed widespread grassroots support in the Tamil areas, separately warned of a split in the LTTE in the eastern province much before it actually happened.

Having achieved the status of a war hero, Karuna had begun to openly express his dislike of both Pottu Amman and S.P. Tamilchelvan, the political head of the LTTE. In his own lair, the eastern province, he undermined both men—an unforgivable audacity as the vengeful Pottu Amman saw it.

The LTTE's Batticaloa political wing leader was Kaushalyan who was theoretically answerable and accountable to Tamilchelvan. Instead, Kaushalyan was forced to clear every schedule from Karuna and even refuse some of Tamilchelvan's directives if Karuna did not endorse them. To Tamilchelvan this was downright humiliating.

Similarly, Reginald, head of the LTTE military intelligence for Batticaloa, was supposed to report to and take orders from Pottu Amman. However, Karuna read his reports first. He would even censor some of the reports and only the edited material went to Pottu Amman. Predictably, Tamilchelvan and Pottu Amman complained against Karuna to the LTTE chief.

Prabhakaran knew what was happening on the ground, from about the middle of 2003—almost nine months before the revolt actually took place. But Prabhakaran thought, mistakenly as it turned out, that this was a personality clash between Karuna on the one hand and Tamilchelvan and Pottu Amman on the other. The LTTE chief had, for long, trusted Karuna immensely and thought that such differences in the highest echelons were inevitable in a large organization like the LTTE.

This turned out to be a horrible blunder. As 2004 dawned, relations soured between Prabhakaran and Karuna. Karuna felt that the boss was lending too much ear to his detractors. According to Karuna, Prabhakaran had refused to heed his advice to give up violence and opt for a sincere and negotiated settlement with Colombo.

Karuna also felt that diplomats and others who called on Tamilchelvan at Kilinochchi, the LTTE hub in the north, should visit him too in Batticaloa. Hadn't he fought more battles than Tamilchelvan? Wasn't he as important as Tamilchelvan in the LTTE pecking order? Wasn't his contribution to the LTTE's growth far greater than that of Tamilchelvan? Karuna did not hide his contempt for two others in the LTTE: B. Nadesan and Tamilendhi, the heads of the LTTE police and financial wings.

Quietly, without fanfare but clearly with Prabhakaran's blessings, Pottu Amman began to sneak his operatives from the intelligence wing into Batticaloa. When Karuna realized this, he knew serious trouble was on hand (Some of these infiltrators would later get killed in Karuna's custody). Already, there had been summons for him to attend a meeting in the Wanni, Prabhakaran's headquarters. Karuna smelt a rat and refused to go. Instead, he decided to go on the offensive.

Karuna called a meeting of his top lieutenants and gave them an unenviable choice. He revealed that he was going to revolt; those who wanted to be with him could stay on in Batticaloa, others should leave for Prabhakaran's fiefdom. Knowing what Pottu Amman was capable of, he stepped up security for himself.

In March 2004 he took another step by shooting off a letter to Prabhakaran asking him to sack Nadesan and Tamilendhi, describing them as unfits for surrendering to the Indian Army instead of biting the cyanide capsules. Karuna knew that the LTTE would never accept this demand. The die was cast.

The LTTE was too stunned by the initial turn of developments to know how to respond. When it did, its long-standing arrogance was evident. It attempted to brush off the unexpected challenge as an "individual problem" and an "internal matter" that it would easily take care of. But it became quickly clear that the unthinkable had happened and that its confidence was misplaced. Barring a few second rung leaders who deserted Karuna and sought sanctuary with Prabhakaran, thousands of LTTE men and women guerrillas remained loyal to their regional chief. Worse, hundreds of young civilians took to the streets in Batticaloa town and elsewhere in Batticaloa, hailing Karuna and denouncing "northern" leaders of the LTTE—a reference to the Jaffna men who held sway in the organization.

Karuna even told Norway that he wanted a separate ceasefire agreement in the eastern province. Norwegian diplomats were taken aback; it was the last thing they had expected to happen. And once the LTTE sacked him, Karuna hurled one accusation after another against the LTTE brass, including Prabhakaran. He flayed the LTTE chief for needlessly killing Rajiv Gandhi, the former Indian Prime Minister and earning the enmity of India. He accused the Tigers of ignoring and discriminating against cadres from the east although they died in larger numbers in the battlefield. No Tamil from eastern province, Karuna pointed out, headed even one of the over 30 departments in the LTTE. Thanks to Karuna, the north-versus-east differences among the Tamils of Sri Lanka, suppressed by years of war, had burst into the open.

For Colombo, the split in the LTTE was a divine gift. (The LTTE's version was more cynical—that Colombo actively fanned Karuna's ambitions and offered him security guarantees before he announced his rebellion.) The Tigers knew this. But like a tiger sneaking slowly towards its prey, Prabhakaran waited for the opportune moment to strike back.

Surprisingly, even as anti-Jaffna and pro-Karuna sentiments gripped Batticaloa, many Tamils in the east insisted that Prabhakaran was not responsible for Karuna's hurt feelings; they blamed the LTTE chief's senior aides instead. Most Tamils elsewhere in Sri Lanka, startled by the break up, predicted rightly that Prabhakaran would never forgive Karuna for his treachery—and would have him killed at the first available opportunity.

Even as Karuna became a hero in the Sinhalese and international media, a David taking on a Goliath, the Tigers hit back on Good Friday at the start of April. Using speed and stealth, its two long-standing weapons, LTTE fighters loyal to Prabhakaran quickly overran Karuna's forces massed along a river in Batticaloa's north. The rout was sudden and total. Karuna fled Batticaloa, with help from a ruling party MP. The military intelligence promptly took him under its wings, protecting a man who had once ordered the slaughter of 600 surrendered policemen but who could now become a deadly weapon to weaken and destroy the wily Prabhakaran.

That's exactly what happened.


## IX

THE LTTE overcame Karuna's open challenge but Sri Lanka's east never saw peace again. Backed covertly by Colombo, Karuna organized his men for hit-and-run attacks to harass the mainstream LTTE. The violence was vicious and neither side gave any quarter. But Karuna went out of sight even as the LTTE launched the biggest manhunt in its history for any one man. Try as they might, the Tigers could never track him down.

This was frustrating to the LTTE, which came down heavily on his supporters, killing some in public to cow down his cadres and sympathizers. The staff of Save the Children NGO was witness to one such cold-blooded execution in Batticaloa's Karadiyanaru village in July 2004. LTTE fighters had caught two young men loyal to Karuna. After gathering the villagers, and forcing the Save the Children staff to watch the spectacle, the LTTE decreed that "Tamil traitors" could only expect death in Tiger land. LTTE gunmen then pumped bullets into the two who collapsed in a pool of blood. So chilling was the effect of this double killing that the Save the Children staff were terrified to return to the village to do development work.

Karuna's younger brother Reggie, another former bodyguard of Prabhakaran, was also gunned down. With the Tamil media mostly siding with the LTTE, scores of cold-blooded killings went unreported. Three middle-rung LTTE leaders who had sided with Karuna were persuaded to return to Prabhakaran's fold by a Bishop in Batticaloa. They were promised they would not be harmed. But when they did what was requested of them, the LTTE quickly executed them for treachery. One of the victims was known by his *nom de guerre* Jim Kelly Thatha.

The string of killings by the LTTE led to an equally macabre retribution. Karuna's men virtually took over parts of interior Batticaloa. Around 40 guerrillas from the Karuna faction entered Batticaloa's Omadiyamadu village and warned its residents not to countenance Prabhakaran's men. To prove that they meant business, they brought bodies of two LTTE cadres tied to tractors.

As months rolled by, there was a marked increase in the activities of the Karuna group. At night, residents would hear heavy exchange of gunfire in Batticaloa's rural areas where much of the Prabhakaran–Karuna war raged. Nobody knew who was targeting whom. The very vocal Kaushalyan, who had remained loyal to Prabhakaran as the LTTE political head in Batticaloa, was killed. Although Prabhakaran mourned his death, the funeral was a low-key affair, mainly because of the terror unleashed by Karuna's armed bands with the backing of Sri Lankan security forces. It was the first major sign that the LTTE's writ was not running in Batticaloa despite the end of Karuna's open rebellion.

The passionately anti-LTTE Eelam People's Democratic Party (EPDP) headed by Douglas Devananda, a militant turned cabinet minister, threw its lot with Karuna. So the LTTE targeted the EPDP too, trying to kill its leader with a suicide bomber in July 2004 in Colombo. Devananda survived, becoming the only Sri Lankan man to survive a string of LTTE assassination attempts. Sri Lanka's military intelligence backed Karuna. In the mêlée, some Muslim traders in the east gathered courage and refused to pay "taxes" to the LTTE—for the first time in years.[36]

In Batticaloa and Amparai, the two districts Karuna had commanded, the LTTE found it difficult to observe the annual Black Tigers day on 5 July 2004, marking the anniversary of the first Tiger suicide attack on that day in 1987. Over time, the LTTE realized to its dismay that Karuna's ambush parties appeared to know in advance about the movements of its fighters, leading to scores of deaths on roads linking Batticaloa. It meant that some of those who had revolted on the side of Karuna and returned to the LTTE fold later were playing a dangerous double game.[37]

The LTTE's failure to catch and kill Karuna, who quietly spent time in India when Sri Lanka became too dangerous for him, infuriated the Tigers. It was the first time the LTTE was finding it difficult to net a sworn enemy despite managing to infiltrate his group. After Mahinda Rajapaksa was elected the President in November 2005, Karuna went on to become a key element in the government's strategy once it was decided to destroy the LTTE. As the tide of the war slowly turned against the Tigers, the LTTE's anger against Karuna only mounted because it knew he was a key reason why it was losing the east.

The LTTE branded Karuna and his supporters "paramilitaries" and demanded that they be disarmed. A section in the West echoed the Tiger demand. Colombo, wiser to the tactics of the LTTE, would have none of it. Karuna's knowledge of the topography and the LTTE mindset helped Sri Lanka capture the entire eastern province from the Tigers in 2007, including areas where Colombo's writ had not prevailed for one and a half decades. Although conventional wisdom held that the military would find it difficult to hold on to the east once soldiers moved to the north, the LTTE failed to regain the eastern province, mainly because it lacked the numbers to confront Colombo.

The wealth of intelligence about the LTTE that Karuna possessed was as astonishing as it was invaluable. It is doubtful if Sri Lanka could have won the war against the LTTE in 2009 so comprehensively, but for the internecine war in the Tiger ranks five years earlier. What the LTTE had contemptuously dismissed as a "one man problem" finally turned into a fireball that eventually consumed Prabhakaran and his once formidable army.

Clearly, the LTTE misread the long-term consequences of Karuna's walking away. It erred in gauging the mood behind the break up. Whatever Karuna's bent of mind and proclivity to violence,[38] he represented a dormant idea that the northern Tamils (read Jaffna Tamils) bossed over the eastern Tamils. This thinking also destabilized a section of the eastern LTTE cadres who were based in Prabhakaran's territory in the north when Karuna revolted.

The LTTE also failed to reconcile with the fact that Karuna's rebellion was qualitatively different compared to the earlier revolt by Mahattaya. Even the two men were different. Karuna was more lethal and more scheming compared to Mahattaya. He was also more ruthless. In sum short, his going away was a dangerous development. But the cocky confidence and ingrained pride in the LTTE's veins did not help it to correctly analyze the Karuna phenomenon. It paid a heavy price for it.

## X

THE aftermath of Karuna's March–April 2004 revolt led to one of the most shameful chapters in the history of the Tamil struggle. Determined to gain back the physical and political space it had lost in the eastern province, the LTTE went on an ugly offensive, urging combatants who had called it quits before and after the rebellion to rejoin the Tigers. While many did respond voluntarily, a majority did not.

Many young men and women had simply dumped their weapons and uniforms and returned to their anxious families, disgusted with the war and the mindless suffering it caused. The more daring ones sold off their weapons for whatever money they fetched, moved quickly to Colombo, where, with help from relatives and friends, they hunted for passports to leave Sri Lanka for good.

The LTTE would not take "no" for an answer—for anything. When it realized that most young fighters were not returning to its fold on their own, it decided to grab them forcibly. Though the Sri Lankan military had been happy over the split in the LTTE, there was no political backing at that point of time to prevent forcible conscription. The pro-LTTE diaspora, its own children tucked away in the safety of the West, looked the other way as Tamil Tiger gangs swooped on children from poor families in numerous villages to make them don the battle fatigues again.[39]

The LTTE-controlled region witnessed mayhem.

On 26 June 2004, over two months after Karuna's challenge had been put down, armed and young female LTTE cadres checking public buses ordered a middle-aged woman and her young daughter to get off a bus in Vakarai area in Batticaloa. It was about 10 in the morning. Vakarai had been held by the LTTE for a long time. The girl had been in the LTTE for about two years and had returned home in April that year. She was from a village close to Panichenkerny and, according to her mother, was only 14 years old.

The frightened mother held her daughter in tight embrace and tried to reason with the LTTE women that the girl was young, had rejoined school and should not be taken away. The girl mustered courage to blurt out that she did not want to return to fighting. This infuriated the uniformed women. As the bus passengers watched in horror, the LTTE fighters kicked the mother and beat her severely. Her crime—she had the audacity to argue!

The daughter was also assaulted. Even as some gang members urged their colleagues to spare the mother, the woman was thrashed until she lost consciousness. Those watching the scene were outraged but there was no stopping the Tigers as they made away with the unwilling and screaming girl—to fight for Tamil Eelam.

Pressed by their leadership to recruit as many fighters as possible, LTTE guerrillas, both men and women, returned that night to the village of the young woman snatched from the bus. They forcibly entered the homes of other young women who too had quit the Tigers in April. In one house, a mother who resisted was beaten along with a 14-year-old girl and her minor sister. When the brother tried to stop the aggressors from taking away his sister, he was threatened with death.

It was as if the LTTE had declared war on the Tamil people.

A female-headed family lived in Panichenkerny, a small village in the LTTE-controlled part of Batticaloa. The son was 14 years old in 1990 when the army had picked him up during a cordon and search operation. He was never seen again. The daughter had served in the Tharavai camp of LTTE at Thoppigala, about 50 km from Batticaloa town, after being abducted by the Tigers in 1999. She too returned home in April. But she could not enjoy her freedom.

Since late May of 2004, LTTE fighters started visiting the family demanding the return of the young woman, now aged 19. The family insisted it had no idea where the girl was. On the third visit, the cadres decided to seize matters by the scruff of the neck. They forced the mother to board a tractor and took her around the village in a public display of what could happen to objectors. They flayed her verbally and physically before other villagers, stopping the tractor in spots where people could gather and silently witness the high-handedness.

It was a chilling warning sign not to follow the woman's methodology of survival. As for the young former guerrilla, she went into hiding in the jungles, determined to avoid re-conscription and firm in her mind that Tamil Eelam was not worth dying for.

For the LTTE, festivals at Hindu temples, which drew large gatherings, provided a happy hunting ground. At the start of August 2004, the Tigers swooped down on a temple festival in Batticaloa's Vavunathivu area, which the LTTE controlled and grabbed up to 40 children at one go. It was a shocking display of high-handedness; but behind the LTTE's iron curtain, there was no court of appeal.

The mothers of the children wailed and wailed, pleading with the LTTE to free their children. That had no effect. The LTTE was simply not bothered about the niceties of human rights and international law—although it would cry foul if Colombo or Karuna violated these. Ironically, this mass abduction took place during a month when the UN Human Rights Adviser to the High Commissioner for Human Rights visited Batticaloa.

The terrible destruction caused by the December 2004 tsunami only triggered further abductions because more Tamil children were rendered orphan and homeless. Since the traumatic disaster had claimed the lives of many LTTE fighters, the Tigers were desperate for recruits. In a major departure from the past, few Tamils were voluntarily joining the Tiger ranks, preferring instead to stay away from the unending conflict even though the LTTE was ready to pay salaries. At one time, an exasperated LTTE Sea Tigers chief, Soosai, made public appeals that the LTTE had enough arms and ammunition to take on Colombo but it was badly short of fighting hands. It was the truth.

Even as the LTTE pretended to respect international law in the main town of Batticaloa district, it ran amok in the interior villages. LTTE guerrillas banged on doors, threatened parents with dire consequences and took hold of unsuspecting and screaming kids from virtually every village, often quickly transporting them in autorickshaws towards the Batticaloa lagoon. From there, the children were put in boats to be taken to the large LTTE camp at Vakarai so as to evade army checkpoints on the land route.

Much of this happened in villages away from the coast, areas that escaped the wrath of the tsunami. The reasoning was simple: kidnappings from relief centres in tsunami hit coastal villages could cause outrage and Western censures. Also, once the tsunami struck, international NGOs and aid workers virtually stopped going to non-tsunami areas. But the Tigers need not have bothered. With the Sri Lankan state looking the other way, poor Tamil parents were left to fend for themselves vis-à-vis the belligerent Tigers. To the distraught Tamil families, this was worse than the tsunami.

A tea stall owner in Koduvamadu village (Chenkalady division) wailed over the abduction of his 15-year-old son, grabbed from nearby fields by a band of LTTE members. The boy used to earn 100 rupees a day as a farm hand to supplement the meagre income of the straitened family. The heart-broken father went to the LTTE intelligence wing office at Illupadichenai as many as nine times over a week to beg for the boy's release. The LTTE procrastinated before finally telling him that his son was being held for an "enquiry". This was a lie because the boy had no previous involvement with any militant group and had no criminal past.

The LTTE refused to free the boy, who was eventually sent to the battlefield to take on the Sri Lankan military. The family had lost to the tsunami several of its members who had lived close to the coast. Now their main livelihood source had been whisked away. The boy's mother was inconsolable and asked aid workers, "Why do we poor people have to be crushed like this?"

There was no one to answer that question or the concerns of the scores of Tamil parents who lost their children—many in their teens—to the LTTE's unending appetite for child soldiers. The LTTE was acutely aware of the asymmetry in the numbers between the Sri Lankan state and its own forces. The situation was made worse by the killer tsunami. In no time, the LTTE fixed quotas for its units in each district in the north and east of the country to make up its lost numbers. After Karuna's revolt, the tsunami was a double blow.

It may have been a coincidence but the brunt of the forced recruitment was borne by Tamils in the eastern province. The overwhelmingly Tamil Batticaloa, the birthplace of Karuna, suffered the worst. Local LTTE commanders repeatedly turned down pleas from impoverished Tamil families to spare their children. The hardened guerrillas would get angry if parents of missing children complained to the UN and other aid agencies or approached LTTE camps and offices in the company of foreign aid workers.

At one such encounter with aid workers, who were aplenty in eastern Sri Lanka, LTTE leader Kaushalyan wanted to know why Tamil families had objections to their children fighting and dying for Tamil Eelam. He talked about the need to understand Tamil history before hectoring the LTTE over human rights. "When I left home on Anna's (Prabhakaran's) call, my mother also felt sad. But she was a brave woman who sacrificed everything for freedom. Please stop encouraging sentimentalism," he told an aid worker as he stood on the road opposite the Thenagam training camp of the LTTE, beyond the Chenkalady black bridge. His devotion to Prabhakaran cost him his life.

Despite promising the UN that it would not go for child combatants, the LTTE finally declared that this was a "Tamil issue" and that outsiders had no role to play in the affair. A mother who went to an LTTE office accompanied by aid workers was told to come the next day. When she did that, the area leader of the LTTE warned her that she would be hung from the nearest tree if she ever came again asking for her son.

Unfortunately, the peace process failed to recognize the enormity of the crime committed against the Tamil population by the LTTE. Once conscription became too rampant to be ignored, the UN and others did become vocal.[40] At their own level, many aid workers were appalled. Many of them were sincerely committed to enforcing human rights. They did what they could to help rescue as many young and unwilling combatants as possible. But sections of the international community appeared to take at face value, numerous explanations trotted out by the LTTE vis-à-vis the children in its ranks. And since the LTTE's continued cooperation was vital for the success of the peace process, not many wanted to rock the boat too violently.

There was also legalese the LTTE cleverly exploited. If the concern of the world was for underage or minor children (aged under 18), then the Tigers only had to prove that the fighters in its ranks were over 18. In some cases, this was simply not possible; those kids were let off. But conscription of those over 18 too was rampant. This was no issue for some international aid and rights groups although it was no less a crime.

Innumerable Tamil teenagers and those in the early 20s were petrified for their lives. The LTTE treated them as high-value targets, more so if they had had training before. Many worried families in Tamil areas married off their young as early as possible in a desperate bid to keep them away from the LTTE's penchant for the unmarried youth.

The LTTE, however, was not the only guilty party in this respect. Once Karuna re-organized his forces, both before and after Mahinda Rajapaksa took over the presidency, he too found it convenient to forcibly recruit children. In any case he had done this and very successfully and ruthlessly, while in the LTTE. So this was not new to him. But this time he had the covert (and overt) backing of a military itching to take advantage of the fissures in the LTTE.

Many young men and women who had escaped from the LTTE after Karuna's revolt suddenly found themselves between the devil and the deep sea. If they took shelter in Sinhalese populated areas at the edge of the east, hoping to get away from the war theatre, they got picked up on suspicion of being LTTE spies. Worse, LTTE's feared "pistol groups",[41] operating under the command of the intelligence wing, were on the constant move to cut down deserters if they refused to re-enlist.

While workers of aid agencies, many from distant lands, performed under trying circumstances to save the missing children, their terrible plight failed to generate enough sympathy in India or in Western countries overseeing the peace process. The pro-LTTE Tamil diaspora of course saw nothing amiss.[42]

Although the children bolstered the badly needed numbers for the LTTE, their military value was always in doubt. Once Colombo took the battle into the east and then the north in real earnest, hordes of young boys and girls gave up and surrendered, unable to face the earth-shaking barrage of artillery and air attacks. They never had the will to fight, in the first place. In any case, those who—had families were desperate to be reunited. However, hundreds, many of whom had been dragged into a war they had no love for, got slaughtered. The LTTE could neither protect them—nor the mass of civilians. Across the northeast of Sri Lanka, particularly in the eastern province, numerous families mourned the numbing loss of their loved sons and daughters. In most cases, they could not even perform the last rites. With no one to come to their rescue, wailing parents cursed the LTTE, the government and themselves.

# XI

IF India played a vital role in the growth of the LTTE in the 1980s, partly consciously and partly unconsciously, it also ended up cold-bloodedly overseeing the decimation of the organization nearly two decades later. As the first country to outlaw the Tigers, New Delhi turned adamantly anti-LTTE from the time a woman suicide bomber acting on Prabhakaran's order stealthily blew up Rajiv Gandhi at a crowded election rally near Chennai on 21 May 1991.

It was a grotesque murder that ultimately cost the LTTE its Tamil Eelam—and Prabhakaran his life.

By the time Norway brokered a truce between Sri Lanka and the LTTE in February 2002, the Tigers had long concluded that India was a resolute foe, one determined not to allow the formation of a Tamil Eelam. New Delhi had no doubt helped the LTTE in many ways and the Tigers had used India in its growth trajectory; but it was more than evident that Prabhakaran had a mind of his own. His was a genuinely homegrown group and the enigmatic and elusive Prabhakaran had built it brick by brick. In its formative years, he would flee to south India whenever things became too hot in Jaffna. But he never was a slave of India, ideological or otherwise.

Prabhakaran realized correctly and early on, that New Delhi's military training to Tamil militant groups, the LTTE included, was not meant to break up Sri Lanka, but to pressure Colombo to talk peace. He also concluded, again accurately, that New Delhi would apply the squeeze one day, leaving the Tamil groups high and dry. So without fanfare, the LTTE boss put in place a well-oiled network to source arms and ammunition from around the world with money donated by the growing number of Tamil expatriates—so that the Indian brakes, when applied, would not halt the Eelam war.

It was one of Prabhakaran's wisest decisions.

The man picked for the task was only one year younger to him. In no time Selvarasa Pathmanathan proved an outstanding choice. He would modify his name to Kumaran Pathmanathan; so everyone addressed him as "KP". Here was a man with a natural talent for secrecy, forgery, business, and sophistication, all rolled into one. He came to acquire multiple identities and as many passports as he could lay his hands on. He reported direct to Prabhakaran, none else.

KP began by acquiring an old Chinese ship that was quickly christened "MV Chola". As the years rolled by, the LTTE added many more ships to its covert fleet, flying flags of countries such as Liberia and Panama. KP presided over a secretive unit whose perennial challenge was to acquire, from all over the world, everything the LTTE needed to pursue its war. This was a never-ending list that included arms and ammunition, aircraft parts, explosive material, sophisticated communication equipment, fibre-glass boats, etc. He also smuggled gold and, possibly, narcotics.[43]

In any country he visited or operated in, he took care not to confine himself to Tamil circles. In New Delhi, for instance, he made friends with north Indians in the hospitality industry, although the city boasts of several thousands of Tamils. For the double life he led, KP was not averse to befriending and having a good time with women if that bolstered the cause. KP subscribed to the view that all is fair in love and war. And the LTTE was waging war, a costly one at that.

Year after year KP remained constantly on the move, flying and sailing to one country after another, always a step or two ahead of law enforcing agencies in several countries. He was now in Southeast Asia, then in Central Asia. He shopped for arms at the Thailand-Cambodia border; he bought weapons from Lebanon. He was in Britain one week and he was elsewhere in Europe, the next. Even after he entered the Interpol's Wanted List, there seemed to be no trace of the man. LTTE supporters saw KP as the most elusive of all Pimpernels—and were proud of him. Few could have matched KP's skills. It would be accurate to say that just as there would have been no LTTE without Prabhakaran, there may have been no Prabhakaran minus KP.

All good things do come to an end.

Coinciding with the tensions surrounding Karuna, Prabhakaran decided around 2003 to clip KP's wings. The LTTE had already signed a Norway-brokered ceasefire agreement with Colombo. The situation looked bright for the LTTE even though it had walked away from the peace talks in April 2003 after the US failed to invite it to an international conference. Prabhakaran was the virtual lord and master of all that he surveyed in the island nation's north and east—perhaps more. Even those who did not support him viewed Prabhakaran as the arbiter of Sri Lanka's destiny.

War had not only come to a halt but its early resumption seemed unlikely, what with the international community keeping a close watch on Sri Lanka and Prime Minister Wickremesinghe strongly wedded to the ceasefire agreement. Now was the time to consolidate. Anyway, KP had held the job too long.[44] And a senior LTTE member, V. Manivannan, who went by his *nom de guerre*, Castro, had been eyeing KP's position. So Prabhakaran made Castro the chief of the international procurement division. There was only one hitch: Castro was ambitious all right, but was no match for the innately talented KP.

The change of guard proved to be a monumental blunder for the LTTE. When people list the follies of Prabhakaran to understand where he went wrong, they tend to overlook this development. Prabhakaran would rue KP's absence once the war picked up lethal speed from 2006 and the LTTE started losing one ship after another and suffering unprecedented battlefield reverses. After his aide Anton Balasingham succumbed to cancer in December 2006, Prabhakaran's loneliness only increased.

The Norwegians began to press the LTTE to name an international interlocutor they could deal with in the absence of the suave Balasingham. They too had concluded by then that Prabhakaran alone mattered in the LTTE, no matter what position others might hold. Unless one had the ability to reach him, even if indirectly, nothing could be achieved. Balasingham was a great asset in that sense. Notwithstanding the fissure that developed over the agreement signed in Oslo, promising to explore a federal solution to the conflict, Balasingham regained the LTTE chief's confidence. He enjoyed a unique proximity to Prabhakaran that afforded him to call a spade a spade when he wanted.[45] So Norway needed a replacement for Balasingham quickly.

Prabhakaran prevaricated—a folly he came to realize only when the situation turned from bad to worse and then to grim for the LTTE. Eventually, as the military began to choke the Tigers from the start of 2009, the LTTE chief dramatically resurrected KP. He was made chief of the newly set up Department of International Relations.

It was too late. There was no miracle KP would be able to unveil in 2009, to save a sinking ship called the LTTE. Although he began interacting with the Norwegians and later the Americans, he was not as astute as the late Balasingham. It was one thing to be an ace smuggler, it was quite another to posses diplomatic and negotiating skills. It was eventually left to KP to make the historic announcement that the LTTE was silencing its guns. KP was also one of the last persons outside Sri Lanka to talk to Prabhakaran before the Tiger chieftain met a chilling death in May 2009.[46] Lacking the charisma and appeal of Prabhakaran and Balasingham even among LTTE supporters, KP tried to resurrect a lifeless LTTE, but ended up getting abducted from Malaysia and landing in Sri Lanka's custody.

## XII

INDIA'S decision to arm, train, and finance Tamil militant groups has led many to believe that there would have been no militancy and no LTTE but for New Delhi and Indira Gandhi, the then Prime Minister. Nothing could be farther from the truth. There is no doubt that India's covert intervention in Sri Lanka's internal turmoil provided valuable oxygen to the militants in the early 1980s. More than the limited weaponry and money India gave away, it was the Indian sympathy and sanctuary that tilted the scales to the advantage of the Tamil rebels vis-à-vis a Sri Lanka not prepared for a full-blown insurgency then.

But if India's covert help was such a determining factor, then the militant groups that would have emerged the strongest, would have been the Tamil Eelam Liberation

Organization (TELO) or the People's Liberation Organization of Tamil Eelam (PLOT). The TELO, the one group that never showed any inclination for Marxism, was the recipient of the most generous Indian assistance. PLOT at one time had the most number of (potential) fighters in its ranks, probably up to 5,000, although it did not enjoy TELO's warm ties with New Delhi. But neither group grew beyond a point, for different reasons. The LTTE eventually crushed the TELO in 1986, accusing it of serving Indian interests, while PLOT suffered mainly due to internal convulsions.[47] Interestingly, when the TELO faced destruction at the hands of the LTTE, the Indian intelligence found, to its dismay, that it had no influence over the Tigers to stop the bloodbath.

Prabhakaran has to be given the main credit for the LTTE's systematic growth from a group of barely 40 men and fewer weapons in 1983 to one of the world's most lethal non-state fighting machines. Even his worst critics admit that the Tamil Eelam dream that Prabhakaran chased, overwhelmed him so much that he was prepared to go to any length to do what he thought was right. And he did just that.

India allowed Prabhakaran to grow (as in the other case of other militant leaders) but the LTTE chief outgrew India very rapidly—and cunningly. He realized the limitations of India vis-à-vis an independent Tamil Eelam. So while Sinhalese hardliners (and many Tamils, at least in the earlier stages) believed that India was committed to breaking up Sri Lanka à la Pakistan/Bangladesh, Prabhakaran understood that this would never happen. He confided this to some of his lieutenants. He decided to get his own crutches. For that, he had to keep away from the Indian strategic worldview while paying lip service to India.

The first major move Prabhakaran made in this direction was to quickly make the LTTE the dominant, if not the sole actor, in the militant arena. He feared that India could play one militant group against the other if there were rival, near-powerful outfits. So he went about systematically destroying other Tamil militants and groups although their members too were loyal to the Eelam cause. This ingrained nihilism was not an Indian gift.

Once the TELO and PLOT were gone, the EPRLF was made non-effective. Its surviving leaders were slaughtered in Chennai in 1990.[48] The Eelam Revolutionary Organizers (EROS) decided to ally with the LTTE. The moderate Tamil United Liberation Front (TULF) had become redundant. That left only the LTTE in the Tamil Eelam field. Once this happened, India had no choice but to deal with Prabhakaran—which is precisely what the Tiger chief wanted. New Delhi's decision not to come hard on the LTTE, when it destroyed the TELO in April–May 1986, was one of India's biggest strategic blunders.

Within months of TELO's destruction, New Delhi was forced to acknowledge the overarching importance of Prabhakaran in the scheme of things. In November 1986, when the South Asian Association of Regional Cooperation (SAARC) summit was held in Bangalore, Indian officials flew Prabhakaran and his aide Anton Balasingham to the city from Chennai, for a meeting with President Junius Jayewardene. But Prabhakaran was not interested in a provincial council; his eyes were set on Tamil Eelam. Predictably, the initiative failed. In less than two months, a bitter Prabhakaran quit India for good.

The 1987 India–Sri Lanka accord may have been a bold diplomatic venture, but it was destined to die because it sought to marginalize the LTTE and Prabhakaran in the long run. Prabhakaran understood quickly that the main aim of the agreement was to make him surrender his weapons—since his was the only group still fighting the military. The euphoria that followed the signing of the agreement by Rajiv Gandhi and Jayewardene in July 1987 was misplaced.[49] While a section of the Sri Lankan state no doubt wanted to sabotage the accord, Prabhakaran's antics contributed in a major way to its collapse.[50] It led to war between the LTTE and the Indian military, with predictable suffering for the civilian population. In the end, the Indian military deployment ended in disaster while the LTTE reigned supreme in Sri Lanka's northeast.

The LTTE no doubt fought the Indians doggedly. But it is doubtful if Rajiv Gandhi would have called off the troops if Sri Lankan President Ranasinghe Premadasa had not publicly insisted on their withdrawal. The Indian decision to end the military intervention in Sri Lanka gave Prabhakaran a false sense of pride that he was invincible. He was—but only in the short run. From then on, he remained uneasy about the Indian establishment and its intentions. It was the fear of Rajiv Gandhi's return to power and another possible confrontation with India that led Prabhakaran to take a decision that he and the LTTE rued till their own destruction: Gandhi's assassination.

The Gandhi killing led India to shut its doors and windows to the LTTE forever. Except to its hardcore supporters in Tamil Nadu, the LTTE became a dirty word. Henceforth, the LTTE cause would never get diplomatic recognition, anywhere. Even when the Norway-brokered peace process got under way, it soon became clear to Prabhakaran that India would never, never make up with the Tigers. His initial I-care-a-damn attitude eventually gave way to frustration.

Prabhakaran mellowed vis-à-vis India as Sri Lanka started to hit him hard. In 2006, when India wanted to send relief material to displaced civilians, the LTTE was happy to cooperate. It agreed to allow vehicles carrying Indian goods to use the A-9 highway without any checks or delays (The highway linked Jaffna to the rest of Sri Lanka and was partly controlled by the Tigers). It even conveyed to the Indian High Commission in Colombo that Indian helicopters could land in Vakarai, a LTTE governed region in the country's east.

After a Sri Lankan air attack in November 2007 killed S.P. Tamilchelvan, the LTTE political head, Prabhakaran went a step further and said he did not desire enmity with India. B. Nadesan, who succeeded Tamilchelvan, conveyed this message to a Tamil National Alliance (TNA) MP. The LTTE, Nadesan went on, would never accept weapons from any country inimical to Indian interests even if the Tigers felt choked. "Our leader (Prabhakaran) wants this conveyed to the Indian government and the Indian people," Nadesan told the MP after Tamilchelvan's funeral.

The message found its way to New Delhi but India remained unmoved.

Years of dealing with the LTTE had made Indian policymakers and strategic thinkers wiser and cautious—vis-à-vis Prabhakaran. The LTTE wallowed under the mistaken impression that it could play Tamil Nadu, where many politicians supported it in varying degrees, against the central Indian government. But the times had changed.

Despite heading a coalition that relied on vital support from political parties in Tamil Nadu, Prime Minister Manmohan Singh (and Congress president Sonia Gandhi) did not allow India's Sri Lanka policy to be torpedoed. New Delhi was well aware that over the years, the LTTE had pointedly killed Tamils deemed pro-India and forced many others to turn against India. Even after the 2002 truce, the LTTE cold-bloodedly killed poor sari traders from Tamil Nadu in Sri Lanka's northeast fearing they could be Indian spies.[51]

In the end, however, the LTTE lost the battle of nerves against India, without even realizing it. Long before it was crushed, the Indian intelligence had developed moles in the LTTE. Although it was RAW the LTTE was in perennial dread of, it was the less assuming Intelligence Bureau—the domestic intelligence agency—that ran rings around the Tigers. It not only thwarted sustained efforts by the LTTE to revive the support base in Tamil Nadu but also played a major role in accurately monitoring the reverses the LTTE suffered during its final retreat—until Prabhakaran lay dead. In the process, it proved the hollowness of LTTE claims that it was withstanding the Sri Lankan military onslaught.

One of the biggest successes the Intelligence Bureau scored was when Soosai, the LTTE Sea Tigers chief, suffered serious wounds in what initially looked like a mysterious accident off Sri Lanka's northeast in 2007, that left his young son and a bodyguard dead.

What really happened?

Soosai had ordered the construction of a 52-feet long vessel and was overseeing its test run close to the coast. He himself was in a 27-feet boat with his five-year-old son and bodyguards. For reasons that never became clear, the bigger vessel suddenly picked up speed and tore into Soosai's boat.

It all happened in a few split seconds. Soosai's vessel broke into two. His son was thrown into the sea and drowned in no time. A weapon held by one of the bodyguards pierced Soosai's ribs from the left. Soosai lost his consciousness and he too fell into the water (One of his bodyguards died in the incident but the LTTE did not reveal this initially).

The incident triggered wild rumours including one that Soosai, wanting to do another Karuna, was trying to flee from the LTTE but Prabhakaran had had him killed. There was also speculation that Soosai's deputies had prevented their boss from escaping and promptly alerted Prabhakaran.

None of this was true. A badly injured Soosai, who grieved a lot over his son's unexpected death, was provided medical care at a house in Pudukudiyarappu. As one of the seniormost commanders, the best of doctors attended on him. He was ordered to rest for three weeks.

The Indian establishment learnt the story from an LTTE insider who managed to call on the convalescing Soosai, who was both amused and alarmed over the rumours surrounding him. The LTTE source also reported that a concerned Prabhakaran had called on Soosai to enquire about his health. The Indians were among the first to know the full story.

## XIII

THE year was 2005. Sri Lanka was in turmoil. War was in the air. Killings were on the rise. An aid worker in the eastern town of Batticaloa casually asked an officer from Sri Lanka's military intelligence: which place in the country could be considered the safest? The major, a Sinhalese, pondered briefly before blurting out: "Come to think of it, it must be Prabhakaran's bunker!" The major and the aid worker had a hearty laugh.

But that was no joke. The answer was apt—in 2005. And it held true even for a couple of years later. Prabhakaran had after all been in the thick of it right from the 1970s and had constantly kept himself many steps ahead of all his foes. The authorities were never able to trap him. And despite a brutal war, Prabhakaran managed to keep himself unscathed and unhurt through many tumultuous years.

Diabetes did catch up with him but neither did the Indian Army nor the Sri Lankan Army until 2009. Only once, when the Indians rained artillery towards his hideout in the Wanni region, did the man come anywhere close to getting hurt. A shell exploded not far from him and threw up dust on his battle fatigues, momentarily stunning him.

No wonder, Prabhakaran became a cult figure for all those who believed in the war he was waging. Even for those who hated him, he was undoubtedly an enigma. How could this man go on and on? Wasn't he a father of three children? How did he manage so much of resources? From where does he procure his arms and ammunition? How does he coax so many Tamil men and women to die at his bidding? How could he command such authority? Where did his appeal come from? Just how does he survive? Where is his family? Can Sri Lanka ever defeat such a formidable foe? Will Prabhakaran ever be caught—or killed?

The questions nagged everyone in Sri Lanka and beyond.

Yet, from 2005 when it was stated that Prabhakaran's bunker was the safest place in Sri Lanka until the rebel chieftain's nemesis in May 2009, the LTTE's slide to destruction was so rapid, that it left those loyal to the Tamil Eelam cause, speechless. Many simply refused to believe that the guerrilla boss they adored was dead. The questions now were very different. How *did* this happen? How *could* this happen? Wasn't he supposed to lead them to Tamil Eelam? Hadn't he promised them victory? How could the LTTE be snuffed out? How could all LTTE leaders die so suddenly? Why did Prabhakaran not escape? How could a Sinhalese army, which the Tamil diaspora and the LTTE despised, manage to trap and kill Prabhakaran?

The reasons for the LTTE's destruction are many. To understand the phenomenon called the Tamil Tigers, it is crucial to understand the man who led it, from its very birth to its very ugly end.

## XIV

WHEN Prabhakaran plunged into militancy,[52] he was a young nobody. He was a product of the times when Sinhalese–Tamil relations were souring and leading to conditions that pushed hotheads in the Tamil community towards violence. The politics of the Tamil United Liberation Front (TULF), at one time *the* party of the Tamils, was their umbrella. Smothered by Sinhalese obduracy, the TULF made aggressive noises that immensely appealed to the restive young Tamils. The thinking was if the elders are ready for battle, why should we, the young, sit idle?

Sri Lanka's inability to heal the ethnic wounds following independence from Britain in 1948, catapulted the island nation from one crisis to another. The nascent militancy in the Tamil areas, particularly in Jaffna, led to iron-fisted steps that only added to the problem. It is to escape police torture and death that Prabhakaran, then a teenager, fled his home for good one night in the early 1970s. Had the police caught up with him then, history would have been different. That was not to be. Luck was on his side.

Prabhakaran's worldview was limited when he founded the LTTE. The year, according to LTTE, was 1976. The killing of Jaffna's Tamil Mayor, Alfred Duriappah, the previous year, arose from a mindset that Tamils and Sinhalese were historical enemies and a Tamil person had no right to be on the side of the Sinhalese establishment. This is not what the majority of the Tamil people thought, but this remained Prabhakaran's central theme all through the years he lived. This worldview prevented him from reaching any settlement with Colombo, even if it seemed fair and just to many, because many of the Tamils he killed had advocated precisely such a negotiated deal.

The ideological foundation on which Prabhakaran's LTTE rested decreed that the Tamils and Sinhalese constituted two nations and that they could not co-exist peacefully. Much like the self-consuming theory that led to the birth of Islamic Pakistan out of Hindu-majority India in 1947, Prabhakaran insisted uncompromisingly that the Tamil nation had to break away from the Sinhalese-majority Sri Lanka.

Prabhakaran considered himself the messiah of the Tamils—and the man ordained to decide the future of the community. Although a poor speaker, he preached Tamil separatism more vocally and more passionately than all others in the militant ranks. Unfortunately for Sri Lanka, ideology and politics did not interest him beyond a point. This led him to give primacy to the gun. Naturally, he came to command many followers who agreed that violence was the only way out. After initial setbacks, Prabhakaran became the LTTE and the LTTE became Prabhakaran. Once he reached that stage, the next step was logical: anyone who disagreed with him was deemed to be disagreeing with the Tamil cause and thus a "traitor" deserving death.

In the process, Tamils, young and old, who were as passionate about the Tamil community, but who thought differently, began to die at the hands of the LTTE. The earliest victims were innocuous Tamils who were simply counted as statistics when they turned into corpses. These included young members of rival groups gunned down like street dogs, even as some of them begged for mercy. When Prabhakaran picked someone to be killed, it did not matter if the person had helped him in the past.[53]

The likes of Appapillai Amirthalingam, the once towering TULF leader, and his colleagues followed. Rajani Thiranagama, a brilliant academic and Tamil nationalist, paid the price for thinking differently and criticizing the Tigers. Men like Neelan Thiruchelvam, a renowned constitutional lawyer, and Lakshman Kadirgamar, the highly regarded foreign minister of Sri Lanka, came later. In Prabhakaran's eyes, all these Tamil men (and women) deserved to die because they had embraced or tried to co-exist with ideas that conflicted with his vision. Finally, after a quarter century of armed struggle that left the world amazed with its military exploits, Prabhakaran could only turn to a man wanted by Interpol when he desired a successor, to the late Anton Balasingham!

One man walked away from the LTTE in its early years and moved to the West when it dawned on him that even disagreeing with Prabhakaran could invite death. He would tell me years later:

I questioned him about something at an LTTE meeting. He didn't like it. He gave me looks that could kill. I knew what it meant. He would kill me for what he thought was my audacity. I wanted to live. I simply left the LTTE.

In the early 1980s, a middle-rung TULF leader in Jaffna had a close brush with death after voicing critical remarks about the LTTE. That very night, a young man armed with a pistol came looking for him at his house. The TULF activist sensed the danger and hid himself until the frustrated to-be assassin retreated.

Violence became the preferred answer to settle disputes and differences. This, in turn, instilled fear about the LTTE in the minds of everyone it confronted.[54] All this helped when Prabhakaran built a formidable military organization, killing at will and turning assassinations into a fine art. Militarily too, few could have achieved what Prabhakaran managed to.

From an era when LTTE members relied on cycles to reach their unsuspecting targets, Prabhakaran went on to acquire a fleet of ships and, much later, a handful of modified light aircraft, that even bombed Colombo. For a man who once craved to see just 100 LTTE members marching in uniform, Prabhakaran came to preside over thousands of heavily armed men and women fighters. He proved repeatedly that he had the ability to come out of the tightest corners. Even those who considered him a foe admitted this.

Away from the battlefield, the LTTE displayed an uncanny ability for Machiavellian politics that tripped even Ranasinghe Premadasa, otherwise a veteran of Sri Lankan politics.[55] By the turn of this century, Sri Lanka appeared to be at its wit's end, vis-à-vis the Tigers. No less a person than General Sarath Fonseka, the army chief, was to tell an Indian journalist: "When I took over (in late 2005), most officers had the mentality that we cannot win this war, as had been the case in the past three Eelam wars."[56]

So how did Prabhakaran fall?

As he galloped from strength to strength, Prabhakaran forgot that his uncompromising strategy based on narrow Tamil nationalism combined with political immaturity and sheer terror could not last forever. He mistakenly concluded from New Delhi's decision to withdraw its army from Sri Lanka and Colombo's recurring failures to overcome the Tigers that the LTTE had become unbeatable. The international community's repeated assertions that the Sri Lankan conflict could only see a negotiated end gave a false sense of superiority and security to Prabhakaran. The de facto Tamil Eelam, that he presided over, came to be perceived by him as a guarantee that the ground situation could never be reversed. He misread Tamil Nadu and misread the West. The University Teachers for Human Rights (Jaffna), a Tamil rights group critical of the war, was perhaps the first to observe that the LTTE, its visible muscles notwithstanding, was hollow from inside.

## XV

WHEN Prabhakaran shifted to India in late 1983, he wanted to have the cake and eat it too. He took material help from India but he would not trust the Indian state. Once he understood Indian officialdom, he played one wing of the government against the other. When it suited him, he contemptuously ignored DMK chief M. Karunanidhi because he wanted to be in the good books of his rival and Chief Minister M.G. Ramachandran or MGR. An amount of Rs 250,000 raised due to Karunanidhi's efforts was to be distributed among five Tamil groups, including the LTTE. Prabhakaran, out to prove his loyalty to MGR, spurned the donation. But when MGR died,[57] the LTTE boss quickly embraced Karunanidhi as if his previous humiliation of him meant nothing.

Karunanidhi had not forgotten the earlier insult, however. One of the first things the LTTE had to do during the 1989–91 DMK regime was to sheepishly accept the Rs 50,000 it had rejected years ago. There was no other way of getting into the good books of Karunanidhi. But the LTTE remained focused on its long-term goal. By the mid-1990s, Tiger literature proudly began proclaiming Prabhakaran as the leader of the Tamils the world over—another quiet snub to Karunanidhi.

Prabhakaran's men prided themselves as a disciplined force on Indian soil. But they had no second thoughts about killing rival Tamils in cold blood in the heart of the state. If that wasn't bad enough, the LTTE chief went on to assassinate Rajiv Gandhi, a former prime minister who had once personally presented him a bulletproof jacket. After the deed was done, Prabhakaran brazenly denied his involvement and dared the Indians to prove his guilt in a court of law! To cap it all, the LTTE chief had the audacity to expect Rajiv Gandhi's widow, Sonia Gandhi, to come to his rescue when the Sri Lankan military cornered him. When she did not do that, she was dubbed anti-Tamil!

Arrogance led the LTTE to commit follies it should have never indulged in. After delivering several near knockout blows to Colombo, the LTTE concluded that Sri Lanka would never be able to stand on its two legs. It was over-confidence that made the LTTE think it could take the Tamil community for granted, despite inflicting so much suffering on it, during the course of the long war. It was political immaturity that pushed the group to turn against India and ignore the sensitivities of an international community that was prepared to invest a lot to help end a seemingly unending conflict. So much so that Prabhakaran even upset Norway that was sympathetic to Tamil aspirations for greater autonomy.

When anti-Tamil violence swept Sri Lanka in 1983, Tamil militancy was widely seen as a legitimate response to a callous state. It was Prabhakaran who took away the moral sheen when he ordered the massacre of innocent Buddhist monks and nuns at the holy site of Anuradhapura in 1985. The next year, in a savage display of brutality that numbed the Tamil community, the LTTE massacred hundreds of guerrillas from the rival TELO group in Jaffna. In no time, a group, claiming to be fighting for the "liberation" of Tamils, ended up holding hundreds of dissenting Tamils in its own prisons.[58] Even LTTE supporters were shocked when it jailed Rajasingham Jayadevan, one of its high profile supporters and a British national, for 62 long days in its fiefdom in February–March 2005 before Scotland Yard's intervention led to his freedom. The slide began a long time ago.

Among the first to realize that the LTTE had become a menace to the Tamils was British scholar David Selbourne, who once sympathized with the Tamil political grievances. After EROS snuffled out the life of a respected Tamil activist,[59] a disgusted Selbourne prophesied that militants such as Prabhakaran were leading the Tamils "towards long term political and moral disaster". He warned: "There will neither be Eelam, nor 'true' federalism, nor genuine devolution, nor anything else which is just and fair to the Tamils this century, if ever." Armed with remarkable political foresight, Selbourne spoke these words in 1988. A good 21 years later, the man was proved incredibly right!

By the time President Mahinda Rajapaksa launched his all out assault on Prabhakaran, the LTTE had become a bundle of contradictions. If the LTTE made peace with the authorities, it was strategy; if other Tamils did so, it was treachery. If the Tigers took arms and ammunition from India, they were clever and scheming; if others did so, they were RAW agents. Premadasa and Rajapaksa were pragmatic if they spoke to the Tigers; they were Sinhalese chauvinists if they waged war. The LTTE had a right to do political work in government territory; others could not enjoy the privilege in Tiger land. Karuna's child conscription was legitimate if he was in the LTTE; it was a crime if he scooped the kids after deserting the group. Prabhakaran would deny involvement in Rajiv Gandhi's killing one day; the LTTE would seek (half-hearted) forgiveness from India another day. Norwegian diplomats were friends if what they did or said helped the LTTE; they were to be shunned if they did not bow to Tiger wishes. Tamil politicians deserved to die if they were independent; they could live if they surrendered to the LTTE. We are not terrorists, Prabhakaran would keep parroting; but he would callously kill innocent civilians whenever he got the chance.

It was amid such discrepancies that Prabhakaran signed the 2002 ceasefire agreement with Prime Minister Wickremesinghe—at a time when he, the perennial rebel, was viewed unbeatable militarily. It was the best opportunity the LTTE had to seek a lasting peace—after the Indian intervention of 1987. In retrospect, it is clear that Prabhakaran never wanted to make peace. He wanted to use the truce to strengthen himself to wage war for Tamil Eelam. And he did that.

So, when Sri Lanka was to elect a new President in 2005, Prabhakaran callously spiked the chances of Wickremesinghe by asking Tamils to boycott the elections. This *alone* led to the victory, albeit by a very narrow margin, of Mahinda Rajapaksa, who was considered a Sinhalese hardliner. The LTTE's grotesque thinking was that a Sinhalese nationalist in Colombo would inevitably widen the Tamil–Sinhalese gulf. This would surely lead to war—and to predictable civilian suffering. The LTTE would then tell the world (read West) that there was no way but to carve out an independent Tamil Eelam—à la East Timor and Kosovo.

It did not happen that way. The world had changed irrevocably since 9/11. The era of terrorism was over, more so if the terrorists had planes to fly. The West and Japan would have generously helped the LTTE if it seriously desired a settlement within Sri Lanka. The Norwegians had virtually handed over federalism on a platter to the LTTE. But no one wanted Sri Lanka to split. That was the bottom line. Prabhakaran did not understand this. Rajapaksa did. And so he proved to be Prabhakaran's nemesis.

## XVI

THOSE who had been with the LTTE and those who knew its working well are unanimous that the 2002 ceasefire agreement laid the foundations for the long-term destruction of the Tigers as a military force.

Way back in 1994–95, Prabhakaran had emphasized to Balasingham that LTTE cadres would get rusted in peace. Maybe his thinking had changed in 2002. But the end result was the same. Once the ceasefire period dragged on and on, many in the LTTE thought it was best to enjoy the de facto state that already existed instead of shedding more and more blood for a mirage called Tamil Eelam. The truce was a badly needed breather for young men and women who, for years, had known nothing but war and suffering. Peace finally allowed them to enjoy life and the power they wielded.

Many got married to colleagues they had been in love with over a period of time. Once that happened, families put pressure on the guerrillas: Enough is enough, how long will you keep fighting? Said a man while describing the life in LTTE territory: "LTTE leaders would go to the market with their wives and children for ice cream. It was a scene unimaginable in the past." Naturally, discipline slackened. There were desertions, which forced the LTTE to go for further child recruitment; this in turn mounted the silent anger in the Tamil community. Ordinary Tamils leading a near primitive life in LTTE zones were aghast on seeing the luxurious lifestyle of Tiger commanders during the ceasefire period. Some commanders had 24-hour running water, uninterrupted power supply, and mansions that could be compared with the best.[60] The alienation was complete.

Then Karuna broke away with thousands of guerrillas, dealing deathblows to the LTTE. His aides have admitted that it was his exposure to the West during the peace talks that opened his eyes to the outside world. One former LTTE woman guerrilla was equally emphatic that, of all the factors that contributed to the LTTE's fall, the Norway-sponsored truce played a key role although that was not its intention. She told me in an interview: "The CFA (ceasefire agreement) destroyed the LTTE."

Unconsciously, the Tamil diaspora, large sections of which were vocally pro-LTTE, added to the slide of the Tamil Tigers. When visits by Tamil expatriates to the LTTE zone shot up following the ceasefire, LTTE leaders suddenly saw what good life was all about. They saw that Tamils coming from abroad were healthier, better dressed, and wealthy too. If the diaspora had wanted, it could have stepped up pressure on the LTTE to make peace with the Sri Lankan government. It may not have succeeded. But at least the world would have realized that sections of the influential Tamil community were serious about a genuine political settlement as opposed to the LTTE's persistent love for war and gore.

Regrettably, that did not happen. The rest, as they say, is history.

# Notes

1. See David Selbourne. 1989. "What Low Brutishness was That?", in *An Untimely Death: A Commemoration of K. Kanthasamy.* Kanthasamy Commemoration Committee, Colombo.

2. Interview to the author, Colombo.

3. The JVP, a Marxist group rooted dominantly in the Sinhalese society, staged two bloody insurrections to capture power—in 1971 and 1988–89. Both were put down violently at the cost of tens of thousands of lives. Most of the dead were young Sinhalese men, mainly from rural areas, the same constituency from which the army recruited soldiers. The latter revolt decimated the established JVP leadership. I was a frequent visitor to Sri Lanka when the second uprising took place. The JVP insurrections showed that Colombo, when faced with deathly crisis, killed at will, no matter who the victims were, ethnically. Indeed, the first mass victims of the Sri Lankan state were the Sinhalese themselves, not Tamils.

4. To know more about the evolution of Prabhakaran, read my unauthorized biography, *Inside an Elusive Mind*, (New Delhi: Konark Publishers, 2003). Unlike my first book, *Tigers of Lanka*, the LTTE did not appreciate *Inside an Elusive Mind*, which quickly become a must read for anyone wanting to understand the Tigers. The first book deals with the origins and evolution of Tamil militancy as well as India's overt and covert involvement in the crisis.

5. Eelam War I was fought from 1983–87; Eelam War II from 1990–94; Eelam War III from 1995–2002 and Eelam War IV from 2006–09. The LTTE fought the Indian Army from 10 October 1987 onwards. The last of Indian soldiers sailed home from Trincomalee on 24 March 1990.

6. My interest in the Sri Lankan conflict followed the anti-Tamil violence of 1983 that truly heralded Tamil militancy. In the early years, most Tamil groups published literature dominantly in Tamil and were constantly on the lookout for journalists in New Delhi who could speak and read Tamil. I recall getting a letter in 1984 from B. Nadesan (who later became the LTTE political wing leader and was killed in May 2009) promising to send me LTTE literature regularly. He never kept the pledge.

   My first and only solo meeting with Prabhakaran took place in a hotel in New Delhi in 1985, courtesy a Chennai-based Indian supporter of another Tamil militant group. I was probably the first journalist to speak to LTTE's Anton Balasingham, its ideologue, after he and Prabhakaran returned to their hotel after meeting Rajiv Gandhi, hours before the Indian Prime Minister flew to Colombo on 29 July 1987 to sign a pact with Sri Lanka that sought to end Tamil separatism.

   My first visit to Sri Lanka was on 5 August 1987, coinciding with the surrender of weapons by the LTTE. Along with several Indian journalists, we flew directly from New Delhi to Jaffna's Palaly air base in a Soviet-built Il–76 transporter. It was a journey that showed India in poor light because none of the journalists had visa to visit the country.

   I visited Colombo for the first time in February 1987 in the aftermath of the assassination of Vijaya Kumaratunga, the hugely popular actor-husband of Chandrika, who would later become the President. Since then I have been to Sri Lanka numerous times and interacted with a very large number of people of all ethnic shades. I have spoken to army officers and LTTE guerrillas, traders and Buddhist monks, academics and politicians, auto-rickshaw drivers and human rights activists, politicians, and journalists.

Unfortunately, some people I knew intimately are no more. Most died violent deaths. In a few cases, I have never been able to guess who the killers were.

One night in October 1988, Indian soldiers took me away from a run down hotel room in Vavuniya (where I had halted en route from Jaffna to Colombo) and made me undergo an identification parade aimed at weeding out LTTE suspects. I revealed my identity to the startled soldiers only after it was all over. I had heard about these cordon-and-search operations and wanted to know how the soldiers dealt with the civilians.

Rajiv Gandhi's assassination brought about a dramatic transformation in the LTTE–India relationship. One fine day in 1995, Nirupama Subramaniam, a gifted Indian journalist who spent many years in Sri Lanka, and I made our way to LTTE-held Vakarai in Batticaloa to meet Tiger leaders in the eastern province. As we entered the LTTE territory in a taxi, a LTTE boy posted as a lookout, no older than 17 years, got into our vehicle. He was angry that India had turned its back on the Eelam struggle. He talked non-stop, occasionally insisting that the LTTE could have never killed Gandhi.

Driving on, we encountered a large group of LTTE men, some of them armed. They were curious about our visit. One of them took the boy aside and whispered something to him. The boy nodded. When we resumed our journey to the LTTE's main office, the boy had gone sullenly silent. He would not even reply to our questions.

The LTTE contacted me from London in November 1998 and offered an advance copy of Prabhakaran's annual speech. I was with AFP. Those days there was no Internet and the LTTE leaked the eagerly awaited policy address first to a friendly media (which thus earned a scoop) and then to others, around the time it was broadcast on its clandestine Voice of Tigers radio. I was surprised I had been chosen for the honour. Since I was never their supporter, I believed it must have been because of my first book on the Tamil conflict that had been published some years before.

I must now reveal why I rejected the speech, a decision that startled the London office of the LTTE. When I got in touch with AFP Sri Lanka bureau chief Amal Jayasinghe, I realized the LTTE was cunningly using me to undermine him. The LTTE had been upset with his reporting for some time and had complained to AFP Paris that Amal was more of a "Sinhalese" than an independent journalist (This was slander because Amal was and is one of the best in wire service journalism). By giving the Prabhakaran speech to me, an AFP journalist in New Delhi, the LTTE wanted to show Amal (who headed the Sri Lanka office) in poor light. After hearing his version, I knew I had a decision to make: stand by a friend or earn a scoop. I chose Amal.

I was among the journalists who attended the 2002 press conference of Prabhakaran at Kilinochchi. It is the first time I saw how the LTTE subtly discriminated between whites and non-whites (both Sri Lankans and Indians). As journalists streamed into LTTE territory, the Tigers allocated different places for them to stay. Most of the whites got plush rooms a little distance away from us, while the rest had to be content with cemented but frog-infested floors for the night. This must have been planned to impress the Western world, which has the power to bestow sovereignty by recognizing some secessionist movements as representatives of independent states.

During the Indian military presence in Sri Lanka, LTTE representatives in Chennai (where the Tigers maintained an office though they were fighting the Indian Army!) contacted me in my Colombo hotel room. They wanted to know if they could get four prints of a photograph AFP had distributed, showing the LTTE releasing a captured Indian soldier in Vavuniya.

AFP gives out its photographs only to subscribers. However, AFP's then South Asia Deputy Bureau Chief in New Delhi, Kate Webb (a fine journalist from New Zealand, who is no more), ruled that we could spare four prints so that we don't lose our ties to the LTTE. I relayed the decision to the LTTE over telephone and added that I would be in Chennai after a week on my way to New Delhi. Could they come to my hotel and pick up the photos? And could they bring some printed LTTE literature as a *quid pro quo*?

Two young LTTE men armed with motorcycle helmets entered my room around 11 in the night. I gave away the photographs and ordered coffee as a mark of courtesy. I then made small talk with them. But the men appeared to be in no mood to leave. I had an early morning flight for New Delhi and I was determined to catch at least a few hours of sleep. Finally, when I suggested to them that it was time they left, one of the men took out his wallet.

I knew what it meant: money was on offer.

I was disgusted and had not expected this. I told my two visitors politely, but sternly, that I had spent no money in taking the photographs or developing the prints. These were AFP property and they were not on sale. The LTTE was not a subscriber either. And I did not need any money. The men mumbled their apologies and left.

All these encounters were valuable lessons to my understanding of the LTTE. I have never had any illusions about the LTTE's inability to live in peace in Sri Lanka. I told Norwegian diplomats at my very first meeting with them in 2003 that they would never be able to bring around the LTTE.

7. At the start of August 2008, the LTTE was in control of about 4,000 sq km of land or 6 per cent of Sri Lanka's territory. And the population under its control was over 250,000, a mere 1.25 per cent of the country's total. This was a far cry from the time when, according to President Chandrika Kumaratunga, the LTTE had controlled a third of all land in Sri Lanka and two-thirds of the winding coastline.

8. More and more accounts of how the LTTE dealt with itself and the Tamil population at large, are beginning to come to light. These are bound to inspire rethinking about a lot of preconceived notions. For one of the most readable versions, in Tamil, of the LTTE's final months, please see Anon. "What happened in the Wanni", Availble online at http://thesamnet.co.uk/?p=15418 (accessed on 26 August 2009).

9. In the process, some families who had originally fled towards Kilinochchi (when it was still with the LTTE) from Mannar in the northwest to escape the advancing army, ended up moving from one place to another as many as 20 times. By the time the fighting ceased in May 2009, many families had lost all their possessions except the clothes they were in. Fearing for their lives, they lived, slept, and ate in hurriedly dug bunkers. But LTTE guerrillas refused to let them go over to government territory. Those who tried were shot.

10. LTTE supporters in the Wanni made telephone calls to New Delhi with this message two days before Prabhakaran was killed.

11. The publication of Prabhakaran's unauthorized biography made the LTTE brand me as an Indian spy—a convenient allegation the Tigers hurled at anyone they didn't like. The charge was made both on select LTTE websites and in person. S. Pulideevan, who headed the LTTE Peace Secretariat and was killed in May 2009, spread the slander to

Colombo-based Western diplomats with whom he was in touch. If the attempt was to prevent people from talking to me, it had the direct opposite effect! The biography opened the most unexpected doors and windows to me—in India and abroad.

12. Outside of the Indian government, no one I know kept such a meticulous record of the refugee arrivals as S.C. Chandrahasan, a Sri Lankan Tamil whose NGO has worked among the refugees for decades. A lawyer by training, the Chennai-based Chandrahasan is the son of the legendary Tamil political leader S.J.V. Chelvanayakam.

13. Karuna, the breakaway LTTE commander, told me in the first half of October 2008 that the Tigers were in "a precarious condition" but no one could predict when they can be overcome militarily. "There can be no deadlines (to defeat the LTTE). In no war can deadlines be set." By then, however, military officials had claimed that the LTTE would be vanquished by 2008-end. They later extended the time frame to mid-2009, which incidentally coincided with Lok Sabha elections in India.

14. BJP leader Atal Bihari Vajpayee became prime minister for a second time in 1998. (His first experiment in government formation collapsed in just 13 days.) His government was voted out by parliament after 13 months. The BJP won the elections that followed in 1999 and went on to become the first non-Congress party government to complete a full term in office.

15. India outlawed the LTTE in 1992; a year after a woman suicide bomber blew up Rajiv Gandhi.

16. Talking about an earlier era, J.N. Dixit, India's High Commissioner to Sri Lanka and later the Foreign Secretary, noted in his book *Assignment Colombo* (New Delhi: Konark Publishers, 1998): "The RAW … had become not just an intelligence and information factor but a political factor directly influencing policy in Sri Lanka since 1980" (p. 233).

17. See Austin Fernando. 2000. *My Belly is White*. Colombo: Vijitha Yapa Publications.

18. Such was the STF's reputation that Indian troops, when they were deployed in Sri Lanka, routinely threatened captured LTTE guerrillas that they would be handed over to the STF if they did not cooperate during interrogation. On most occasions, particularly in the eastern province where the STF had a bigger presence, the trick worked.

19. In his book *My Belly is White* (see p. 34), Austin Fernando, Sri Lanka's Defence Secretary during the peace process, criticizes President Chandrika Kumaratunga for doing nothing concrete to weaken the LTTE. He then says of Prime Minister Ranil Wickremesinghe: "Our approach was different. It was to corner the LTTE through negotiations and international pressures."

20. According to one published account, the casualty rate of soldiers-LTTE was about 1:1 in 2002. See University Teachers for Human Rights (Jaffna) document, *Rajani's Vision for Lanka*, 18 September 2009. Available online at http://www.uthr.org/Rajani/Tribute_Reflections.htm

21. France was Kumaratunga's first choice as peace facilitator but the LTTE vetoed the idea. Kumaratunga had many friends in Paris, where she had studied. So the LTTE suspected the impartiality of France although its own International Secretariat was based in Paris after moving out of London in the 1990s.

22. No Indian envoy to Sri Lanka evoked so much hostile reaction as Dixit. Former Defence Secretary Cyril Ranatunga calls Dixit "the worst high commissioner India has ever sent" to Colombo. Dixit (who served in Colombo during 1985–89) was perhaps the only

Indian diplomat who dealt directly with Prime Minister Rajiv Gandhi when he wanted to, bypassing the foreign minister. One Sri Lankan who intensely hated Dixit was Ranasinghe Premadasa, the prime minister in President Junius Jayewardene's government. When Premadasa became the president in December 1988, he drastically cut Dixit's access to him. In contrast, Dixit was a frequent visitor both at Jayewardene's office and residence.

23. See Dixit's book, *Assignment Colombo*. Whatever one might say about Dixit's personality, he was among the few who had the courage to admit that he had been in the wrong when he wielded power. Since Dixit was a key policymaker vis-à-vis Sri Lanka, the candid admission meant that at least some of the government decisions during the troubled 1980s were based on his flawed assessments. Indian Army officers deployed in Sri Lanka disagreed with Dixit's overall understanding of the LTTE and India's military-cum-diplomatic capabilities in the island nation.

24. It was a Sri Lankan leader who informed J.N. Dixit about India's deep involvement in the peace process. According to one account provided to this author, Dixit's eyes almost popped out when he heard the full details of what RAW had achieved—and so quietly. As far as Dixit was concerned, this was not the RAW he knew, when he was India's envoy to Sri Lanka.

25. Support for the LTTE and other militants began to wane at the popular level in Tamil Nadu even before the Tigers took on the Indian Army in October 1987. The LTTE–India war of 1987–90 and Rajiv Gandhi's assassination in 1991 together destroyed mass sympathy for the LTTE in the state. A section of its politicians, however, continued to vocally back the Tigers, giving an impression to outsiders that the LTTE still enjoyed popular support. In contrast to 1983, when genuine grief engulfed Tamil Nadu over the killings of Tamils in Colombo, there was hardly a whimper, outside of known pro-LTTE forces, when the Tigers were crushed and Prabhakaran was killed in 2009.

26. As one who has covered the subject for a long time, I realized that Indian concerns about the situation in Sri Lanka were often conveyed to leaders (including ministers) from Colombo, but rarely revealed to the media. If and when there was an announcement, it would be a tame version of what transpired in closed-door meetings. It was clear to those on the Sri Lanka beat that India had forged a mature bilateral relationship compared to the 1980s and there was far greater understanding in New Delhi of the constraints Colombo faced, vis-à-vis the war. Additionally, all wings of the Indian government without exception were ranged against the LTTE. There existed differences in the outlook of the two countries and these were not glossed over.

27. The ENDLF was a constituent of the provincial administration that presided over the northeast of Sri Lanka in 1988–90. When the Indian military was deployed in Sri Lanka, some surrendered LTTE militants joined the ENDLF. Later, when it was forced to withdraw from the island after the LTTE virtually took over the northeast, the ENDLF opened a camp for its members and their families at Malkangiri in India's Orissa state. (The unlikely destination followed Tamil Nadu Chief Minister M. Karunanidhi's churlish refusal to allow a ship ferrying fleeing EPRLF and ENDLF members from Sri Lanka to berth in Chennai.) The ENDLF later opened a school for Sri Lankan Tamils in Bangalore. After the ENDLF threw its lot with Karuna, one of its key operatives, Pakyanathan Rajarattinam alias Mano Master, who was based in India, mysteriously disappeared during a visit to Colombo. Some say the LTTE abducted and possibly killed him; others said

that he was a long-time LTTE mole in the ENDLF who quietly rejoined the Tigers. I would prefer to believe the former version. Before undertaking what turned out to be his last trip to Sri Lanka, Mano Master had visited the Norwegian embassy in New Delhi to submit a memorandum criticizing the LTTE.

28. Once fighting erupted between the Indian military and the LTTE in October 1987, the Tigers unleashed a propaganda war against India. LTTE media accused New Delhi of "suppressing" its various "nationalities" such as Kashmiris, Sikhs, and Gurkhas. One man who aired such views openly was LTTE's Gopalasamy Mahendrarajah alias Mahattaya, the designated number two in the group. Ironically, the LTTE later killed Mahattaya after accusing him of being an Indian spy! For instance, *Tamil Nation*, a pro-LTTE journal originally published from India, took a brazenly anti-India line after Rajiv Gandhi's killing.

29. An ULFA member who underwent LTTE training surrendered to Indian security forces on his return. He is now a moderately successful businessman in a north Indian city. At the same time, LTTE leaders kept denying that it was anyway linked to Indian insurgents. Balasingham told India's *Outlook* magazine ( 8 November 1995):

> As far as the LTTE is concerned, we consider India a friendly ally. Even now, we don't have any animosity towards the Indian government and people. We are not involved in any insurrectionary or terrorist movements in India. The LTTE will not contribute to or get involved in the Indian secessionist politics. It is not going to act in any manner inimical to the national and the geo-political interests of India.

Amid its own contradictory statements, the LTTE never hid its contempt for India. Asked about Rajiv Gandhi's killing, Balasingham told *The Hindu* (30 May 1991) that it did not involve any sophisticated technology. "It was just a matter of joining two wires together."

30. For all practical purposes, successive Indian governments never deviated from Rajiv Gandhi's assessment of the LTTE, which he made public in a speech at Pudukkottai in Tamil Nadu on 21 December 1987:

> The LTTE represents no one but itself. It has not been ready to come into a democratic framework and it has been responsible for the killing of most of the militant Tamils who have been killed and many hundreds, thousands of innocent Tamils... The LTTE has gone back on every promise that it made. It has gone back on every commitment. It has shown itself, and proved itself, to be untrustworthy and unreliable. It has shown that it does not have the interests of the Tamils at heart. (See, Satyamurthy, *Patriot of Dignity and Dedication*. 1988. New Delhi: DAVP, Government of India.)

31. When Tamil militancy erupted in a major way in 1983, there were five frontline groups: the LTTE led by Prabhakaran, the EPRLF led by K. Pathmanabha, the People's Liberation Organisation of Tamil Eelam (PLOT) led by Uma Maheshwaran, the Tamil Eelam Liberation Organization (TELO) led by Sri Sabarattinam and the Eelam Revolutionary Organizers (EROS) led by V. Balakumar. The LTTE killed Sabarattinam in 1986 and Pathmanabha in 1990. Maheshwaran was killed in 1989 in an internal PLOT feud. Prabhakaran fell to the military in 2009. Balakumar was among those who disbanded the EROS and joined the LTTE in 1990. He may have perished with other LTTE leaders in 2009.

32. While the Tamils and Sinhalese in Sri Lanka are predominantly Hindu and Buddhist respectively, both communities boast of a large number of Christians. Almost all Muslims in the country speak Tamil (many speak Sinhalese too) but they see themselves as a distinct community. This was not so for a long time, at least in the north and east where Muslims took active part in the peaceful anti-government struggles led by Tamils of an earlier era. Later, many young Muslims joined Tamil militant groups. Although it is fashionable for some Tamil apologists to blame Colombo for Tamil–Muslim fissures, the LTTE contributed in a major way to fomenting anti-Muslim sentiments and violence. This led to Muslims leaving militant groups. The LTTE eventually expelled hundreds of thousands of Muslims from Jaffna in 1990, callously disregarding the fact that they had lived there for generations. It followed it up with the cold-blooded massacres of Muslim worshippers, that too inside mosques, in Batticaloa. The LTTE subsequently admitted that it was wrong in forcing Muslims out of Jaffna but it never allowed them to return.

33. In a 1991 interview to *The Indian Express* (May 1991), Sathasivan Krishnakumar, alias Kittu, then head of the LTTE International Secretariat in London and formerly its Jaffna commander, put the number of guerrillas who had left the group until then at around 3,000. It was the first time the LTTE gave out a statistic of this kind. Kittu spoke in the aftermath of Rajiv Gandhi's assassination. His argument was that since a large number of LTTE cadres had quit, the organization could not be blamed for the Gandhi killing even if the killers were found to be linked to the Tigers. It was a dubious argument and Indian investigators proved it to be so. After the early 1990s, quitting the LTTE became more and more difficult. But people continued to leave, taking the number until the Karuna rebellion to an estimated 5,000. I knew a Jaffna family that had known Prabhakaran from his younger days and which wanted their son, who was in LTTE, to migrate to Denmark. The boy's father became desperate as the 1990s drew to a close because the LTTE would not release his son. Eventually, the approval came, to the family's delight.

34. I have spoken to Karuna on more than one occasion. Much of my information has come from those who were close to him and those who witnessed his revolt first hand in Batticaloa. What is significant about his rebellion is the popular acceptance it got in no time among very many ordinary Tamils in the east. Karuna's complaint that the "northern" LTTE was lording over the "eastern" Tamils had touched a sympathetic chord. After Karuna fled Batticaloa, the LTTE carried out a systematic purging of his known and suspected sympathizers in the civil society in the region. One man who was picked up by the LTTE intelligence was an academic who survived only because he was a relative of D. Sivaram, alias Taraki, a Tamil militant turned journalist. The academic is still alive but the once anti-LTTE Taraki, who eventually became a staunch LTTE supporter, was abducted and murdered in Colombo, apparently by those linked to the government.

35. Interview with the author.

36. When it ran a de facto state in Sri Lanka's north, the LTTE charged "duty" on goods brought into "Tamil Eelam". This ranged from a low of 5 per cent on agriculture machinery, outboard motors and Anchor milk powder to a high of 25 per cent on items such as furniture, electronic and electrical items, building material, lead, lubricating oil, cigarettes, matches, camphor, candle, bakery items, and liquor. Owners of bicycles and motorcycles were charged over 70 per cent duty. An LTTE announcement said:

Government and non-government employees coming on transfer from Sri Lanka can bring items used by them, free of duty. Duty exemption would be given for used items brought by persons from Sri Lanka and other countries coming to Tamil Eelam with the intention of taking up permanent residence.

37. Interviews with residents of Batticaloa.

38. I am ignoring charges of financial embezzlement hurled at Karuna after he broke away. Even if the charges were true, he was not the lone sinner in the LTTE. Although the LTTE maintained meticulous accounts of expenditure, thefts from the Tiger kitty were not uncommon. Incidentally, some LTTE guerrillas turned against the group after being wrongly accused of corruption.

39. What follows here is mostly unpublished information. Aid workers in the eastern province kept me informed about child recruitment, as the LTTE forced kids to join its ranks, particularly from remote rural parts. The information I got was precise—including names of villages, victims and their parents. But precisely because of this reason, I was urged not to go public with the details. Aid workers feared then that publicity might spoil whatever chances they had of rescuing the abducted children.

40. An aid worker told me that he and his colleagues reached an LTTE camp in Batticaloa in 2004 to demand the release of an abducted young boy. To their surprise, a young uniformed Tiger at the camp gate said he would bring out the boy and they could take him away in their vehicle; the guard promised to concoct a story about the boy's escape to his seniors. The aid workers could not believe their ears. But they did not fall for the temptation. Even if the sentry meant what he said, they knew it would lead to trouble. The LTTE could chase and catch up with them. In any case, this was against their organization's charter. They politely turned down the offer. This was a rare, but not the only instance, when LTTE militants in camps and prisons acted or volunteered to act, against the interests of their own group, out of humanitarian concerns. A rival Tamil militant once held in an LTTE prison recalled that a young Tiger guard offered him water from the toilet to drink, but on the condition that this should not be reported to his seniors, who were holding the prisoner hungry and thirsty. In another instance, a young LTTE woman guerrilla scolded a group of girls who reached her camp to enlist. Why did you come here, she asked in disgust. "*Ithu thooimayana iyakkam ellai*" (This is not a pure organization), she remarked.

41. The "pistol groups" were mostly controlled by the LTTE intelligence—and drew their name from the weapon wielded by their members, dominantly young men. They were akin to the hit men in the mafia. If the LTTE wanted to kill someone who was not a VIP, a member of the "pistol group" would be assigned the task. Who would suspect an innocent looking young man on the street? The assassin would approach the victim, shoot, and quickly escape, if necessary after dumping the weapon. As for the LTTE, it would play innocent and not claim responsibility for the murder.

42. The University Teachers for Human Rights (Jaffna), which over the years, issued numerous eminently researched reports on the human rights situation in Sri Lanka, particularly in the northeast, repeatedly pointed out that many Tamils who left with their families for greener pastures in the West had no hesitation in approving the LTTE's recruitment of kids from poor families to fight and die for Tamil Eelam. It is highly doubtful if they would have ever allowed their own children to be conscripted in this manner.

43. Allegations that the LTTE was into drugs to finance its war, are as old as the LTTE. I recently asked a senior official of the Narcotics Control Bureau (NCB) in India if this was true. The response was: It might have been but we have never had any conclusive evidence. The official added that men from all religions and ethnic groups (including the well-heeled) were into Sri Lanka's drug trade. There is no doubt that narcotics, heroin included, are smuggled into and out of Sri Lanka in large quantities. And it is difficult to believe that this could have happened without at least the LTTE's approval if not participation when it reigned supreme in the north of the country.

44. Despite dethroning him, Prabhakaran continued to share secrets with KP. When Anton Balasingham fell from Prabhakaran's grace after signing a pact in Oslo in December 2002 promising to explore a federal solution to the conflict, the LTTE, chief complained bitterly against him to KP.

45. When Balasingham died, Erik Solheim, the Norwegian Special Envoy to Sri Lanka who met the LTTE ideologue more than 100 times, described him as an honest man. The comment was erroneously, but widely, seen as endorsing the politics of one committed to violence. Solheim was actually referring to Balasingham's ability to speak the bitter truth (in private) on matters related to Tamil militancy, LTTE and Prabhakaran, even if these were unpalatable to the Tigers.

46. KP told a Tamil politician before his own abduction from Malaysia that he learnt about Prabhakaran's death from Soosai, the Sea Tigers chief, on 17 May. Soosai was reportedly calm when he broke the news over satellite phone. Unless KP was confused or lying about the date, this contradicts the official versions that Prabhakaran was killed on 18 May.

47. Remnants of both TELO and PLOT exist. After being decimated by LTTE, surviving TELO members sided with the Sri Lankan military against the Tigers for a long time before dramatically joining the pro-LTTE Tamil National Alliance (TNA). The PLOT has remained steadfastly anti-LTTE and its leader is Dharmalingam Sitharthan, who has known Prabhakaran from their younger days. A section of PLOT broke away to form the Eelam National Democratic Liberation Front (ENDLF).

48. The LTTE intelligence member who oversaw the assassination of EPRLF chief K. Pathmanabha and his close aides in Chennai was none other than Sivarasan, who later headed the cell that killed Rajiv Gandhi. The failure of the Indian authorities to take the investigation into the Pathmanabha killing to its logical conclusion emboldened the LTTE to send Sivarasan again to Tamil Nadu to target Gandhi.

49. While most Indians thought the 1987 pact would herald peace in Sri Lanka, one Indian who knew better, disagreed. This was P. Jayaram, a seasoned journalist then with United News of India. Based in Colombo since 1983, Jayaram went on to live there for 14 long years. He was not taken seriously when he insisted in July–August 1987 that the LTTE would sabotage the accord. Jayaram was also the first journalist to report that the LTTE had taken a vocal anti-India stand while destroying TELO in 1986. Alarmed by Jayaram's reporting, which was a revelation to Indian policymakers, the LTTE took the unusual step of issuing a press statement denouncing him by name.

50. Prabhakaran told Indian journalist P.S. Suryanarayana (whom he had known well since his Chennai days; the interview of Prabhakaran was conducted by P.S. Suryanarayana at Jaffna, Sri Lanka on 7 September 1987) that he would "play politics" to counter the Indian military presence in Sri Lanka. He would also provoke the Indian troops to attack

Tamil civilians. "The provocation should be so fine-tuned as not to arouse suspicion." (See Suryanarayana. 1988. *The Peace Trap*, p. 22. New Delhi, Madras, Bangalore, Hyderabad: Affiliated East–West Press Private Ltd.)

51. Interestingly, the murders of the sari traders evoked no protest from Tamil Nadu's political parties, whose leaders were always quick to condemn the killings of Sri Lankan Tamils by security forces. In the end, families of the dead men were left to fend for themselves. This itself could be taken as implicit evidence that the killings were committed by the LTTE.

52. This is not meant to be a biographical sketch of Prabhakaran. Those wanting to understand the man in detail, can read my unauthorized biography, *Inside an Elusive Mind*. There is plenty of other informative literature too on the subject.

53. A case in point is Tamil MP M.K. Shivaji Lingam, who, like Prabhakaran, hailed from Velvettiturai in Jaffna. But Shivaji Lingam joined TELO. In the early 1980s, Shivaji Lingam provided Prabhakaran a hideout close to the coast when the latter wanted to escape to India. In 1986, when the LTTE sought to destroy TELO, Tiger gunmen reached the very same hideout looking for Shivaji Lingam. He was not there and so survived. Similarly, in the early years of militancy, EPRLF's Annamali Varadaraja Perumal provided a hideout in Jaffna for Prabhakaran. That did not deter the LTTE chief from targeting Varadaraja Perumal in later years.

54. Aid workers recall attending a LTTE cultural programme in a rural area of Batticaloa one night during the ceasefire period. One of them told me:

> The LTTE put up this skit. There were many people in the audience, mostly men though. But they looked artificial, like some kind of zombies. They lacked any lively expression on their faces. In contrast, there were stern looking LTTE guerrillas in uniform. They stood around the audience. When one man clapped, everyone clapped. They had to clap. The people had no choice. I asked myself: "Hey, am in Sri Lanka or North Korea?"

55. President Premadasa's decision to give weapons and other material to the LTTE (besides a free run in Colombo) during the war against the Indian Army is seen by many in Sri Lanka as treachery. The latest to express his disgust is General Cyril Ranatunga, who was then the Defence Secretary but was not consulted about the arms transfer (See Ranatunga, Cyril. 2009. *From Peace to War, Insurgency to Terrorism*. Colombo: Vijitha Yapa Publications). During the Premadasa presidency, the LTTE "arrested" Tamils in Colombo who it saw as foes and took them away to the country's north in buses with tinted glass in which the prisoners were handcuffed and bound to the seats with ropes. The buses went past police and military checkpoints that had orders not to stop or check them.

56. See Gokhale, Nitin A. 2009. *Sri Lanka: From War to Peace*, p. 54. New Delhi: Har-Anand Publications Private Ltd.

57. MGR and his AIADMK ruled Tamil Nadu when Tamil insurgency erupted in Sri Lanka in 1983. MGR held the reins in the state, until his Christmas-eve death in 1987. This was just over two months after the LTTE began fighting the Indian Army in Sri Lanka.

58. LTTE's prisons form another sad story of the Tamil militant movement. When it did not want to kill, the LTTE imprisoned and tortured its real and perceived foes in the most horrific manner. Unable to face the pain and humiliation, some prisoners went insane. All this began even when the Tigers enjoyed Indian patronage. I have met ex-LTTE prisoners

who recalled the savagery they underwent in these jails, often at the hands of sadistic young men (women too) who appeared to enjoy seeing others suffer.

59. EROS abducted and killed Kandiah Kanthasamy, a Tamil human rights activist, in Jaffna in June 1988, triggering widespread condemnation. Kanthasamy had given up an outstanding legal career to devote his life to human rights work. EROS wanted to lord over Kanthasamy's NGO, the Tamil Refugee Rehabilitation Organization (TRRO), but he refused to bow to the militant group. The meticulous Kanthasamy quietly made detailed notes of all his meetings with EROS representatives. These became public knowledge after his death, exposing the killers. Cornered, EROS denied killing him; but a previously unheard of group, Tamil Eelam Pasari Movement, claimed responsibility for his death. David Selbourne's moving tribute to the dead man is part of a book, *An Untimely Death: A Commemoration of K. Kanthasamy*, published by the Kanthasamy Commemoration Committee, Colombo, on his first death anniversary in 1989.

60. Interviews with former LTTE guerrillas.

# Testimonies of LTTE cadres

THE LTTE stood out in comparison to other insurgent groups because of the large number of women it had on its rolls although Tamil society was deeply patriarchal. Young women began joining the group in right earnest in 1984. It took about two years before they fought their first battle, in Mannar. Since then, women combatants have taken part in almost all military offensives, in varying degrees, at times displaying ferocious courage. They also played a key role in suicide attacks, the most significant of them being the assassination of former Indian Prime Minister Rajiv Gandhi. Unfortunately, many of the women imbibed the LTTE's fascistic streak. This was evident when they took part in forcible conscription of young combatants, girls included. The women's role in the Tamil Eelam war should not be taken to mean—as some believe—that the LTTE emancipated or elevated the status of women by making them fighters and killers. Aid workers who saw the LTTE from close quarters, post 2002, say that many in the women's wing would slip away or stand back when male cadres passed by in the villages of Trincomalee and Batticaloa. I present here the stories of two young women who joined the LTTE in different periods and fled Sri Lanka just before the war ended in 2009.

## Testament I—Saroja's story[1]

I was born into a lower middle class family in a village in Kilinochchi district. My father was a farmer. Besides my mother, I had three brothers and two sisters. My brothers used to help my father in the fields. We were a hard working family. The war was around us.

The year was 1999. I had passed the 9th standard examination and had just gone into the 10th standard. This was the time when the LTTE was on the winning streak—or so it seemed. Their members used to come to schools and address students about the armed struggle. They would speak about "Sinhalese atrocities" and the need to fight for an independent Tamil Eelam. They would call out for 16-year-olds and above to join them. Sometimes, if students, they specifically beckoned, insisted that they were only 15-years-old, then they would be spared. The forced recruitment began much later, at least in our area.

We had a deer in our house. One day, there was a row in our house over the upkeep of the animal. My mother beat me badly. This hurt me a lot. I became emotionally disturbed. I simply left the house and walked towards the fields on the outskirts of the village. There I was spotted by a group of LTTE guerrillas. They consoled me and asked me to join their ranks. I consented. I was not in a frame of mind to say no although I had never agreed to join the LTTE when such appeals were made in school.

Thus began my life in the LTTE. The initial training was not difficult. It was a three-month capsule. Since I was always interested in sports, I took to it easily.

One of the first things we did was to pick a name for ourselves in our organization. This was our "*iyakka peru*" (*nom de guerre*). The only condition was that it had to be a typical Tamil name. We were told that these names would be sent to our higher ups for approval. Most names got the go ahead. Some names, which the leadership thought was not Tamil enough, were changed.[2] We did not mind it. After all we were all Tamils and the feeling of Tamil identity ran deep in us. This was our first introduction to the LTTE.

Quickly everyone in the camp became a family. All of us in our unit were more or less of the same age group. I was in the women's unit. But our instructors were not necessarily female. There were males too. In some cases, there were joint classes for males and females. One thing that made us happy was the peace in the camp. There was discipline too. In fact, there was a sense of peace wherever the LTTE ruled.

We would run every day for several kilometres. We would also cross hurdles of various kinds. We did all kinds of physical exercise. Then came firing practice. Those who passed the firing test were promoted in the training regimen. Those who failed had to pass it before going ahead with the training.

Even as they trained us, the LTTE would spot out those with leadership potential. They were very good spotters of talent. The instructors always observed us closely. Those who, the LTTE concluded, had the ability to grow as leaders would be asked to head a unit of 10 people, then 20, then 30, and so on. This is how leaders were born in the LTTE from among the mass of its members. This process kept the LTTE alive.

Although we slowly became immersed in our new lives in the LTTE, we did not forget our family. Our memories about our family would get rekindled whenever we stepped out of our camps. On the streets, we would see mothers and daughters walk past us. On those occasions, I would fondly recall my family, my mother, and father in particular. We would get occasionally homesick. But we knew where we were.

There was no question of deserting the LTTE. It was utterly dangerous and we knew what happened to deserters. So we would return to the camp.

Occasionally we would be assigned sentry duty. There would be just the three of us the whole night. Frankly speaking, this was the one time fear did creep into us. This was partly because we were young and largely inexperienced and partly because of the feeling of isolation at night. During daytime, there were so many of us that the fear factor disappeared.

My first major battle was the war for Elephant Pass. Whenever the LTTE conducted a major operation, they would gather all the fighters in large groups and show them battle maps. But they would never reveal which place was to be attacked. They would say for example—"Suppose, if this building is to be attacked, then you must take up positions in these spots." They would not tell us which building they were referring to or where it was located. Nor would they tell us when and where the fighting would begin or take place. It was always a hush-hush affair even if the operation included hundreds of fighters. No one asked needless questions.

But it would become evident that a major operation was under way. There would be these sudden coming and going of trucks. There would be a general atmosphere of excitement. These were tell-tale signs of impending major military operations.

Within days we realized that the LTTE wanted to capture Jaffna.[3]

As I was forging ahead with others towards the Elephant Pass, a Sri Lankan artillery shell landed nearby and a splinter struck my back. There was piercing pain but I carried on. Suddenly a bullet grazed my right hand. It was damn painful but I carried on, now holding my AK-47 with my left hand. Before long, another bullet tore through my left hand as well. This was worse.

My rifle fell as my left hand almost got twisted. I could not walk any more. I collapsed in pain. On the fourth day of the battle, I was back in an LTTE camp as a wounded soldier.

Doctors took several X-Rays of my hands, my left one in particular. They feared that there was a chance of paralysis. So they had to act quickly and carefully. I was in terrible pain. The LTTE medical unit had arranged for elderly women to take care of us. As for the doctors in the camp, they were among the best, perhaps, in the whole of Sri Lanka. The best of doctors always had to work for the LTTE. The other doctors in Kilinochchi were ordinary. I was bedded for 15 days but I got excellent medical care.

When we learnt that the LTTE had halted its advance towards Jaffna after capturing the Elephant Pass, we were very, very disappointed. We kept asking one another why stop when we have come this far. Why don't we press ahead? Will this halt in war lead us to Tamil Eelam?

During training, we would wake up at 4 a.m. whatever the weather and whether we liked it or not. Only the badly sick could escape the training schedule. For about two hours, we had to run in the open field and do various types of physical exercises. We also had to learn and practice judo and karate. We would get a cup of tea at 6 a.m.

The lunch was always sumptuous. There would be "pittu", vegetables, a curry, and fish. The vegetables came from a section of the market reserved for the LTTE. Some of us would go there with a special card. The shopkeeper would give us what was prescribed in the card (for our camp). There would be various chores to do at the camp. Weapons had to be cleaned and errands had to be run. We also had to cook by turns. All this kept us busy for the better part of the day.

Before the day got over, there would be more training. We would also listen to the LTTE radio and watch TV.[4] We were always in uniform, morning to night. We stepped out of it only when we slept.

On one occasion, Prabhakaran came to our camp. He used to make these sudden visits to various camps. Sometimes we were told that he would come but he would not. His movements were kept very secret. But he would certainly come on the anniversary day of our unit. On those occasions, he would sit through the entire function the unit organized. On such days, he came with his family at times.

Death was constantly in the air. But frankly we never feared death. Four or five of my best friends died in battles. I was very moved on those occasions. They were people I had become very good friends with. We had shared many things in common. We ate, slept, and trained together. When they died, I would be overcome with emotions. But such martyrdom only steeled our resolve. We would vow to avenge their death by deepening our struggle.

Without doubt, the best fighters came from the eastern province. The reason was simple. While we had only heard of Sinhalese atrocities, these people would have experienced it. That made them really hard boiled and vicious fighters. Some of them related to us how soldiers had shot dead their family members and friends, occasionally right in front of their eyes. Most of them were from Batticaloa. When they told us their horror stories, it made us doubly loyal to the LTTE cause. Some of the eastern guerrillas were orphans and would have taken days of trekking through impregnable forests to reach the Wanni. They came looking for the LTTE. They had nowhere to go. They never bothered about death. They would keep saying that it is better to fight and die rather than live like slaves; at least we would get a free state where Tamils can live a life of dignity.

During training, we were first given wooden rifles to handle and hold. They were prototypes of rifles. But we had to treat them like real rifles. These could never be placed on the ground. Then came the AK-47.

If we did any wrong, we faced punishment. We could be asked to stand on a barrel, holding a rifle and under the hot sun, for hours together. On other occasions we would be asked to run for miles holding our rifles.[5] Sometimes cooking was turned into punishment. Normally we would cook for 30 to 40 people by turns in our camp. Punishment cooking included making food for 400 to 500 people.

We knew nothing about the CFA (ceasefire agreement of 2002) until it happened. We were taken aback by the development. We had been told in our political classes about the history of our struggle and the need to fight on and on for Tamil Eelam. So, what was the need for CFA?

One of my brothers came to our camp after the CFA and asked me to return to the family. I was very fond of that particular brother. I too badly wanted to rejoin my family. I left the camp quietly one day and proceeded with him to Jaffna. He had readied a Sri Lankan ID[6] card for me. I used it to travel to Colombo.

When I look back, I think the CFA destroyed the LTTE. Once the ceasefire happened and fighting ceased, the LTTE became very relaxed. The discipline slackened. The daily rough and tough life gave way to easy life. This was something the LTTE was not used to. Many colleagues got married within the ranks. These included some leaders too. Clearly, people had fallen in love over a period of time and were waiting for the first opportunity to tie the knot.

Family life then became the dominant factor for many. Once the CFA was signed, desertions shot up. Like me, many left the camps, never to return to the LTTE. The LTTE did come looking for me but failed to trace me. I had told them earlier that I had no relatives in Jaffna. So they never thought of looking for me there.

When I look back, I am thoroughly disgusted with everything, including the LTTE.

After so many years of fighting for Tamil Eelam, after losing so many fighters and people, after so much of destruction, where are we? Tamils have nothing today. This long, long war has helped us gain nothing. On the contrary, we have lost whatever little we had when militancy started. Either the LTTE should have made permanent peace with Sri Lanka or it should not have rested until attaining Tamil Eelam. Today, the Tamils are nowhere.

Will the end of war lead to peace? I am not so sure. The LTTE may not rise again but there would never be permanent peace in Sri Lanka. The Sinhalese would never accept Tamils as their equals. They will always look down upon us. That is for sure.

In December 2006, my brother who had helped me escape from the LTTE was shot dead in Jaffna by the military.[7] He was a (car) mechanic and led a quiet life. He had nothing to do with the LTTE or any other group of any kind. But for reasons that are unclear (to this day), Sinhalese soldiers shot and killed my brother. I can understand the army killing LTTE guerrillas but why kill innocent Tamils? Why kill my brother?

## Testament II—Vani's story[8]

I was 13 years of age when I joined the LTTE. The year was 1991. My house was at Thondamanar, near VVT.[9] I knew I was a minor but I approached the LTTE on my own. I was attracted to the LTTE and the weapons they held. My family was shocked by my decision. My father in particular was deeply unhappy. But I had made up my mind. Yes, it is true that in later years, the LTTE abducted many underage children into its ranks, but I went to them voluntarily. So did many others like me.

We were immediately inducted into their training programme. This included physical exercises and firing practice. We had to run around fields and do various other things to toughen our bodies and mind. It was difficult in the beginning. A days passed, the number of kilometres we had to run kept increasing.

During my time, the LTTE did not provide too much ammunition for rifle practice.[10] We were given only a limited number of bullets to fire. If we hit the target, i was good; too bad otherwise.

Political ideas followed. This was very important in the LTTE. Once, Anton Balasingham presided over a political class. Usually the teachers were our own instructors. They told us about Tamil history, about the history of our armed struggle about the LTTE's growth, about its aims and aspirations. They showed us inspirational movies. This teaching was considered very important because it brought us closer to the LTTE worldview and ideology. The LTTE knew that many of us had no real moorings in Tamil nationalism. Without that, our loyalty to LTTE would always be tenuous. These classes helped us understand and appreciate our Tamil identity vis-à-vis the Sinhalese.

After about two years, I was selected for the computer wing of the LTTE. I had never seen a computer in my life. Initially we were given theoretical lessons about computers. We were shown pictures of computers and taught about CPU, ROM MS Word, and so on. We were not told about the Internet. I got to know that much later. To initiate me into computers, I was given typing lessons. It helped.

Eventually, the computers arrived, about 10 of them. We were a total of 15 people Once the computers came, we had to practice more and more. Most of us fell in love with computers very quickly.

Our main task was to translate books and literature from other languages into Tamil. I didn't know English well. I had learnt computers with Tamil keyboards. was good at Tamil typing. There were experienced translators who would read out

English books and dictate in Tamil. This we took down in computers. One book I was involved in was a thick one about Germany and Russia and related to World War II. I don't recall it very well though.

Life in the LTTE was very regimented. Although I did not take part in any battle, our training programme was no different compared to guerrillas who took part in battles. We had to wake up between 4 and 4.30 in the morning and start running. There were physical exercises. Once that got over, we would bathe, followed by various chores in the camp. By 9 or 10, we would be in the computer room and start work. After lunch, we would be back at the computers. In the evening, there was more work at the camp. Sentry duty was given to us all by rotation. This involved guarding our camp at night.

The LTTE had no religion although most of us were Hindus.[11] None of us worshipped any God or went to temples. However, the LTTE did celebrate certain important festivals. We got sweet *pongal* to eat on Pongal day and sweets on Deepawali. We all celebrated Christmas. When it was our individual birthday, there would be little gatherings in the camp. All this brought us closer emotionally since we were living away from the families. On Prabhakaran's birthday, we all got cakes to eat.

I saw Prabhakaran only once. He came to our camp. We were told that someone important was coming, but the identity was not disclosed to us. This, I realized later, was due to security reasons. The meeting took place in a hall. We were overawed by his presence. We could hardly speak. He spoke softly. He asked us if we had any complaints about life in the LTTE and whether there was anything that was lacking in the camp. None of us replied. I think we could not get the courage to speak before him. He spent about 30 minutes and left. We were all held back at the venue for a while after he left. It was only later that we got to stir.[12]

I remained with the LTTE through the tumultuous 1990s, seeing many ups and downs. After the fall of Jaffna to the military in December 1995, we moved to Kilinochchi area. From there, we had to move again before the LTTE recaptured Kilinochchi and made it its administrative and political hub.

I decided to quit the LTTE after the CFA of 2002. The reason was personal. I had problems with my camp commander who was my immediate superior. The differences escalated after the CFA, when there were no more prospects of war.

I sought permission to quit. The LTTE heard my case and ruled against me, saying I would have to serve another five years in a punishment posting before they could discharge me. This was too much and I argued against it. So they cut the punishment posting to two years. I served that period quietly cooking for hundreds of cadres, day after day, night after night, waiting for the two years to be over. Finally, in 2004, I called it quits.

I remained in Kilinochchi till late 2008 when the military began to advance menacingly. I then became a part of the mass of civilians numbering thousands who retreated deep into the Wanni along with the LTTE. The military assaults were relentless. I can never, never forget this period of my life. I can say without hesitation that if there was any hell on this earth, it was this.

From March/April, we were on the run every single day. Each day and night, indeed each hour, was passed in fear and terror. We never knew when the military would rain MBRLs (Multi Barrel Rocket Launchers) and artillery or bomb us from the air. Our only concern was survival. We kept on praying that we should be alive with our extended family members, including two children.

We spent most of our life during the last two months of the war (until May 2009) with nothing except the clothes we were in. We lost everything. I lost all my educational certificates, including those related to computer learning. Many people lived virtually in bunkers. When shells fell, people died instantly. They were the lucky ones. There were others who were maimed, suffered in pain, and died in agony due to deep cuts and excessive blood loss. There was no medical care and there was nothing we could do. My cousin, who was with me, lost her father and mother. She saw them die in front of her eyes. It was an extremely painful sight. Even today, she has not recovered from that horrifying moment.

Eventually, my family and I were trapped at Mullivaykkal, where the LTTE put up its last ditch fighting before going down. Frankly, I had been afraid of crossing over to the government side fearing they would kill me due to my past LTTE links. Would they believe that I had no relationship with the LTTE since 2004 and indeed had served the last two years undergoing punishment in the LTTE?

At Mullivaykkal, I stayed put till 15 May before deciding that we had no choice but to escape from the LTTE territory. Bombs were falling all around us. The sound of gunfire and explosions were perennial and deafening. It was frightening. It made us numb at times. I saw young LTTE boys and girls, who I could make out were forcible recruits, drop their weapons and run for their lives. Their war ended in distress. They mingled with the civilians in a desperate bid to escape. By then, the LTTE was in such a bad shape that they could not even hit back. They were busy fending for themselves.

Why did the LTTE lose so badly? As I see it, there were two reasons. One was the frenzied forcible recruitment of children that took place in LTTE areas on a large scale, particularly after the revolt by Karuna. The LTTE had to make up the lost numbers. But it completely turned ordinary Tamil civilians against the LTTE. Who will not get angry when they see their young sons and daughters being taken away, against their will, to fight and die? Even I would have been furious if my siblings had been kidnapped. But the LTTE didn't care and paid a heavy price for this folly.

Then came the deaths of various leaders. Balasingham died in 2006, Tamilchelvan in 2007. So many died one by one. Many of them were key people. Once you lose important people, what is left of you?

As for me, I am thoroughly disgusted. I feel it has all been a total waste. All these years of fighting, of dying, of war, of violence, everything has gone down the drain. Today I cannot bear to see even war movies. I am disgusted with everything that has happened in the past. My only aim now is to live in peace.

## Notes

1. Saroja is neither the real nor the "organizational" name of the LTTE guerrilla interviewed here. The interview was conducted in Tamil in a congenial atmosphere, and the young woman spoke her heart out about her life in the LTTE. This is a slightly condensed version of the interview. I have, over the years, observed that LTTE guerrillas speak a language that borders on artificial when they are in their lair or in a large group. They, however, become free and frank if they are alone and if you are able to win their trust. Like others who were with or linked to the LTTE I spoke to for this book, Saroja remains a Tamil to the core but, unlike the Tamil diaspora dispersed mostly in the West, has no illusions that the Tigers can make a comeback. Given the choice, she would not want them to. It is possible that in the interview she may have glossed over aspects of her life as a guerrilla that could land her in trouble now.

2. The system of giving a *nom de guerre* (or alias) to fighters is as old as Tamil militancy. This became an obsession in the LTTE. In its early stages, the group picked aliases for its fighters. Religious differences were glossed over for this purpose. Thus, a Hindu fighter could be called "Raheem" or "Antony". As the numbers swelled in the LTTE ranks, it ran out of easy aliases and it asked its entrants to choose short names for themselves. Thus a whole lot of bizarre *nom de guerre* cropped up: Reagan, Castro, Gadaffi, Newton, and so on. Indian troops chasing the LTTE were surprised to know that one of their quarries was a Gavaskar! It was deemed a crime in the LTTE to try finding out the real names of guerrillas. In the 1990s, the LTTE became insistent that aliases should be very Tamil sounding.

3. Jaffna, the Tamil heartland in the very north of Sri Lanka, is where Tamil militancy began. The LTTE ruled over Jaffna from early 1990, when the Indian troops returned home, to December 1995, when the Sri Lankan military recaptured it after a 50-day operation. Prabhakaran had vowed to recapture Jaffna come what may, but the dream remained unfulfilled. The LTTE mounted a major offensive in 2000 to take control of Jaffna. In the process, it overran and captured the strategic and heavily defended Elephant Pass, the narrow isthmus linking Jaffna with the rest of Sri Lanka. But even as panic gripped Colombo about the fate of thousands of soldiers trapped in Jaffna peninsula, the LTTE suddenly halted its offensive. It has never been conclusively clear why.

4. Saroja was referring to the Voice of Tigers radio, which operated secretly in Sri Lanka's north, initially on FM frequency. It must have had a powerful transmitter because it could be monitored even in northern India. From the start of this century, Voice of Tigers began beaming advertisements. Its correspondents were daring and reported from the frontlines

when the LTTE waged war. The LTTE also had a TV station but it was not as popul.
as its radio. In later years, several radio and TV stations (besides websites) emerged in th
West. Most of them were brazenly pro-LTTE. The Tigers encouraged their guerrillas
tune in to BBC Tamil Service as well as Radio Vertias, a Catholic radio station based i
the Philippines. After the 1991 assassination of Rajiv Gandhi, the LTTE "banned" A
India Radio (AIR), accusing it of bias. AIR had been hugely popular among the Tami
of Sri Lanka between 1983 and 1987.

5. It is here that the LTTE stood out vis-à-vis numerous militant groups in the worl
Punishment was swift, often lethal. Matters related to corruption and illicit sex ofte
resulted in capital punishment. This was surprising considering that the only Marxi
hero Prabhakaran looked up to was Che Guevera, who, when he was in the jungle
ordered minimal punishment to his erring colleagues.

6. It is mandatory for all Sri Lankans to have a national identity card. The lack of it coul
lead people to prison. In later years, the LTTE issued its own "national" ID cards.

7. Saroja appeared to be sure that it was the military (in uniform), not the LTTE, whic
killed her brother.

8. Like in the case of Saroja, Vani too is neither the real nor the "organizational" name of th
guerrilla who was interviewed. Surprisingly, despite years of interaction with compute
and English translators, her grasp of English language remains poor. She too spoke i
Tamil.

9. VVT is short for Velvettiturai, the birthplace of Prabhakaran. This is a coastal villag
located in the northern tip of Jaffna.

10. This could have been because the war against Sri Lanka had resumed in June 1990, an
the LTTE may have faced an ammunition crunch in 1991.

11. Despite its overwhelmingly Hindu membership and the Prabhakaran family's assc
ciation with Hindu temples in VVT when he was young, the LTTE buried its falle
comrades instead of cremating them. But it is known that many LTTE Sea Tiger guerrilla
would quietly pray in the direction of the Velankanni Church on Tamil Nadu's coa
when they took to the sea. In February 2002, when I was frisked ahead of the Prabhakara
press conference in Kilinochchi, a young guerrilla noticed photos of Hindu gods in m
wallet. I also had a small packet of "vibuthi" (sacred ash) given by my mother-in-law a
my wedding. When I asked him not to spill the "vibuthi", the young man replied: "Don
worry, Sir, the gods you worship are the same gods we too worship."

12. This is how it happened at the 2002 Prabhakaran press conference too. Journalists wei
prevented from leaving the venue until the LTTE chief had got into bulletproof vehicle
and had been driven away. In the process, there was a great deal of jostling at the mai
gate because journalists were desperate to file their stories ahead of their deadlines. Thos
lacking satellite phones had to drive back all the way to Colombo to communicate. Arme
LTTE guerrillas, who had no knowledge about journalism, had a tough time handling
crowd they had never encountered earlier.

2003–2005

# 1

(As 2003 was coming to a close, the LTTE began to sound pro-India yet again. The reasons were not far to seek. Even as the West appeared to accept a LTTE that had signed a ceasefire agreement, India remained steadfastly anti-Tiger. Prabhakaran and his ideologue Balasingham understood this needed to change.)

## Why does LTTE make pro-India noises?

WITH just eight months to go for the Indian government to decide whether or not it should extend its two-yearly ban on the LTTE, the insurgent group has again started singing pro-India tunes.

The last time we heard this was in April 2002 when the LTTE chief, Velupillai Prabhakaran, held his first press conference in over a decade at the Tiger-held northern Sri Lankan town of Kilinochchi. Sitting beside him, both as a translator and an ideologue, Anton Balasingham—the longest-surviving high-profile Prabhakaran aide—described India as a "fatherland" of Tamils. Tamils wanted good relations with India, he said. Prabhakaran did not back what Balasingham said but did not contradict him either. The LTTE numero uno, however, made it clear he did not want to see India militarily intervening in Sri Lankan affairs ever again. New Delhi was not impressed.

Four months later, the Indian government extended its ban on the LTTE, first imposed in 1992 after the Tigers assassinated the former Prime Minister, Rajiv Gandhi, the previous year. Once the ban was extended, Balasingham could not hide his anger and disgust vis-à-vis India.

Now, once again, Balasingham has made comments that amount to requesting India to lift the ban on the LTTE. Speaking at a gathering of Sri Lankan Tamils in

3

London in early December 2003, he reiterated what has become a pet LTTE theme since New Delhi's crackdown a decade ago:

> We want a healthy relationship with India. We will not act in any way prejudicial to India's geo-political, strategic and economic interests. We want to establish friendly relations with the government of India. As such, we are seeking a radical change in India's attitude.

Balasingham went on, making one significant departure from all his previous comments:

> If India wishes to play a significant role in the current peace process, then she should not treat the LTTE as a hostile force. Both sides have made mistakes in the past. Let us put the past behind us and look forward. We urge India to adopt a new, creative approach and initiate friendly relations with our organization.

There can be no doubt that the LTTE, whatever it might say publicly, continues to feel the pinch of India's policy decision to treat the Tigers as an outcaste. In the immediate aftermath of the 1992 ban, the LTTE was somewhat cocky about its ability to set right its fractured ties with India. Having meddled in Indian politics for too long, the LTTE was under the impression that the after-effects of Rajiv Gandhi's killing would not outlast a regime led or influenced by the Congress party in New Delhi. By assassinating Rajiv Gandhi, the LTTE failed to realize that it had rubbed the Indian security establishment the wrong way—and gravely at that.

Since then the Tigers have tried various ways to get into the good books of New Delhi but in vain. If the Indian government continues to view the LTTE as a group capable of posing security threats (as it now does), it is highly unlikely the ban on it would be lifted even in 2004, whatever be Balasingham's protestations.

This is where Balasingham's admission that the LTTE has made mistakes assumes significance. The LTTE theoretician—a British national who mainly lives in London—did not elaborate what "mistakes" he was referring to. Of course we know that in the LTTE's eyes India has made numerous "mistakes"—most of which the Tigers have publicized over the years. But what are the "mistakes" he feels the LTTE committed? He does not say. The obvious inference is the killing of Rajiv Gandhi.

I have said it before and say it again: the assassination of the former Indian prime minister was Prabhakaran's biggest blunder. As a Sri Lankan Tamil politician remarked, using Hindu religious idioms:

> The Saturn takes hold of you for seven and a half years during every cycle, making you undergo great hardships. In the case of Prabhakaran, the Saturn gripped him on 21 May 1991 (when Rajiv Gandhi was killed) and it is unlikely to leave him.

The Indian security establishment now considers the Tigers an unfriendly force, one that can never be trusted, and one that is unlikely to be ever genuinely friendly towards India. Though suspicions about the LTTE started to originate as early as the 1980s, the group retained a measure of sympathy in India for a variety of reasons, even while fighting Indian troops in Sri Lankan's northeast. But as the investigation into Rajiv Gandhi's meticulously planned killing showed, the Tigers could go to any length to exterminate a key player of the Indian political establishment (a possible second time Prime Minister at that)—a cold-blooded act that even the perennially hostile Pakistani intelligence agencies would have dreaded to undertake.

This was in line with the LTTE's publicized thinking that the group has its right to use anyone for its goals, but it reserved the right to strike back, in whatever way, if it felt it had been "betrayed". Such thinking means there is nothing to stop the LTTE from doing another Rajiv Gandhi-like operation vis-à-vis India, a country whose leadership, whatever the party at the helm of affairs in New Delhi, is highly unlikely to ever back the break up of Sri Lanka and support the establishment of an LTTE-led Tamil Eelam state. So, even though the LTTE has in recent years tried to influence Shiv Sena chief Bal Thackeray and has allowed the Vishwa Hindu Parishad (VHP) to operate in the country's east (where LTTE-backed anti-Muslim violence keeps occurring), there seems to be no place for the Tigers in New Delhi's strategic worldview.

The LTTE probably realizes this. Which is why Balasingham has referred publicly to the unspecified "mistakes" committed by the group. But even while making such seemingly conciliatory statements, there is a certain undertone in LTTE thinking that only reinforces fears in New Delhi about the group's long-standing goals and strategy.

A few days after Balasingham made his London speech, the International Students Association of Thamileelam (ISAT), a pro-LTTE body, issued a statement, also calling upon India to adopt a positive stance that would help the Tamils to arrive at a fair and just political solution meeting their legitimate aspirations.

It went on to say that at no stage had the Tamil freedom struggle targeted India's geo-political interest, its economic and political stability or even its sovereignty.

And then the student body made a bizarre charge, probably giving a hint to the LTTE's mindset:

The Sri Lankan Tamils have suspicions that India might be behind the current constitutional crisis in Sri Lanka. Sri Lankan Tamils are also holding the view that India has been attempting to promote a new Tamil leadership comprising Tamil groups which earlier worked under the Indian Army and later had been working with the Sri Lankan Army.

After a decade of hands-off policy vis-à-vis Sri Lanka, some changes are beginning to take place in New Delhi. None of this, even remotely, has a pro-LTTE shadow. This should worry the Tigers. One is India's public decision that it would favour only such a solution to Sri Lanka's ethnic conflict that keeps that island nation physically intact—in other words, an independent Tamil Eelam would not be acceptable to New Delhi, however much the LTTE might insist that Tamils (read the LTTE) alone have a right to decide their future. India has of course always held this view—even when it trained the Tamil militants in the 1980s. But this was reiterated in October this year for the first time in years, just when the LTTE was preparing to submit its much-awaited proposals for an interim set-up for the north and east of Sri Lanka.

Increasingly unhappy with the kind of role being played by Norway and countries like Japan in the Oslo-brokered peace process, New Delhi has decided to forge a military relationship with Colombo. When President Chandrika Kumaratunga took on Prime Minister Ranil Wickremesinghe in November (shortly after the Indian statement referred to above), triggering a major political crisis, India used diplomatic channels to convey to both leaders that Colombo's interests would be better served if they worked together—a view that does not serve the LTTE's purpose.

Indian opinion makers are also beginning to take the view that the LTTE has been treated with velvet gloves for too long. About a year ago, one of India's foremost experts on terrorism, B. Raman, formerly of the Cabinet Secretariat, said it was important for New Delhi

keep up the pressure for Prabhakaran's extradition (he is wanted in India for Rajiv Gandhi's assassination) and to encourage the emergence of a moderate leadership in the LTTE. At this moment, such an alternate leadership is nowhere in the horizon and appears to be a pipedream. This does not mean that India should not try for it. In fact, India should have started looking for such alternate leadership immediately after the assassination of Rajiv Gandhi. It has already wasted 11 years. It should not waste more.

And in December 2003, M.K. Rasgotra, a former Indian Foreign Secretary, publicly warned the LTTE not to provoke India by taking fishermen from Tamil Nadu captive in the sea. This is one of the strongest statements made on the subject by any Indian. Tamil Nadu Chief Minister Jayaram Jayalalitha, who has emerged as the most influential and thoroughly uncompromising anti-LTTE political force in India, has now called for joint training by the Indian and Sri Lankan navies in the Palk Strait to send a message to the LTTE that its brazenness on the sea would not be tolerated.

What has irked Indian policy makers is the LTTE decision to impound and its audacious refusal to release the boats of the fishermen it detained (the men were freed following Norwegian intervention) until "compensation" was paid for their trespass into waters supposedly belonging to the Sea Tigers, the group's naval wing. These are some of the very fishermen who once upon a time, like many in Tamil Nadu, supported the Tamil cause in Sri Lanka and some of whom even sold diesel to the LTTE!

The Norwegian-sponsored peace process has also led to a situation whereby the LTTE has almost legitimized its control of the north and the east. Since the February 2002 truce between the Tigers and Colombo, several countries and international bodies have begun to treat the LTTE as if it was a legal, legitimate entity. It is no wonder the LTTE has sought to legitimize the Sea Tigers, demanding that it be treated as the third navy of the region. Some Indian officials and policy makers feel the Norwegians are needlessly indulgent towards the LTTE (although it has been branded a terrorist group in countries ranging from the US to Britain to India) and are very hesitant to criticize it despite its continued killing of opponents, abduction of children as well as various acts of illegality.

The LTTE of course thinks the north and east of Sri Lanka belongs to it and that it alone can decide what is good for that region—and for the Tamil people. And with the kind of dubious links the LTTE has forged over the years around the world to buy arms and ammunition, India is extremely wary of having in its neighbourhood an armed force in control of a large swathe of territory. In any case, the bottom line is that New Delhi cannot condone the terrorism of the LTTE variety while crying hoarse over acts of terror perpetrated against India by other groups with roots within and outside the region.

This is where the Sri Lankan political crisis comes in. Whatever the merits/demerits of the way President Kumaratunga sacked on November 4 three key ministers and took over the Defence Ministry, the political stalemate has led to a freeze on the kind of unilateral concessions that were being made by Prime Minister Wickremesinghe to the LTTE—some of them sanctified by the ceasefire agreement. And despite the widespread criticism of Kumaratunga, the Sri Lankan military is happy with her intervention. Her actions have, however, given the LTTE the moral high ground to argue that Sri Lankan politicians will never give any meaningful concessions to the Tamil community, come what may. This in turn reinforces the LTTE worldview that Sri Lanka is made up of two nations, the Sinhala nation and the Tamil nation, and that these two nations cannot co-exist in peace and in one territorial unit.

It is not without significance that Prabhakaran's annual speech of November 2003 is replete with references to the "Sinhala nation", the "Sinhala political parties", the "Sinhala chauvinistic ruling elites", the "Sinhala racist forces" and "Sinhala racism". There are few references to Sri Lanka. The speech also made it clear (to those who have had doubts) that the Tigers have not given up their avowed goal of Tamil Eelam, to be gained through armed struggle. What they are now seeking is an interim administration. This does not mean that they will not one day break away from

Sri Lanka. Indian policy makers are convinced that the proposals for an interim set up advanced by the LTTE can only be an eventual stepping stone for a Tamil Eelam. In a situation where the Tigers are getting entrenched in the north and the east and Sri Lanka's two main political parties are squabbling over the peace process, India has a delicate and difficult situation on hand. It has to be very observant and focused and tread slowly and carefully vis-à-vis Sri Lanka.

(*Mainstream*, 27 December 2003)


# 2

(This was one of the most exhaustive commentaries written on the split in the LTTE, within two weeks of the event. It is based on information that came largely from Batticaloa where Karuna was based. I had predicted that irrespective of how the Karuna revolt ends, it would seriously weaken the LTTE.)


## Turmoil in Tiger land

ALMOST three decades after the LTTE was set up with nothing more than a handful of weapons, the world's reputedly most well-organized and well-armed insurgent group is facing its gravest crisis. Despite the LTTE's public assertions to the contrary, it is a challenge LTTE chief Velupillai Prabhakaran has never faced. The decision by V. Muralitharan alias Colonel Karuna to break away from the LTTE with over 5,000 fighters in the eastern districts of Batticaloa and Amparai is something that even the most hardened Sri Lanka watchers had never thought would happen one day. It is an event of monumental importance, and it will certainly leave the LTTE seriously weakened, whichever way the crisis ends.

The most striking thing about the revolt by Karuna, the longest-serving regional commander in the LTTE, is that it has already lasted well over a fortnight. And since the LTTE leadership may not risk an attack on Karuna's forces (although this too cannot be ruled out), it is increasingly clear that the LTTE will try to create confusion in Karuna's ranks and assassinate him to bring the unprecedented revolt to a quick end. This could well happen before 2 April when Sri Lanka will hold its parliamentary elections. It is no wonder that the London-based LTTE ideologue, Anton Balasingham, claims that Prabhakaran has a strategy to overcome the situation without armed violence and bloodshed and that the rebellion "is a temporary aberration, which will pass away in time". However, since Karuna is a battle hardened fighter who must have learnt the Prabhakaran mindset in the past two decades he has been with the LTTE, these are risks he must have hopefully prepared himself for.

Published reports say that Karuna's forces, numbering 5,000 to 8,000 men and women guerrillas, are massed in the northern zone of Batticaloa, ready for an aggression that the LTTE forces might undertake from Trincomalee district, further north. Karuna's men are also keeping a close watch on possible infiltration by LTTE fighters from adjoining areas controlled by Prabhakaran. The LTTE chief has not commented on Karuna's defiance, but the various statements that have come so far from his camp show a certain confusion bordering on uncertainty. This has never happened in the LTTE earlier.

It was on 3 March that Karuna's stinging revolt came out in the open. The tough-talking, tough-looking man, who until recently had been a member of the LTTE delegations in the peace talks with Colombo, suddenly informed the Norwegian facilitators that he was breaking away from the Tigers ranks and wanted a separate peace pact with Colombo. A stunned Sri Lankan government of Prime Minister Ranil Wickremesinghe quickly turned down the request. While Norwegian Special Envoy Erik Solheim—who is being increasingly criticized by many Tamils for reportedly glossing over the LTTE's continuing violations of the ceasefire terms—rushed to the northern town of Kilinochchi to meet the LTTE leaders, he refused to intervene in the LTTE crisis. But his comparing Karuna's move with Wickremesinghe's spat with President Chandrika Kumaratunga would have been surely jarring for Prabhakaran.

Once Karuna came out in the open, events moved at remarkable speed. In the first reaction to the media, a spokesman for Karuna said that LTTE fighters in both Batticaloa and Amparai would henceforth take orders only from Karuna. The 4 March issue of *Thamil Alai* (Tamil Wave) newspaper, published from Kokkaddicholai, a large village controlled by Karuna about 15 km from Batticaloa town, quoted a Karuna aide as saying:

We are functioning with commitment to our cause under the command of our national leader Prabhakaran and the guidance of commander Colonel Karuna.

But the next day, the same daily carried an open letter from Karuna to Prabhakaran that almost mocked the LTTE chief. In the letter, Karuna brought to public knowledge, for the first time, his complaints that the Tamils of Sri Lanka's east were being discriminated against by the northern Tamils. He feigned loyalty to Prabhakaran but underlined that he did not consider the guerrilla chief above the problem. In what can only be described as a carefully worded communication, Karuna said:

> Please let us function independently under your direct leadership. We are not leaving you. We are not opposed to you.

But the taunt followed:

> If you love the people here (eastern Sri Lanka) and if you trust the fighters here, please let us function independently and directly under your leadership. In the current situation, I want to do my duty by the people of southern Tamil Eelam. It is my final goal that I should fight for these people and die at their feet. I do not want anyone to interfere in this.

By then, pamphlets were being distributed in Batticaloa in the name of Karuna calling upon Prabhakaran to sack three of his closest aides if he desired reconciliation with the renegade commander. One of the three was Pottu Amman, the feared LTTE intelligence chief who serves as Prabhakaran's eyes and ears. Karuna would have surely known that Prabhakaran would never accept this demand. Published reports say that Karuna—one of the LTTE's most respected military strategists—had been bothered by the activities of the LTTE intelligence chief in his Batticaloa–Amparai area and had become convinced that Pottu Amman was targeting him with the ultimate objective of killing him. So, to avoid a repetition of what happened to G. Mahendrarajah alias Mahattaya, the former LTTE number 2 who was executed in 1994 on charges of being an Indian spy after a sting operation by the LTTE intelligence, Karuna struck—employing to his advantage—the long-held differences between the Jaffna and Batticaloa Tamils with devastating effect.

Finally, on 6 March, the LTTE retaliated. A full 72 hours after Karuna's rebellion erupted, the LTTE sacked him, accusing him of "acting traitorously to the Tamil people and to the Tamil Eelam national leadership". The gloves were off—from both sides now. Karuna's supporters, in an act symbolizing the formal snapping of ties with Prabhakaran, burnt the LTTE leader's effigies at Valaichenai and Thirukkovil towns in Batticaloa district. This would have been unthinkable in the past. As tensions escalated, students from Jaffna studying in Batticaloa town fled the university fearing death at the hands of Karuna's men. LTTE police stations and kangaroo courts, which did not come under the direct control of Karuna, were ordered to stop functioning in his domain. A peeved LTTE announced a new command for Batticaloa and Amparai and presented before journalists Karuna's most senior aides who, it said, were siding with Prabhakaran. But they were far removed from where they should have been based and with no indication if they would be able to return to Batticaloa. No wonder, even on 8 March, the LTTE chose to receive at Kilinochchi, where it has its political headquarters, a delegation of senior citizens from Batticaloa who wanted Prabhakaran and Karuna to make up even now.

But it was too late. A war of words had now begun. S. Karikalan, a former head of the LTTE's Batticaloa–Amparai political division, for the first time blamed "external forces" for Karuna's "confused state of mind". Speaking to the London-based IBC Tamil Radio, Karikalan—who is also from the country's east—accused Karuna of acting without consulting any of his commanders or political aides. Yet, in the same breath, Karikalan indicated that Karuna's upsurge might not have been that sudden. "I struggled to resolve the crisis by talking to him several times," Karikalan explained. He added:

Our leader (Prabhakaran) invited me to come to Kilinochchi at the very start of the crisis. But I wanted to find an amicable solution and (I) stayed in Batticaloa to talk with Karuna in an attempt to keep him under the national leadership.

Clearly, Karuna had discussed his discontent with some of his commanders—this probably explains why some of his closest aides, realizing what was to come, managed to flee to the Prabhakaran-controlled north.

In a strategic move, Karuna kept escalating the tempo. He accused the LTTE of asking him to provide 1,000 fighters from the east and claimed it showed Prabhakaran wanted to resume his separatist campaign. The LTTE, under international scrutiny, quickly denied the charge. It also warned that it also had plans to retake the vast area under Karuna's control. "By refusing to abide by our movement's ruling, he is pushing himself into a dangerous corner," thundered S.P. Tamilchelvan, the LTTE's political head and a Prabhakaran confidant. Karuna's men scoffed at him. They asserted that they had complete control on the Batticaloa–Amparai region and that there was no LTTE in the area any more.

Allegations and counter-allegations were now aired thick and fast. In a hard-hitting interview to *The Hindu* at his lair, Karuna hit out at Prabhakaran, accusing him of refusing to share power with his colleagues ("this is his monumental mistake") and of preventing others from "growing up as an equal to him". "In the beginning he was a good man," the rebel said. But he added that once Prabhakaran came under the influence of people like Pottu Amman, he moved away from the leadership qualities and started behaving differently. Pottu Amman, who along with Prabhakaran is wanted in India and by the Interpol, is a terrorist, alleged Karuna. None of the work done by him is acceptable to the international community.

Although not blaming Prabhakaran for the crime, Karuna described the gory 1991 assassination of former Indian Prime Minister Rajiv Gandhi as the LTTE's biggest blunder. It is because of the assassination that we have such a bad reputation, he said.

And in comments that could only be dubbed sacrilegious, he said Tamil nationalism in Sri Lanka would survive only "when the northern Tamil Eelam people discard the Wanni leadership". It was a clear reference to Prabhakaran, whose headquarters are based in the thickly forested region.

Stung, the LTTE hit back with a well-coordinated counter attack. Tamil newspapers took an anti-Karuna line, and the once admired Batticaloa–Amparai boss began to do to the Tamil media what the LTTE had done when it suited it—muzzling its voice. Tamil journalists in Batticaloa were told to accept Karuna as the new god of the region. Most Tamil media organizations around the world echoed the allegations levelled by the LTTE against Karuna, who was dubbed a "traitor" to the Tamil cause. In the LTTE's lingua franca, calling someone a traitor is tantamount to passing a death sentence against him.

The LTTE also accused Karuna of embezzling money and of poisoning his driver who was aware of the wrongdoings. In comments that could only be aimed at India, the LTTE's Karikalan—now in the forefront of the anti-Karuna campaign—accused "a foreign force hostile to Tamil struggle" of covertly backing the rebel commander. "Karuna could not have acted traitorously without external backing," he said. "He has been brought over by an external power that is intent on destroying our liberation struggle and our leadership."

The developments in the LTTE have caused an unprecedented rift in the world's most ruthless and, until now, the most regimented insurgent group and raised doubts about Sri Lanka's fragile peace process. Even in the realm of the impossible, probably only Karuna could have dared anything like this. To understand what is going on within the LTTE, it is vital to know and understand Karuna.

A native of Kiran village in Batticaloa district, Karuna was a former bodyguard of Prabhakaran (only the most trusted men are allowed to protect the LTTE chief) who rose rapidly in a group that combines terrorism with the classical tenets of war and insurgency. Karuna joined the LTTE after the anti-Tamil pogrom of 1983 and came to head the Batticaloa–Amparai division in 1987, the year when India deployed troops in Sri Lanka's north and east. The Indians never managed to catch him, but the man came on his own only after the war for Tamil Eelam resumed in June 1990. One of his most brutal acts was gunning down some 600 policemen, mostly Sinhalese, who had surrendered to the LTTE in Batticaloa.

As the years rolled by, Prabhakaran came to depend more and more on Karuna. Very soon he came to be recognized as a brilliant military strategist, one who knew how to win even against impossible odds and was fiercely loyal to the LTTE boss. He played a key role in reversing the Sri Lankan military gains that forced President Kumaratunga to sue for peace with the LTTE with the help of the Norwegians.

After the LTTE signed a truce with Colombo in February 2002, Karuna was a leading member of the LTTE delegation at the peace talks. In April that year, when Prabhakaran met the media for the first time in a decade, Karuna was seated by him. Last year, Karuna was named the Special Commander of the Batticaloa–Amparai region. In retrospect, it is evident the man was deeply unhappy with the activities of the LTTE intelligence wing, which reported directly only to Pottu Amman and who in turn reported directly to Prabhakaran. It was this that finally forced him to break away.

Even when Mahattaya was executed, there were murmurs of discontent in the Tamil society. But Prabhakaran never felt militarily challenged. That has now happened for the first time. If Karuna does have thousands of fighters with him, it would meant the LTTE's fighting strength—estimated at some 12,000 to 18,000—has been seriously eroded. This is bound to have major consequences for Prabhakaran's ability to wage war again and also put a question mark on the future of the Norwegian-sponsored peace process, even if both Colombo and Oslo refuse to deal with Karuna.

(*Mainstream*, 27 March 2004)

# 3

(Once the LTTE crushed the Karuna rebellion in April 2004, the rebel commander quickly went out of sight. In July 2004, he spoke over the telephone in Tamil from an undisclosed location to three Sri Lankan journalists and to me. He claimed he was still in Sri Lanka and that his break up had seriously weakened the LTTE.)

## "Only a snake understands a snake"

**Why are you forming a political party?**

People have lost hope in the (armed) struggle. We can achieve our objectives only through the democratic process. Death and destruction cannot go on.

**When will it be formed?**

Prabhakaran has killed or tried to kill everyone who chose the democratic path to oppose him. At an appropriate time we will come out openly with our party. We cannot do that now.

**Will your party have an armed wing?**

We are not interested in an armed wing. After all I had 6,000 (guerrillas) with me. But I dismissed them. But if the situation demands, we will be forced to set up an armed wing.

**Is not Prabhakaran also for peace?**

Prabhakaran had told us he is not interested in talks. He was interested only in the procurement of weapons. When I went to Thailand (for peace talks), he told me meet KP's people (the LTTE's chief arms procurer is a Jaffna man known as KP). I met them and gave them a list of weapons we needed. I can say with certainty that a lot of arms shipments have arrived during the peace period.

**Do you think Sri Lanka will see war again?**

President Chandrika Kumaratunga seems sincere. But Prabhakaran does not share her belief (in peace). The talks are a ruse for him to fool people and the international community.

**How do you know all this?**

Only a snake understands a snake. He has always been preparing to resume the war. This demand (for autonomy in Sri Lanka's north and east) is a drama.

**What about the Tamil people?**

Our people are sick and tired of fighting. They want peace.

**What effect has your action had on LTTE?**

(Because of my split), they are very weak and they will continue to get weaker.

**What role do you envisage for yourself?**

Earlier they told Norway that I was an internal problem for them. Now things have changed. Now they tell the government there cannot be talks until the Karuna problem is resolved.

**What about India?**

We need India's support. We strongly believe that without India's support, nothing is possible; peace won't come to Sri Lanka. The killing of Rajiv Gandhi was a blunder. It killed the Tamil Eelam struggle. The killing has ensured that an independent Tamil state will never be possible.

**By the way, where are you?**

We are in Batticaloa. Their (LTTE) propaganda is that I have gone abroad. I have not gone anywhere. I am here.

*(The Week*, 25 July 2004)

# 4

(Sri Lanka was the worst victim of the December 2004 tsunami after Indonesia. For a brief while, it seemed that the colossal human tragedy would perhaps help heal the festering wounds of the ethnic conflict. I argued, within a week of the tragedy, that this was most unlikely. Unfortunately, I was proved to be right.)

## Can tsunami bring peace to Sri Lanka?

PARTLY due to ignorance and partly because of misplaced optimism, there is a feeling that the killer tsunami that ravaged Sri Lanka may push the Tamil Tiger guerrillas to sue for peace with the government.

Nothing could be further from the truth.

There is no doubt that the LTTE suffered heavily when mammoth waves rising up to 40 feet swept away many thousands in the island's northeast—the war theatre.

In just two hours of Black Sunday, Sri Lanka lost close to 30,000 people—half the numbers killed by the ethnic conflict in over two decades. While civilians, as elsewhere in Sri Lanka, suffered the maximum in the northeast, an unspecified number of LTTE fighters also perished. The estimates range from "many dozens" to "hundreds".

But military experts feel the losses to the Sea Tigers, the LTTE's naval wing, may not be very high because they keep their vessels inland, far away from the coastline, as a matter of routine.

After the tragedy, some sources in Colombo speculated that the Tigers may have lost up to 1,500 fighters, perhaps even more, in Batticaloa and Trincomalee districts and that most of these would be from the Sea Tigers.

However, residents in Batticaloa town insist that panic did grip local LTTE cadres in the immediate aftermath of the 26 December killer waves that Tamil Tigers chief Velupillai Prabhakaran described as the deadliest of nature's furies to hit the northeast.

"For the first time we saw fear on their faces," one resident told IANS over telephone. "They always look and act fearless, giving an impression that they are invincible. But that day I saw them frantically stopping vans belonging to aid agencies and pleading with them to do something."

Another source said that numerous small villages on the Batticaloa coast were still under water, with no news of their residents.

So how many cadres did the LTTE lose?

The LTTE has thrown no light on the subject and its websites have spoken mainly of civilian losses, which indeed are colossal.

According to "Colonel" Soosai, the Sea Tigers he heads lost just over half-a-dozen fighters and suffered "some property damage. In Trincomalee and Batticaloa two observation posts were washed away. The losses are not that significant".

One source in Batticaloa said he went to a LTTE camp four days after the disaster and found new faces. "My belief is most of the earlier inmates died but were quickly replaced from inland. But they are not admitting any of this."

The LTTE can only be expected to underplay its losses. When the LTTE's former regional commander Karuna split with thousands of fighters, the rebels insisted on calling it a "one man problem" until it became embarrassing to say so.

But one military analyst said: "I don't think the LTTE has suffered very major military losses. But they have taken some serious blows. One, the large-scale deaths and civilian displacement means the numbers they can recruit from has fallen drastically. Also, the economy of the region they taxed has been almost shattered. They also don't have the resources to face a crisis of this sort."

What must be bothering the LTTE is its inability to get direct international assistance the way it would have wanted, forcing it to publicly declare that it could take help from the very Sri Lankan state it has vowed to break up.

Soosai has publicly said that Colombo should not differentiate between the Tamils and Sinhalese and that Sri Lanka's navy must emulate the example of its Indian counterpart and come to the aid of the beleaguered Tamil population.

Rebuilding the battered northeast, in particular areas held by LTTE, will not be easy. The Tigers have deployed two "battalions", including elite units, in relief and rescue efforts. It has sought trucks from Colombo, and is urging Tamil expatriates to contribute generously.

There are complaints that LTTE cadres have commandeered at gunpoint half-a-dozen trucks packed with food and drugs meant for civilians. And with hundreds of buried land mines getting displaced because of the tsunami, foreign aid agencies fear to venture into some areas.

But even if LTTE's political head S.P. Tamilchelvan is making conciliatory noises during this hour of crisis, this can only be a strategic move. When the Sri Lankan prime minister went to Jaffna, LTTE-sponsored protests forced him to cut short his trip. The Tigers don't want Colombo to get credit for relief and rehabilitation; at the same time they cannot provide a new lease of life to the displaced on their own. International aid agencies will not find it easy to bypass Colombo and deal with LTTE. This will be the rebels' biggest dilemma.

But the LTTE remains fixated on its stated goal of Tamil Eelam, tsunami or no tsunami. What the killer waves have done is to put off for an unspecified period a war that seemed, until Christmas, imminent. For now, there will be no war.

(IANS, 2 January 2005)

# 5

(When the tsunami struck in December 2004, causing unprecedented death and destruction in Sri Lanka, it initially brought out the best in people, the Sinhalese, Tamils, and Muslims. Forgetting their ethnic differences, ordinary folks helped one another in distress, providing immense relief when there was only darkness. Unfortunately, this was quickly overtaken by the disaster of war politics.)

## The tsunami, and Prabhakaran

TSUNAMI or no tsunami, the irrepressible Vellupillai Prabhakaran remains committed to an independent Tamil Eelam.

Tsunami has, however, postponed a fresh conflict that had seemed imminent. The LTTE had been belligerent ever since the humiliation of a split in its ranks in March–April 2004. That event was followed by escalating violence in Sri Lanka, with the Tigers claiming responsibility for some killings in brazen defiance of the February 2002 ceasefire pact. By December 2004, both the LTTE and Sri Lankan troops had advanced menacingly towards one another in parts of the east. The Tigers had also deployed their artillery in frontline areas, and Western diplomats in Colombo were wringing their hands in despair.

That was when tsunami struck, shattering the war plans and Sri Lanka alike.

The December 26 disaster that ravaged Sri Lanka, claiming in just 30 minutes more than half the number of lives lost during two decades of ethnic conflict, unsettled both the government in Colombo and the LTTE. In the immediate aftermath, even as a numbed Sri Lankan government desperately sought international assistance, the LTTE showed an uncharacteristic nervous streak. As residents fled their homes in the thousands, aid workers in Sri Lanka's eastern province of Batticaloa reported that visibly shaken LTTE cadres had stopped their vehicles and pleaded with them to do something. The cockiness was gone.

International aid poured in as the scale of devastation came to be known. As it normally happens in any disaster, the tsunami brought out the best in human beings. In the worst hit eastern province, as Tamils and Muslims reeled under the impact, ordinary Sinhalese citizens, Buddhist monks included, rushed in from adjoining areas with relief material. Even local LTTE leaders and at least one pro-LTTE Tamil MP admitted as much. Stories from the tsunami-devastated east spoke of Sinhalese soldiers—whose camps along the winding coast were as badly hit as the LTTE bases—doing what they could to save civilian lives.

A paralysed government in Colombo, however, did not wake up immediately. When it did, its concentration was more on the Sinhalese-majority areas in the southern shores, although it would be an exaggeration to say that it neglected the Tamil region.

By then, the LTTE had recovered from the initial shock and, as is its wont, launched a diatribe against Colombo. Despite suffering heavy losses, the Tigers asserted themselves in the areas of the north and east they controlled. The LTTE quickly made it clear to Colombo and the world at large that no one else would be allowed to call the shots in that region.

It unleashed a massive effort to dispose of bodies, treat the wounded, and provide succour. The government was accused of discriminating against the Tamils in the relief effort. LTTE-fronted "youth clubs" soon took control of places sheltering displaced Tamils, even as the government deployed soldiers in other camps. In the LTTE's ideology, Sri Lanka will always comprise a Sinhalese nation and a Tamil nation, and an ethnic rapprochement is out of question, whatever misplaced faith the international community might have on Norway's ability to arbitrate the end of two decades of conflict.

When Colombo announced a "state of emergency", the LTTE echoed a "national emergency". In tune with its ultimate secessionist goal, the Tigers insisted that foreign governments and international aid agencies would have to deal directly with it and not via Colombo. It made the Tamil Rehabilitation Organisation (TRO), an LTTE front, the nodal body for relief and rehabilitation in Tamil areas and forbade anyone else, even the LTTE-backed Tamil MPs (because they are paid by Colombo), to intervene. When Sri Lanka denied UN Secretary General Kofi Annan permission to make a trip to the LTTE-held north, the Tigers deployed counter-pressure to ensure that at least a special representative of Annan visited Kilinochchi, where the LTTE maintains its administrative headquarters.

The LTTE also launched a massive fund-collection drive from the Tamil diaspora. However unfortunate the tragedy was, LTTE chief Vellupillai Prabhakaran (whose reported death turned out to be a rumour) had exploited the tsunami to show that he was the undisputed head of a de facto separate nation. The Sri Lankan government's aid to Tamil areas did not matter: if help came from Colombo, it would be treated on par with assistance coming from any other country. After the initial burst of help-lessness, the LTTE leader called the natural disaster "another tsunami" for the Tamil people. Nothing, he meant, has happened to alter the ground realities in the Tamil north and east.

(*Hard News*, February 2005)

# 6

(Shankar Rajee was one of the best-informed Sri Lankan Tamils when it came to Tamil militancy. There was nothing that escaped his eye. And he was generous in sharing his understanding of the situation with those who cared to seek him out. I did that often. I wrote this after his death.)

## Tribute: Shankar Rajee

SHANKAR RAJEE, who died of a heart attack in Colombo on 10 January 2005, was one of the earliest entrants into Tamil militancy in Sri Lanka, one who closely witnessed the growth of the movement from its nascent days to the frightening proportions it has now assumed. In the last years of his life, Shankar (real name Nesadurai Thirunesan) had bowed out of the Indian media scene and led a largely low key, though not quiet, life, hopping between Chennai, where his mother lived, and Colombo, where he was a consultant with the state-run Cashew Corporation. He was also the leader of whatever was left of the EROS, the oldest of all Tamil militant groups that came up in the 1970s in response to growing Sinhala chauvinism. Shankar, who was educated in Jaffna and London, was among the earliest Tamils who took military training from Palestinian guerrillas in the Middle East, probably in the hope that their own community would some day produce a Yasser Arafat.

In the years I covered the Sri Lankan ethnic conflict, I came into close contact with Shankar and he helped me gain valuable insight into the Tamil society. Our first meeting took place at the EROS office in a middle-class Chennai neighbourhood where I had gone to interview its best-known leader, V. Balakumar. As the latter spoke to me, I saw Shankar seated by his side, studying a map of Jaffna and making a note or two. EROS had a collective leadership in which Balakumar and Shankar were the first among equals. They had contrasting personalities. Balakumar was the quite one, almost inaudible and at home in Tamil, while Shankar spoke Tamil and English with equal ease, was outgoing and felt comfortable dealing with Indian bureaucracy and diplomats. Shankar was designated the head of the EROS Military Unit and maintained liaison with revolutionary groups from around the world.

Like so many Sri Lankan Tamils of that era, Shankar was a Marxist during his student days. In London, he and like-minded students formed a student group and then in 1975 set up EROS. It was a path-breaking development in Tamil history. Some EROS members enjoyed a warm relationship with the local PLO representative who helped them to fly to Lebanon and Syria to get military training from Arafat's Fatah guerrilla group. Shankar valued this training although nothing much came out of it. It was EROS that introduced the LTTE, then a virtually unknown group, to the Palestinians. But this produced frictions between him and the LTTE chief Velupillai Prabhakaran. The row was over money, which Shankar paid up. But their relations never improved and years later, LTTE's Anton Balasingham, probably reflecting Prabhakaran's view, accused Shankar of being an Indian spy, a charge the latter vehemently denied.

Much before that, Shankar recalled meeting Prabhakaran sometime in 1975–76 in the Tamil Nadu town of Trichy. Shankar had flown into India from London carrying air gun pellets, batteries and film rolls. He had been told to deliver them to a man but was not given his identity. It turned out to be Prabhakaran, a young and largely unknown entity who turned up at a small hotel across the Trichy bus station where Shankar was putting up. When I researched for the LTTE chief's biography *Inside an Elusive Mind*, Shankar told me: "It was Prabhakaran who came to take the delivery. Honestly, I was not impressed with him. He did not seem happy with what I had brought. He obviously was expecting some other things. Just what I do not know."

Years later, before the souring of ties, Shankar had a more fruitful meeting in an LTTE hideout in Sri Lanka's north with Prabhakaran who by then had begun to acquire a stature in the militant ranks. Shankar had a vivid memory, and in 2001 could recall what really happened. "Prabhakaran was eager to know what training the Palestinians imparted. His eyes sparkled at the mention of M-16s, AK-47s and anti-aircraft guns. But he was keen to hear about pistols and revolvers."

But Prabhakaran was not a man of theory. He invited Shankar to display his shooting skills. The target was an empty *Milk Maid* can. From 20 feet away, Shankar took aim and grazed the can, toppling it. Prabhakaran walked up to the fallen can, picked it up and put it back on the wall. He then returned to where the Fatah-trained Shankar was standing and fired. He hit the can smack in the middle. Shankar was naturally impressed.

Despite the Palestinian training, Shankar and his friends in EROS did not carry out any military action in Sri Lanka. There were also differences within EROS, leading to a split and the birth of the EPRLF. When Tamil militancy galloped from 1983, EROS was among the first groups to secure Indian military training. Shankar was also among the first to understand that New Delhi would never allow an independent Tamil Eelam to come up.

During the years leading up to the 1987 India–Sri Lanka peace agreement that sought to end Tamil separatism, Shankar, as the EROS Military Wing leader, masterminded some deadly bomb attacks in the island nation that claimed many innocent lives. He also developed close ties with the Indian establishment but this was not enough to save him from a jail term in Chennai that may have contributed to his early death.

Shankar and Balakumar met the then Prime Minister, Rajiv Gandhi, just before the latter flew to Colombo in July 1987 to sign the India–Sri Lanka accord. Prabhakaran, however, continued to mistrust him. Shankar and Balakumar met the LTTE chief at New Delhi's Ashok Hotel at that time; but on a second occasion, Prabhakaran told Balakumar that he did not want to see Shankar.

Shankar had a keen understanding of the Sri Lankan Tamil society and of LTTE. When the Tigers took on the Indian Army, he prophesied to friends that Prabhakaran would never, ever give up his Eelam goal. He was proved right. In March 1990, the

Indian troops came home and the now powerful LTTE ordered EROS to disband or merge with the Tigers. Some disgusted EROS members drifted away from politics; other (Balakumar included) joined LTTE while a small band led by Shankar kept the outfit's flag flying for whatever it was worth.

Shankar was arrested in 1997 on charges of smuggling foreign currency and was jailed. None of his contacts in the Indian establishment came to his rescue. He spent over a year in prison where, his mother recalled later, he developed a good rapport with the other, mostly Indian, prisoners and became their leader. But despite the bitterness the detention caused, Shankar considered himself a friend of India. The imprisonment, however, affected his health, and he was never the same old self again.

Shankar never underestimated the LTTE or Prabhakaran. At the same time, he could not think of giving up his independent existence. Once the Sri Lankan military took control of Jaffna from LTTE in December 1995, Shankar visited the town to see a relative. The LTTE—which controlled a small part of Jaffna peninsula but had many eyes and ears in the region—came to know about the visit. The Tigers wanted to know if Shankar was merely calling on the relative or trying to resurrect EROS. Shankar got the message and promptly left Jaffna. More than once he told me that Prabhakaran's personality would never allow him to compromise with Colombo, Norway or no Norway. It is a viewpoint that many have come to share now. But in February 2002, when the LTTE and the Sri Lankan government signed a ceasefire, only a few like Shankar asserted, with confidence that comes with experience, that it would not lead to Prabhakaran embracing Colombo, never ever.

(*The Mainstream*, 15–21 April 2005)

# 7

(On 12 August 2005, an LTTE sniper shot dead Kadirgamar as he approached the swimming pool in his well-guarded house in the heart of Colombo. It was one of those meticulous killings the LTTE was notorious for. It irrevocably turned the West against the Tigers and eventually killed the ceasefire pact.)

## Kadirgamar assassination will kill peace process

THE cold-blooded assassination of Sri Lankan Foreign Minister Lakshman Kadirgamar, who for a long time figured high on the Tamil Tigers' hit list, is a death blow to the already floundering peace process. The killing may or may not lead to the immediate resumption of war, but it is clear that the Norway-mediated ceasefire agreement (CFA) of 2002 will henceforth remain alive only on paper.

Three features stand out in the chilling Friday killing: one, the LTTE's ability to kill, and kill anyone anywhere, to achieve its goal of Tamil Eelam; two, the persisting inability of the Sri Lankan political establishment to understand the sheer determination of its foe; and three, the now very visible failing of Norway and the West to herald genuine peace in the island nation.

The LTTE has not claimed responsibility for the killing, and its vast diplomatic and strategic interests will prevent it from doing so. Even if the Norwegians lodge a "protest" with the LTTE against the killing (as they most probably will), the Tigers will simply wash their hands off saying they are not aware who cut down Kadirgamar. It is unlikely the assassins will ever be caught.

It may be pertinent to recall that in a 1991 BBC TV programme, the group's political ideologue, Anton Balasingham, admitted the LTTE does not claim responsibility for all the killings it does. His comments came soon after the grotesque assassination of former Indian Prime Minister Rajiv Gandhi, blown up by a LTTE woman suicide bomber.

By last year it was known to Sri Lankan authorities that the LTTE, taking advantage of the peace process, had laid a strong network of killer squads in Colombo. This is a proven LTTE tactic and has paid dividends in the past. LTTE sympathizers were letting it be known that in the event the war again erupted in Sri Lanka, Colombo— the country's heart and capital—would see death and destruction like never before. The ominous warning is already coming true.

Kadirgamar's killing is a tribute, if one may say so, to the LTTE's meticulous killing machine. Kadirgamar, who was a Jaffna Tamil married to a Sinhalese, knew he was living on borrowed time because the LTTE had a long time ago branded him a "traitor" for the Tamil cause. In the LTTE's blood-soaked dictionary, a "traitor" deserves to die. He was passionately anti-LTTE and never stopped propagating in the West (where the LTTE maintains a string of offices) that the Tigers were a terrorist force and needed to be dealt with as such.

There is no doubt that he did contribute to the hardening of positions vis-à-vis the LTTE in countries such as Australia, Britain, Canada and the US. To the LTTE, he was a thorn who had to be removed. And it proved by gunning him down that no Sri Lankan was safe anywhere in the country even if he or she lived in a high-security neighbourhood.

The Sri Lankan political establishment is not just a badly divided house; any democratic society is bound to see sparring divisions. But it is clear the top political leaders have, despite two decades of blood and gore, not understood the LTTE's cold-blooded will to break up the island and achieve a free state called Tamil Eelam. Having failed to overcome the Tigers militarily, Sri Lankan politicians believe that Western mediation would somehow force the group to capitulate in some form or the other.

Kadirgamar, the man who led the foreign ministry for years, was a party to such wishful thinking.

LTTE chief Velupillai Prabhakaran, whether one likes it or not, is determined to achieve what he set out to secure when he fled his home way back in 1973 armed with nothing more than a fanciful dream. Over the years and decades, the LTTE has grown from a rag-tag outfit to the world's most awesome and well-knit insurgent group.

Those who feel the Tigers have given up or will ever renounce the path of secession are living in a fool's paradise. Sri Lankan politicians who think that Western mediation would provide them an "international safety net" against Tamil Eelam have failed to come to grips with Prabhakaran. Colombo's inability to come to a consensus on what constitutes the Tamil grievances and how to go about it has already led to a de facto Tamil Eelam, with its own distinct identity completely different from that of Sri Lanka.

In a way, this inability to understand the LTTE and Prabhakaran extends to the West. Norwegian diplomats admit they did think their job in Sri Lanka would be an easy one when they took their first initial steps in 1999. By last year the Norwegians were confessing the LTTE was not amenable. Contrary to what many in Sri Lanka think, the Norwegians have taken up with the LTTE the many killings the group has committed since February 2002. But the LTTE is just not bothered, and unlikely to heed anything the West might say because it knows the West will be unable to act against it.

(IANS, 13 August 2005)

# 8

(With the LTTE provoking Colombo and a new hardliner President in office, Norway found itself on very delicate ground as 2005 neared its end. This piece examined Norway's predicament—and the likely path ahead in Sri Lanka.)

## Norway has to recalibrate Sri Lanka peace process

AS Norway resumes its role as facilitator in Sri Lanka's stalled peace talks, it is clear things will never be the same again. Norwegian diplomats will not find it easy to establish a rapport with new President Mahinda Rajapaksa after his public attacks on them.

His Sinhalese–Buddhist hardliners remain distrustful of Oslo but need to be taken on board for the peace process to succeed. The LTTE is belligerent—and increasingly wary of global players. And India wants its sensitivities vis-à-vis the LTTE to be taken seriously.

Norwegian diplomats are also sick and tired of the criticism they have faced since the 2002 truce between the LTTE and Colombo. And they want some ground rules in place: (*i*) Sri Lankan leaders must stop flaying Norway in public while privately seeking its help; (*ii*) LTTE must give access to its chief Velupillai Prabhakaran, as easily as one meets the powers that be in Colombo; and (*iii*) both Colombo and the LTTE must respect the ceasefire sincerely; the latter has to end all killings.

At the same time, the Norwegians are emphasizing the need for human rights and pluralism in the island's north and east, parts of which are held by the LTTE, and saying they are not in the game to be a midwife for a free Tamil Eelam.

But all this is pointless until Colombo and the LTTE decide that they indeed want a negotiated settlement that takes care of their interests but without breaking up Sri Lanka. As Norwegian Prime Minister Jens Stoltenberg said in New Delhi: "We are interested in facilitating talks only if both parties are serious about reaching a resolution. If they are not willing, there is no role for Norway."

It is very easy to attack Norway, as indeed many have done, on grounds of its overt and covert bias towards the LTTE or being just plain naive vis-à-vis the latter's long-term intentions. There is no doubt some of the criticisms are valid. But no peace process can be perfect because it is aimed at bringing together deeply antagonistic parties and helping them find common grounds that can unite them or at least drastically reduce the gulf between them.

What is striking is that despite distinct differences, there are some remarkable parallels between the Norwegian role and the much less successful peace accord signed by New Delhi and Colombo in 1987. Both initiatives, despite divergent approaches, led to euphoria. The United National Party (UNP) initiated both moves; in both cases, the Sri Lanka Freedom Party (SLFP) either fully or partly came out in opposition.

Both India (quickly) and Norway (slowly) came under attack from Sinhalese–Buddhist nationalists on charges of being soft towards the Tigers. As is happening now, extremist rhetoric and actions on both sides pushed the peace that followed the 1987 pact into uncertainty and later to war.

On both occasions, the LTTE received covert funding from the peace brokers but refused to accept the peace process in full. When the LTTE started killing Tamil rivals in August/September 1987, Colombo bluntly told the Indians to move against the Tigers or get out. Norway has faced a similar situation.

One main difference between the Indian and Norwegian peace processes was that in 1987 the LTTE accepted the peace pact half-heartedly before jettisoning it with contempt. But because it signed an agreement in 2002 with Colombo, it was an enthusiastic partner for peace as long as it got a free run in the northeast.

Norway's biggest success has been that it has halted fighting in Sri Lanka for the longest duration since Tamil insurgency erupted in 1983. Norway's involvement also led to high-profile talks between the two sides. But, as in 1987, once the LTTE concluded that the peace process was undermining its interests, it backtracked.

In 1987, the LTTE accused India of secretly arming other Tamil groups; this time it blamed Colombo for backing its former regional commander Karuna. Both India and Norway, to somehow bring around the LTTE, made concessions to the group that not only hurt their credibility but made them suspects in the eyes of the Sinhalese majority.

But unlike in 1987, when the LTTE was promised a dominant but not exclusive say in an interim administration, the 2002 pact is tilted towards the group. While the accord allows the LTTE to do "political work" in government areas, Colombo gets no such reciprocity. But the Norwegians argue, and rightly, that the Tigers would have never agreed to a ceasefire if this was not so. The LTTE in 2002 was not of the 1987 vintage.

Today Norway has the backing of the West: this is its biggest strength. Norway also has no historical baggage to carry. Norwegian diplomats have shown great ability to withstand stringent and even personal attacks and still carry on.

The most important question is: can Norway succeed where India failed? Will and can the LTTE give up its separatist goal at some point of time? Whatever may be the LTTE's other faults, Prabhakaran has been candid in admitting that his target is Tamil Eelam and his participation in peace talks is only a strategic affair. Can the Sri Lankan state, which seems confused in its approach to peace, give concessions that satisfy the LTTE chief? Can there be a genuine rapprochement between the Tamils and Sinhalese?

Will Norway's new conditions for being a facilitator be accepted—and lead to a recalibration of its role? Or will it, like India, unwittingly end up making the LTTE more powerful? Norway has a daunting task ahead in Sri Lanka, one that will test its diplomatic skills to the limit.

(IANS, 11 December 2005)

2006

# 9

(The active international involvement was a key factor in Sri Lanka's peace process. But when it all began, the LTTE probably did not reckon with two factors. One was India's continuing veto power over any settlement that did not accept Sri Lanka's territorial integrity. The second was the West's loyalty to democracy and human rights, which the LTTE did not subscribe to. Nevertheless, the West continued to hope that the LTTE could be reformed and somehow persuaded to accept a political package that fell short of Tamil Eelam. That did not happen. Eventually, like India in an earlier era, several Western countries got disgusted with the Tigers. After Sri Lanka objected to peace facilitator Norway as a venue for talks in February 2006, Switzerland stepped in.)

## Switzerland taking deep interest in Sri Lanka

SWITZERLAND, which hosts this week's talks between Colombo and Tamil Tiger guerrillas, is one of the world's oldest democracies and has been taking a deep interest in Sri Lanka's ethnic conflict for years. It is precisely this reason that made Berne let the Sri Lankan government and the LTTE meet in Geneva between 22–23 February for their highest-level dialogue in three years after they squabbled over a venue.

Since Switzerland is not a member of the European Union, it was not bound by the latter's decision taken in September 2005 not to host LTTE delegations any more after Sri Lankan Foreign Minister Lakshman Kadirgamar's assassination.

Switzerland is one of the Western countries home to a large number of Sri Lankans, the majority of whom are Tamils. The LTTE also maintains offices in the country, including in Berne and Zurich. In 2003, a year after the LTTE and Colombo signed a Norway-sponsored ceasefire agreement, Switzerland invited the LTTE Political Affairs Committee as well as a group of MPs, ministers and journalists from Sri Lanka.

31

They had long sessions at the Institute of Federalism on the complex Swiss system of governance and visited municipalities and bilingual schools. The LTTE delegation was impressed by Swiss federalism. In its previous interactions, Switzerland has advised the LTTE to stop political killings and end child recruitment to its ranks and tried to convince the Tigers that a federal solution was in the best interests of the Tamil minority.

In the same breath, Swiss authorities keep a close eye on LTTE activities within the country, particularly to see if the outfit extorts money from Tamils. In 1996, many LTTE members were arrested in Switzerland but they were let off later. After Norway, Switzerland has thus shown the most active interest in the European region in Sri Lanka's dragging bloody ethnic conflict.

After the talks with Colombo, the LTTE delegation members, led by Anton Balasingham, the London-based ideologue of the group, will stay on in Geneva to meet members of the Tamil community. It is not clear if the Swiss foreign ministry will hold informal talks with the LTTE on the sidelines of the Geneva summit this time.

Norwegian peace envoy Erik Solheim told IANS: "Switzerland has been extremely constructive all the way. The parties chose Switzerland because of its continuous positive support to the peace process." That is what the Swiss government itself said when it agreed to let Geneva be the venue for the LTTE-Colombo dialogue.

Switzerland ... will do its utmost to ensure that the talks take place in an environment that is conducive to reaching a mutually acceptable solution, the foreign ministry said. Switzerland calls on the parties to the conflict to do all within their powers to ensure that the talks can start in a constructive atmosphere.

A Western diplomat told IANS: "There is no mystery about Switzerland's interest in Sri Lanka. It is keen to see that the peace process moves forward and the ceasefire agreement is properly implemented." But Switzerland, located in central Europe and a federal state since 1848, will only be the host at Geneva; Norway will remain the facilitator.

(IANS, 19 February 2006)

# 10

(Erik Solheim, Norway's Special Envoy to Sri Lanka, was the face of a peace process that failed. Unfortunately, his role brought him too close to the LTTE, earning him many critics, both among the Sinhalese and non-LTTE Tamils. This clouded his painstaking contribution to a process that did bring unprecedented peace to Sri Lanka before things went wrong. While some of the criticism was no doubt right, he suffered vicious personal attacks. But Solheim told me in March 2006 that he was not running away.)

## Solheim not to quit peace process

NORWEGIAN International Development Minister Erik Solheim has no intention of quitting as the main facilitator of Sri Lanka's peace process—at least for now. Oslo's search for a new special envoy for Sri Lanka is aimed at finding someone who can assist Solheim, not replace him.

Despite the intense objection among Sinhalese hardliners in Sri Lanka to Solheim's continuation as facilitator, the minister will remain in charge of the four-year-old peace process. IANS reported this on 29 December 2005, but speculation about his possible departure or playing a backroom role rekindled following a media report that Solheim planned to stand aside as a Special Envoy.

The 51-year-old was quoted as saying in Oslo: "You can't do this day and night and look after my other government responsibilities. It's always good to bring in some fresh blood and it may help the cause too." But an informed source made it clear to IANS: "Solheim has not stepped down. He will continue to lead Norway's efforts in the peace process. A special envoy, under Solheim's leadership, will be appointed shortly."

The broad understanding among the co-chairs to the faltering peace process is that Solheim is best suited for the job for now as he has been involved since the beginning.

He played a key role in framing the 2002 ceasefire pact between the Sri Lankan government and the LTTE. And his ability to bring Colombo and the Tigers to the negotiating table in Geneva last month amid escalating violence won him kudos even among sections of those in Sri Lanka who are intensely opposed to him. If the LTTE and the Sri Lankan government meet again in Geneva next month, Solheim will mediate the fresh round of talks between the two sides that remain poles apart despite four years of peace on the battlefield.

Solheim is from Norway's Socialist Party and was named development minister in addition to being the Sri Lanka peace envoy after a coalition of centrist and leftwing parties took power in September 2005.

But diplomatic sources in Colombo admit that despite the Geneva talks and the Western total backing to Norway, opposition to Oslo as well as Solheim remains high among Sinhalese hardliners in Sri Lanka. Many in Sri Lanka allege that Solheim is too close to the LTTE and is perceived as someone sympathetic to them vis-à-vis Colombo. Others argue that it is this relationship, more so his close ties with the London-based Tiger ideologue Anton Balasingham, that has helped Solheim keep the LTTE glued to the peace process even amid continuing uncertainty. Solheim is known to enjoy a personal rapport with Balasingham as opposed to S.P. Tamilchelvan, the head of the LTTE's political wing.

(IANS, 17 March 2006)

# 11

(Despite its bitter experience, India never lost its focus vis-à-vis Sri Lanka. After a hands-off approach for many years following Rajiv Gandhi's assassination, New Delhi resumed its active interest in the affairs of the country. While adamantly refusing to support any break up of Sri Lanka, India made it clear that it will remain an interested party in the affairs of the Tamil minority.)

## India clawing back to Sri Lanka's northeast

INDIA is slowly, patiently and with a clear agenda finding its way back into Sri Lanka's northeast, after having almost washed its hands off the Tamil scene following Rajiv Gandhi's assassination in 1991. In just a year after Foreign Secretary Shyam Saran declared in Trincomalee that the "northeast is very close to India's heart", New Delhi is making its presence felt again in a troubled region where it once enjoyed tremendous goodwill.

Unlike in the 1980s when it was accused of covertly arming Tamil guerrillas, India is maintaining a safe distance from the LTTE, which New Delhi outlawed in 1992 on charges of killing Gandhi. The objective this time is to reach out to the predominantly Tamil and Muslim people of the northeast with development projects, which have the full backing of the Sri Lankan government.

Early in March 2006, India's ambassador in Colombo, Nirupama Rao, visited the eastern district of Amparai and discussed the needs of the local South Eastern University as well as ways of making perennially flooded areas suitable for paddy cultivation. She visited a cultural museum and met Tamil and Muslim leaders besides government officials.

On 20 March Rao was in Kotagala, in Sri Lanka's hill country that is home to "Indian Tamils", when President Mahinda Rajapaksa ceremonially opened a bio-technology institute set up with help from an Indian agriculture expert. The institute is developing a model farm with sections on floriculture, vegetable growing, beekeeping and herbal-aromatic plants cultivation as well as a farm implements workshop and a tissue culture laboratory. A similar project is in operation in the mainly Sinhalese Gampaha district.

In November 2005, a month before Rajapaksa visited New Delhi, Rao handed over medicines urgently needed by the Kilinochchi district hospital in Sri Lanka's LTTE-controlled north at a simple function held in her office in Colombo.

All these come on top of New Delhi's decisions to build a hospital and a vocational training centre in Trincomalee, another hospital in central hills, re-build small schools in the northeast destroyed by the 2004 tsunami, and also provide aid like fishing boats and nets and sewing kits to the northeast.

Indian officials say they have no problems attending to the humanitarian needs of the people living in LTTE control but they will not deal with the Tigers, whose leader Velupillai Prabhakaran is wanted in India for the Gandhi killing. This was stated unambiguously by India's former envoy to Sri Lanka, Nirupam Sen, in May 2004: "Our rehabilitation and assistance is for the people of Sri Lanka irrespective of where they live... (But) there is no question of India engaging the LTTE."

Even while meeting politicians of the pro-LTTE Tamil National Alliance, Indian diplomats seek to avoid those who come from the ranks of the Tigers.

When a suicide bomber from the LTTE blew up Prime Minister Rajiv Gandhi near Chennai in May 1991, India went into a shell, virtually withdrawing itself from Sri Lanka. At the same time, New Delhi cracked down on the Tigers, who once enjoyed sanctuary in India.

India threw its weight behind the 2002 Norway-brokered and Western-backed ceasefire agreement between Colombo and the LTTE. It has no intention of taking the place of Norway or even becoming a co-chair to the peace process because that would involve dealing with the Tigers.

However, there was a feeling in recent times that it was being edged out of the Sri Lankan scene. The December 2004 tsunami gave India an opportunity to get involved in gigantic relief efforts in Sri Lanka. In the northeast, Indian army and navy teams helped restore communications, provide medical relief and drinking water, restore the functioning of hospitals and rebuild the damaged bridge at Arugam Bay.

In April 2005 Shyam Saran visited Sri Lanka and summed up New Delhi's thinking: "The welfare and well-being of the people living in the northeast is very close to India's heart." He also made it clear that India firmly stood for the unity and territorial integrity of Sri Lanka and, with the northeast in mind, emphasized the need to promote democracy, pluralism and human rights.

At the same time, Indian military commanders have in recent times visited Sri Lanka. Despite protests from a section of politicians in Tamil Nadu, New Delhi has continued to assist Colombo militarily. It has also urged Sri Lanka to go for a federal settlement to meet Tamil aspirations.

(IANS, 22 March 2006)

# 12

(Even as media reports quoted President Mahinda Rajapaksa as recommending my biography of Prabhakaran to his senior officials, I came under some uncomfortable scanner in Sri Lanka. I wrote this piece in response.)

## A book is a window to knowledge

AHEAD of the 22–23 February Geneva peace talks between the LTTE and Colombo, my biography of the Tamil Tigers chief Velupillai Prabhakaran (*Inside an Elusive Mind*) unexpectedly and suddenly came into renewed focus in Sri Lanka, propelling some media attention on me. A section of the Sri Lankan media reported that I was to address a workshop for government negotiators on their way to Geneva and that I had chickened out due to premature publicity! Had matters ended here I would have considered the reports as no more than a joke in poor taste and taken them in my stride. But very unfairly and needlessly, a senior Sri Lankan officer has chosen to cast aspersions on my professional integrity.

It all began with a recommendation by Sri Lankan President Mahinda Rajapaksa that those going to Geneva for the talks should read my book in order to understand the LTTE better. A PTI report from Colombo dated 5 February quoted official sources as saying that the president was himself going through the book and "has ordered seven copies" for his officials. The report went on: "Officials said the government at the highest level believed that there were valuable insights to be gained from the book."

I must confess I was pleased but somewhat taken aback. The book was the first independent attempt to string together the compelling story of Prabhakaran, the man who holds the key to war or peace in Sri Lanka. It came out in late 2003 and immediately won raving reviews in India and abroad. I am told it is a must read for diplomats in and dealing with Sri Lanka and for officials of the Sri Lanka Monitoring Mission, the Nordic body that oversees the 2002 ceasefire between the LTTE and Colombo.

The only other person who had written on Prabhakaran's life was P. Nedumaran, a senior political figure in Tamil Nadu and an avowed supporter of the LTTE leader. His book was in Tamil and published way back—in 1989. The low-key person that I am, I had never gone out of the way to promote my book. So Rajapaksa's reported comments came out of the blue for me.

What followed later was somewhat bizarre. A Colombo newspaper quoted a Sri Lankan intelligence officer as trashing the biography. He reportedly spoke at a meeting of government officials going to Geneva. Criticism is fine by me, and if someone thinks it is a bad book, he has every right to his view. I have no problems with that. One remark of him, however, dismayed me: that I had never met Prabhakaran.

Two questions arise here. One, can a biography be plausibly authored without meeting the person one is profiling? Two, did I ever meet the LTTE chief or not?

My answer to the first is an emphatic yes. How do you write biographies of people who are long dead? Is it anyone's case that we cannot write biographies of persons like Mahatma Gandhi, simply because one has not met him? There is a related aspect. What if a person at the centre of the biography is inaccessible or does not wish to be met or, say, even does not want to be written about? Can one still attempt an unauthorized but fair and independently researched biography?

Partly because I worked in New Delhi, I did not have the access to Prabhakaran that many journalists had when he lived in Tamil Nadu. In any case, I have never claimed interviewing Prabhakaran. In the introduction to my book, I recall, in some detail, the one instance when I did meet the man face-to-face briefly at a room in Hotel Diplomat when he came to New Delhi in 1985. I used to work for UNI then and Sri Lanka was incidentally not my beat. The LTTE chief's intriguing personality is what led me to the hotel and it was an Indian supporter of the EPRLF who introduced me to him. (The LTTE and EPRLF were then part of an umbrella grouping called the ENLF.)

In any case that meeting had nothing to do with *Inside an Elusive Mind*, the idea for which was born only after my first book, *Tigers of Lanka*, was published in 1994. Even if I had not met Prabhakaran that day, I would still have profiled his life as a guerrilla leader. What point was the Sri Lankan officer trying to make?

When I set out to write Prabhakaran's biography, it was evident to me that I would not have access to the man. That only made the project all the more challenging.

To tide over the difficulty of not meeting the subject in person, and all the more since there was nothing much available other than Nedumaran's book to go by (in terms of life history), I did (*a*) extensive reading in Tamil and English, and (*b*) met or talked to a wide variety of people who had known him from his childhood, his father included.

Some of the Tamil sources had met him only once or twice but every bit of information they recalled contributed to the bank of knowledge I was building, brick by brick. The research could veritably have gone on and one but I had to draw a line. What was arguably more difficult was to conjecture (crosschecking was nearly impossible) as to who were telling me the truth, who were exaggerating, who were downright making false statements or who were recalling impressions of and encounters with the LTTE chief accurately and with objectivity. *Inside an Elusive Mind* should be seen for what it is: a window to Prabhakaran. It is just one window. If I dare to claim anything more, that would be a lie.

The book's importance should lie in the fact that it is the first exhaustive study of Prabhakaran, and his evolution as a guerrilla. What did strike me (even when I wrote my first book) was that no one had tried to profile a man who has been at the centre of a struggle that began well over three decades ago and shows no signs of ending. It is immaterial whether one likes or dislikes Prabhakaran. The reality is that he cannot be wished away, and as things stand today, he matters utmost in the geopolitical situation of Sri Lanka. I do hope that if and when a more complete story of Prabhakaran is written one day, *Inside an Elusive Mind* would have offered some insights.

Rajapaksa's comments coincided with the time when I secured an interview with the president. My office, IANS, had bought tickets for me to travel to Colombo for what was to be a two-night trip. There was nothing hush-hush about my trip. Between New Delhi, Chennai and Colombo, close to 15 people (excluding my family but including some Western diplomats and my editors) knew I was to fly to Sri Lanka. At least eight among them were aware that I was to interview the president and even helped me with the questions I could ask. I was to meet one more person on the day of my travel. So I must disappoint those who thought I was planning to fly down to Katunayake furtively. However when friends in Colombo alerted me that my name had been put on the workshop for government negotiators, without my knowledge, I called off the visit after offering my apologies to the Sri Lankan source who helped arrange the interview.

Like other Indian journalists who have covered or still cover Sri Lanka, I am used to occasional spiteful mail. I take them in my professional stride, never bothering to reply to any that is even slightly rude. I have been called a RAW agent, even an LTTE agent! Fortunately or unfortunately, I am neither!

A final word: my own understanding of the LTTE and Prabhakaran is simple, if not simplistic. I believe the Tigers, as I know them, are irrevocably committed to achieving an independent Tamil Eelam state. Whether they succeed or not is a different matter. When the Norway-brokered truce came into effect in February 2002, I was reduced to a minority of one in my office when I opined that the agreement would not end the ethnic conflict.

Needless to say I was disparaged and dubbed a pessimist. A European diplomat who left New Delhi after finishing her posting in 2004 told me at the farewell meeting: "I wish I had believed you then. I do now believe what you told me two years ago!" Indeed, few Sri Lanka watchers today see any silver lining.

The LTTE is not the only reason for this. There are faultlines in the Sri Lankan establishment as well. The no-war situation that now holds is prone to break down unless there is a genuine desire on both sides to make up, backed up with concerted action. Despite the criticism heaped against him, I admire the tenacity of Erik Solheim, Norway's peace facilitator. He and I have chosen to disagree on Sri Lanka's prognosis. I pray his efforts are successful and I hope my worst fears are proved wrong.

(*Mainstream*, 24–30 March 2006)

# 13

(India has, over the years, played a significant behind-the-scenes role in Sri Lanka. Indian and Sri Lankan leaders often exchanged views on the telephone while the war against the LTTE raged. A rare conversation in April 2006 got leaked to a section of the media. The telephonic talk is linked to the larger situation in Sri Lanka.)

## Indian PM urges Rajapaksa to save Tamils in Trincomalee

AS anti-Tamil violence erupted in Sri Lanka's Trincomalee town, Indian Prime Minister Manmohan Singh urged President Mahinda Rajapaksa to intervene and prevent any further loss of lives. In a 10-minute conversation late Wednesday, the prime minister

xpressed grief over the death of some 15 Sri Lankan soldiers in claymore mine attacks
ince 7 April for which the LTTE was blamed. But he focused on the anti-Tamil
iolence in the eastern port town of Trincomalee after a bomb blast in a market on
Wednesday, also linked to the LTTE, left several people dead and injured and sparked
ttacks on Tamil civilians and property.

An official in Rajapaksa's office told IANS over telephone: "Your prime minister's
1ain talking point was the situation in Trincomalee. He also offered condolences
ver the death of soldiers." The official added that it was Rajapaksa who telephoned
Manmohan Singh.

The prime minister also gave a timely backing to Sri Lanka's blood-splattered
eace process amid growing violence in that country and uncertainty about peace
ilks between the LTTE and Colombo due in Geneva.

Trincomalee, a traditional communal tinderbox, has been put under curfew. The
iolence there has left at least 15 people dead. Most victims are believed to be Tamils.
he Indian leader urged the president to take necessary steps to bring the situation
nder control and voiced support to the Norway-brokered peace process that has
ome under unprecedented strain.

Significantly, the Indian government has chosen not to make any official
1nouncement about the telephonic talk, allowing Colombo to put out a statement.
spokesman for the Indian prime minister told IANS he had no idea of the Singh–
ajapaksa conversation.

Trincomalee town is a major Sri Lankan naval base whose security is of major con-
rn to India. Attacks by Sinhalese mobs on Tamil civilians invariably end up pushing
e latter into the arms of the LTTE. A dramatic spurt in killings and counter-killings
the gunning down on Friday of pro-LTTE activist V. Vigneswaran at Trincomalee
is left scores dead on both sides of the ethnic divide in Sri Lanka.

The fatalities in the last six days include at least 15 soldiers and sailors, two po-
:emen and members and supporters of the LTTE and its breakaway group led by
aruna besides innocent civilians. The violence and a flaming row between the LTTE
id Colombo over the latter's refusal to provide a military helicopter to ferry Tiger
»mmanders from the east to the north has put question marks on the second round
˙ peace talks due on 19–21 April in Geneva.

(IANS, 13 April 2006)

# 14

(This was written within hours after Sri Lanka's tough-talking army chief narrowl escaped an assassination attempt by the LTTE at the military headquarters i Colombo. It discussed the possible motives behind the killing and the likely repei cussions the murder attempt would have on the battered peace process. On bot counts, the analysis proved correct. The army chief oversaw the liquidation of th LTTE in 2009.)

## Suicide bomber blows up Sri Lanka's peace process

LESS than 24 hours after India urged Sri Lanka and the Tamil Tiger guerrillas t strictly adhere to the Norwegian-brokered ceasefire, a woman suicide bomber almo killed the island's army chief in a meticulous operation that was capable of beir carried out only by the LTTE.

The fireball of red and orange that left General Sarath Fonseka battling for life al: killed several people, including the woman strapped with explosives and pretending t be pregnant. But the biggest casualty of the Tuesday strike was the Norway-brokere peace process.

If the LTTE did carry out the suicide attack, the seeds for it would have been la: a long time ago, even while it was seriously engaged with the various players in t peace process.

General Fonseka was picked for the post soon after Mahinda Rajapaksa becan president in November 2005. The army chief was described as one who desired a ha: line vis-à-vis the Tigers. He advocated a strategy that advocated suffocating the LTT by teaming up with the breakaway Tiger group led by Karuna. He would have be targeted only for this reason.

From previous cases it can be safely assumed that LTTE operatives would have made a thorough study of Gen. Fonseka's movements and concluded that the best way to take him out was at his own supposedly secure army headquarters.

The suicide bomber (who would have belonged to the Black Tigers) would have been told about the layout of the army headquarters and the car the army chief uses. In line with the LTTE folklore, she would have had one last supper with Tigers chief Velupillai Prabhakaran before making her way to Colombo for her final mission.

The suicide attack came just weeks after Canada outlawed the LTTE as a terrorist organization and days after Sri Lanka publicly called upon the 25-nation European Union to follow suit. A European Union ban would undoubtedly be a blow to the Tigers, whose International Secretariat is located in Paris and who have a string of offices all over the continent. Europe is also home to thousands of Sri Lankan Tamils, many of who fund the Tigers.

But if the LTTE still carried out the suicide bombing, then it only proves what has been long suspected: beyond a point, the Tigers care two hoots about international opinion. The US, one of the key members of the co-chairs to Sri Lanka's peace process (besides the European Union, Japan and Norway), has in recent times taken a particularly tough stand vis-à-vis the LTTE. Western countries have in recent times repeatedly denounced the LTTE as terrorist.

Since the London tube bombings of July 2005, Britain has banned even public events linked to LTTE. And since the assassination in August of Sri Lankan foreign minister Lakshman Kadirgamar, countries like Switzerland have cut the number of visas given to Sri Lankan Tamils. As for India, it has made clear its anathema to the LTTE. For the LTTE there is thus nothing to be gained further from the peace process diplomatically. Militarily and financially, the four years of peace process have proved a windfall for the Tigers. On both counts, the LTTE has strengthened itself enormously although Karuna's split has weakened it.

But those mocking at the LTTE's incipient air force forget that its naval wing, Sea Tigers, also began with a handful of boats—before emerging as a serious threat to the Sri Lankan military. Look at it from the LTTE's point of view: it has not evolved from a ragtag group in the 1970s to what it is now, merely to accept Sri Lanka's sovereignty.

When Norway began its mediation in Sri Lanka, India's then foreign minister Jaswant Singh had a friendly warning for the Norwegians. "We wish you all the best. But please remember that it is not going to be an easy job." An Indian diplomat was more blunt with Erik Solheim, Norway's Special Envoy. "The Tigers took us for a ride, the same may happen to you."

The reality is that Prabhakaran is determined to carve out Tamil Eelam, knowing fully well that no country is going to come to Sri Lanka's aid if a full-scale war erupt again. The LTTE is not going to allow anyone, the international community included to preside over the liquidation of the de facto Tamil Eelam that exists today in the north of Sri Lanka.

(IANS, 26 April 2006

# 15

(The LTTE's most predictable trait was its unpredictability. Prabhakaran at time took decisions that made no sense. One reason why many failed to read the LTTE correctly was because they viewed it from a rational prism. But the LTTE often acted irrationally. Prabhakaran's adamant refusal to meet Japan's Special Envoy to S Lanka, Yasushi Akashi, was one such irrational decision.)

## Prabhakaran's pride: Or why he refused to meet Akashi

TAMIL Tigers chief Velupillai Prabhakaran's curt refusal to meet Japan's Special Envoy, Yasushi Akashi, is a well thought out public snub that will not surprise those who have seen the Tigers grow from a ragtag group to be the world's most powerful insurgent outfit. Pride, dignity and self-respect are immensely important to Prabhakaran and closely linked to the struggle for Tamil Eelam even if others consider the goal a mirage.

Almost two decades ago, in early 1987, Prabhakaran met V. Balakumar, a leader of another Tamil group and now with the LTTE, in Jaffna. Prabhakaran had quit India for good after a tumultuous three and a half years in Tamil Nadu. Balakumar asked Prabhakaran if he would go back to India, a country Sri Lankan Tamils then almost worshipped as their motherland.

"If India needs me, they can send a chopper and invite me. Otherwise I won't go," was Prabhakaran's response. Balakumar argued that this would never happen and that India did not need the Tamils as much as the Tamils needed India. The LTTE chief said: "I don't agree. If they need us, they can invite us."

Coincidentally, that is exactly what happened. In July 1987, after a complex interplay of fighting and diplomacy, India dispatched two military helicopters to Jaffna to pick up Prabhakaran to ferry him to New Delhi for a meeting with the then Prime Minister Rajiv Gandhi. Once things went sour for him, Prabhakaran swore vengeance. Gandhi got killed in May 1991.

After the assassination of Sri Lankan Foreign Minister Lakshman Kadirgamar in August 2005, peace facilitator Norway changed gears. It decided, among other things, not to settle in future for meetings with just S.P. Tamilchelvan, the LTTE political wing leader, but insist on direct talks with Prabhakaran. The argument was: since Sri Lankan leaders met Norwegian Special Envoy Erik Solheim whenever the latter desired, why should Prabhakaran be so choosy?

But that is not going to happen. Although Solheim met Prabhakaran in January this year, it is the latter who will continue to pick who he wants to meet—and when. Western players who think that Prabhakaran will be eager to court them so as to gain some sort of legitimacy are sadly mistaken.

Not long ago, a once-high-profile Colombo-based diplomat insisted on meeting Prabhakaran. The LTTE politely turned down the request and asked him to meet Tamilchelvan instead. When the diplomat persisted, he was told, politely but firmly, that he should either settle for Tamilchelvan or someone more junior!

Prabhakaran was just another player in Tamil militancy when he began to live in India in late 1983. But the man grew rapidly in stature as the LTTE took on the Sri Lankan state and positioned himself within years as the sole player in the battlefield. On his way back to Jaffna from India in August 1987, Prabhakaran took off his slippers (a Tamil trait to show courtesy) while entering the office of an Indian general in Chennai. It is the same man who has refused to meet Akashi though Japan is one of the co-chairs to the peace process. Why?

A safe—and logical—guess is that Prabhakaran feels there is nothing for him to gain from such a meeting. From the LTTE's perspective, the Norway-brokered peace process is unlikely to generate further dividends. The outgoing chief of the Sri Lanka Monitoring Mission has already declared that the international community recognized the LTTE only for the sake of the peace process, which, like the 1987 India–Sri Lanka accord, has become a "peace trap" for the Tigers.

Significantly, while some Western diplomats think that Prabhakaran is only isolating himself by putting himself in a cage, the fact is he interacts with a fairly large number of people including from Tamil Nadu. In Prabhakaran's eyes, a Tamil Nadu politician is a more valuable ally than a Western player despite the fact that the LTTE has a string of offices in the West. If war breaks out again in Sri Lanka, the reactions in Tamil Nadu and India would be more crucial to its outcome than anything Tokyo might feel or do.

(IANS, 8 May 2006)

# 16

(As Sri Lanka slid towards war, the international community overseeing the tottering peace issued one of its most important statements ever. They made it abundantly clear to the LTTE that an independent Tamil Eelam was an absolute no-no. This was done so as to remove any suspicion in the minds of the people in Sri Lanka vis-à-vis the West. India quietly contributed inputs to this statement.)

## Co-chairs' forthright Sri Lanka edict will please India

INDIAN policy makers will feel mighty pleased that their uncompromising stand on Sri Lanka has been echoed for the first time by international players to the island's now precarious peace process. There is no certainty, however, if Colombo and the Tamil Tigers will fully grasp the import of the unambiguous statement from the co-chairs to the peace process and radically change their ways.

Tuesday's statement issued in Tokyo by the US, Japan, the European Union and peace facilitator Norway is one of the most important documents to emerge on Sri Lanka since the peace process was unveiled four years ago. It is a strong indictment of both Colombo and the LTTE for failing to make peace despite the strong support of the global community.

Although India, Sri Lanka's key neighbour and a country with great stakes in a final resolution of the ethnic conflict, finds no mention in the statement, it is clear that there is substantial Indian input, and New Delhi's concerns have been duly addressed. As one Sri Lanka watcher with access to decision makers said: "Ninety-nine per cent of what India desires is there in the statement."

The co-chairs have made it abundantly clear that there is no scope for an independent state of Tamil Eelam, the LTTE's stated goal. The LTTE has been called upon to re-enter the negotiating process by renouncing terrorism and violence. "It must show that it is willing to make the political compromises needed for a political solution within a united Sri Lanka."

Expanding the theme, and avoiding the row over a "federal" versus "unitary" state, the statement says:

> The co-chairs will support any solution agreed by the parties that safeguards the territorial integrity of Sri Lanka, assures protection and fulfils the legitimate aspirations of the Tamil people and indeed of the Muslim people, guarantees democracy and human rights, and is acceptable to all communities.

In the same breath, the Sri Lankan government has been called upon to address "the legitimate grievances of the Tamils", prevent armed groups operating in its territory from "carrying out violence and acts of terrorism", protect the rights and security of Tamils all over the island and ensure that violators of law are prosecuted.

> It (Colombo) must show that it is ready to make the dramatic political changes to bring about a new system of governance which will enhance the rights of all Sri Lankans including Muslims... The Tamil and Muslim people of Sri Lanka have justified and substantial grievances that have not yet been adequately addressed.

Most of these are issues that India has been, mostly quietly, emphasizing for years, particularly since the Norway-brokered ceasefire agreement was signed in 2002, more so from the time New Delhi started to feel that the LTTE was viewing the peace process as a vehicle to turn its de facto Tamil Eelam state into a de jure one. At the same time, India has been unhappy over the Sri Lankan leadership's failure to address genuine Tamil grievances although these are not articulated publicly so as not to embarrass Colombo.

The co-chairs have declared that solutions to Sri Lanka's problems "cannot be brought through conflict" and that "war is not winnable for either side". Both the LTTE and the Sri Lankan government have been reminded that they "have agreed to the basic principles of any future peace during the successful period of negotiation in 2002–03" and asked to recommit to these principles as well as to the Geneva peace talks of February 2006.

While making it amply clear that Norway will keep steering the peace process, the Tokyo declaration makes three important points: one, Sri Lanka is on the brink of war; two, Colombo and the LTTE do not seem to be able to prevent the slide back into violence; and three, nevertheless ingredients for a peaceful settlement remain.

The conclusion in the statement: "The international community can only support but cannot deliver peace. Peace can only be delivered by Sri Lankans themselves." India has been saying this for years. Can the co-chairs succeed where India failed in the past?

(IANS, 31 May 2006)

# 17

(I was perhaps the first journalist to write about the mysterious murder of a sari trader from Tamil Nadu in Sri Lanka's east. Both the LTTE and the Karuna faction were suspected for the killing; the Tigers frequently branded Indians to be spies. Despite their penchant for vocal protests, Tamil Nadu politicians did not take up the issue. The Indian government made some noise—and then the victims were forgotten.)

## Indian trader brutally killed, two missing in Sri Lanka

AN Indian sari trader from Tamil Nadu has been tortured to death and two other are missing in Sri Lanka's east in a horror saga that some are linking to business rivalr and others to the Tamil Tigers or its breakaway faction.

Locally, both the LTTE and its rival group led by Karuna have denied any involve ment in the murder of Mahalingam Vijaykumar, whose decomposed body with tell tale torture marks and a gaping bullet wound on the head was found in Batticaloa' Valaichenai area in December 2005.

Police in Valaichenai, some 35 km from Batticaloa town, blame the LTTE for the grisly killing. But Vijaykumar's distraught father-in-law, who gave his name as Nagarajan, insists that the Karuna faction is most probably the culprit.

"That's what local people told me," Nagarajan told IANS on telephone from near Dindigal town, 380 km southwest of Chennai. "Seeing the body was a shock to me. I just cannot tell you how badly he had been tortured. It is terrible." According to Nagarajan, two other sari traders from Tamil Nadu, Murugesan and Radhakrishnan, also went missing last month in Batticaloa and are believed to be dead.

But a Tamil journalist in Batticaloa who did not wish to be named told IANS that the authorities had found and cremated two bodies after no one identified or claimed them. He said they were believed to be of the missing Indians.

Several theories are doing the rounds in Batticaloa about the likely identity of the killers.

Since the February 2002 ceasefire in Sri Lanka, and thanks in part to a liberalized visa regime, many traders from Tamil Nadu have been touring the island's Tamil and Muslim areas in the northeast as well as tea-growing hills selling saris and salwar kameez.

Vijaykumar, father of a four-month-old child, went with his father-in-law and other Indians to Sri Lanka for the first time on 21 February and returned on 10 April. They again left on 10 May and soon checked into a small lodge near the police station in the eastern town of Batticaloa.

As was the custom, they would take separate buses every morning from Batticaloa town to go to the interior to peddle their wares, going from house to house. All of them would return to the lodge by 4 p.m. Vijaykumar failed to return one day. Nagarajan tried to reach him on his mobile phone but it was switched off.

Early next morning, Nagarajan and his friends went looking for him at Valaichenai, a Muslim-majority town, only to be told at a shop near the bus station that Vijaykumar did have tea there around 11 a.m. the previous day but had left an hour later.

As Nagarajan roamed around seeking information about his son-in-law, a young man drove up on a motorcycle and asked them to get lost. A frightened Nagarajan came back to Batticaloa town. The next day, on a tip off from a woman, Nagarajan returned to Valaichenai. This time he learnt that his son-in-law had been taken to a place about six kilometres away, robbed of his saris and threatened by four or five men that they would kill him if he moved from there.

Very soon, a white colour van drove up and took away Vijaykumar. "Thinking he had been kidnapped, I spread the word that I was ready to pay ransom," Nagarajan said. "I went looking for him to the local Karuna people, but they did not give me a proper reply. I then went to the EPDP (Eelam People's Democratic Party) office. They also did not give me a satisfactory reply. I then went to the LTTE office at Karadiyanaru. There one man took down a written complaint from me and said: "We don't do these things. We don't harm any Indian".

That day I was called to the police station and shown a pant and keys and I identified them as my son-in-law's. The police asked us to sign some papers but I refused to until I saw the body. So my (Indian) friends and I went in police vans to Vinayagapuram, about 30 km away.

There, close to a school, between some houses and a forested area, we found the body. Vijaykumar had been brutally tortured and then shot. He had been repeatedly stabbed with sharp instruments. We wanted to cremate the body, but no one gave us wood. Finally we decided cut down some trees. But the police officer would not let us do that. He insisted that we had to leave immediately. We got into a row. Eventually, I gave money to some locals to cremate the body. As we left, the police vehicles came under attack. A bomb exploded and suddenly everyone was firing away. It was like a movie. The vans picked up speed and came on to the main road some distance away. It was a miracle we survived.

Asked who he thought were the killers, Nagarajan said: "In Batticaloa the LTTE and Karuna group are known as 'periyavar' (elder) and 'chinnavar' (junior). One or two Tamils told me it was the job of the 'chinnavar' (junior). I also think so."

Nagarajan later filed a complaint with the Indian high commission in Colombo. Valaichenai officer-in-charge K.G. Dharmavardana, however, told IANS that he believed the LTTE had killed Vijaykumar.

Of course we have no evidence. This (Indian) man had come here before also. He had apparently been told not to come again. But he came. People are saying that it is LTTE's work. I know of only one Indian was murdered. But I did hear that two other Indians are missing. But not in my area … elsewhere.

A Tamil source in Colombo with contacts in Sri Lanka's northeast insisted that the LTTE had killed the other two Indians at Santhiveli near Valaichenai.

He pointed out that the LTTE had for some time been insinuating that some of the Indian traders were Indian spies.

But a Batticaloa resident told IANS that the Tamil Nadu traders also went to LTTE areas and were not harmed. "Why would the Tigers let them in if they were spies? In any case Vijaykumar got kidnapped in government-controlled territory. He was also killed there."

This resident and two others alleged that the murder might have been committed by someone on the urging of local Muslim businessmen who they said had suffered ever since the Tamil Nadu traders began visiting Sri Lanka's northeast.

While they could not explain why Vijaykumar was so badly tortured, they admitted that only the LTTE could have ambushed the police vehicles ferrying Nagarajan and other Indians.

A Muslim resident in Batticaloa told IANS: "One sari trader from India comes to our house every three months. They can't be spies. They never ask any unwanted questions. They even give saris on credit. It is a mystery why anyone would want to kill them."

(IANS, 4 June 2006)

# 18

(Although many viewed Karunanidhi as a strong supporter of the LTTE, he was anything but that—at least after Rajiv Gandhi's assassination, notwithstanding some of his public pronouncements. It is no wonder that Karunanidhi did nothing dramatic when the LTTE went down fighting even though he was the chief minister of Tamil Nadu and a key ally of Prime Minister Manmohan Singh. Naturally, not everyone in the Tamil Eelam ranks liked Karunanidhi.)

## Pro-LTTE website attacks Karunanidhi

A website that supports Tamil Tiger guerrillas has come out with a stinging attack on Tamil Nadu Chief Minister M. Karunanidhi over his government's alleged support to the breakaway faction of Karuna. In a hard-hitting commentary in Tamil, www. webeelam.com has accused the DMK government of allowing Karuna loyalists to recruit members from among Tamil civilians fleeing Sri Lanka to Tamil Nadu and called it a "very big betrayal". It has also warned ominously: "This will not be forgiven by world Tamils."

The website is one of the many that is either run by or closely linked to the LTTE, whose 2002 ceasefire with the Sri Lankan government is now on the brink of a formal collapse. The LTTE has accused Colombo of covertly backing Karuna, the Tigers' former regional commander who broke away in early 2004.

Attributing its information to "highly reliable sources", the commentary has alleged that the Tamil Nadu government, which took office last month, had allowed a Karuna supporter, Paranthan Rajan, to woo destitute Sri Lankan Tamils reaching Tamil Nadu with offers of money. The commentary does not refer to Karunanidhi, one of India's most senior politicians, by name and addresses him by his hugely popular title "kalaingar" (artist).

Paranthan Rajan heads the anti-LTTE Eelam National Democratic Liberation Front (ENDLF), which was a key member of the provincial administration in Sri Lanka's northeast when Indian troops were deployed there in the late 1980s. After Karuna broke away from the LTTE, Paranthan Rajan—who has been based in India for long—joined hands with him to form a new political group known as TMVP, which is registered with the Election Commission in Sri Lanka.

The commentary says that Paranthan Rajan was jailed over a year ago when J. Jayalalitha was Tamil Nadu's chief minister but was eventually freed and returned to Sri Lanka with a promise not to return to India. According to the commentary, Paranthan Rajan did come back to India but lived in Bangalore. He moved to Tamil Nadu after the Karunanidhi-led alliance won the state elections in 2006. The commentary says that allowing Paranthan Rajan to recruit Tamils from refugee camps in Tamil Nadu is a "very big betrayal" of "Tamil people".

The LTTE and Karunanidhi have for long enjoyed a love-hate relationship. LTTE chief Velupillai Prabhakaran avoided Karunanidhi during his 1983–87 stay in Tamil Nadu so as not to offend then Chief Minister M.G. Ramachandran or MGR. However, after MGR's death in December 1987 and the outbreak of war with Indian troops, the LTTE cultivated Karunanidhi, who spoke out in favour of the Tigers. He also refused to receive Indian troops when they returned home from Sri Lanka in 1990.

New Delhi sacked the DMK government in January 1991 on charges of failure to curb LTTE activities. In the state elections following former Prime Minister Rajiv Gandhi's May 1991 assassination by the LTTE, the DMK was crushed. Since then both the DMK and Jayalalitha's AIADMK had distanced themselves from the Tamil Tigers.

In December 2005, then Tamil Nadu Chief Minister Jayalalitha—who for years remained vocally anti-LTTE—refused to meet Sri Lankan President Mahinda

Rajapaksa on his way home from New Delhi. But in May 2006, Karunanidhi—who for long had a soft corner for Tamil militancy—met Sri Lankan Tamil politician Arumugam Thondaman (who has no sympathy for the LTTE) when he flew to Chennai as a special representative of Rajapaksa.

(IANS, 15 June 2006)

# 19

(This is a touching human story. Tamils began fleeing to India in large numbers from early 2006, to escape escalating violence. Their arrival in Tamil Nadu rarely made news. But when a girl landed on the shores with parrots perched on her shoulders, everyone was curious—and pleasantly surprised.)

## Armed with parrots, Tamil girl flees to India

A Sri Lankan Tamil girl who braved choppy seas for five long hours to flee to India is making waves with her two parrots. But cats at the refugee camp are posing fresh threats to her pets and giving her sleepless nights.

Like thousands of others before her, Nishanthani Lombert, 15, came to Tamil Nadu, crossing the rough sea dividing the two countries in a fishing vessel that was packed with 18 people and battered suitcases with their life belongings.

The group included her parents and three brothers and the birds, which were put into a cardboard box to keep them from flying away during the five-hour journey. But the birds—which her father B. Lombert bought for her about 18 months ago for Rs 50 each—got drenched when the boat was repeatedly lapped by huge waves. Consequently, when they reached the shores of Rameswaram in Tamil Nadu, the birds came perched on the shoulders of Nishanthani, who her parents said adores the birds more than anything else.

"When the (Indian) officials saw my daughter and the parrots, they were pleasantly surprised," B. Lombert told IANS over telephone from near the refugee camp in Tamil Nadu. "Everyone started talking to us about the birds. There was real excitement."

Like most of the 4,000 Tamils who have fled to India since January 2006 to escape rising violence in Sri Lanka, the Lomberts are poor. They lived in the Pesalai area of Mannar in the northwest of the island. Pesalai has in recent times seen some bitter violence, for which Sri Lankan security forces are blamed. Lombert said he paid the boatman 1,000 Sri Lankan Rupees and a pair of earrings and a ring, all made of gold, to sail to India.

"Sometimes these boatmen charge as much as 10,000–12,000 rupees. But we did not have that kind of money."

Lombert said his daughter Nishanthani had dropped out of school some time ago "due to some earlier trouble". One day, he saw a man selling parrots at Pesalai. Promptly, he bought a pair for his daughter. "I cannot tell you how fond of the birds my daughter is. She cannot live without them."

His wife, who also spoke to IANS, added: "The parrots were really small when we got them. My daughter is in love with them. She would never leave home without the birds. When we decided to leave for India, she made it clear that the parrots would come with her."

We are very happy to be in India. We did not even have food to eat in Pesalai. We could not live in our own homes. We used to spend the evenings and nights in a (Hindu) temple, fearing violence. Here (in Tamil Nadu) we feel safe. We get food. The officials are taking good care of us. But there is one problem. There are cats in our refugee camp. Naturally Nishanthani is very worried for her birds. She doesn't sleep at night fearing the cats would attack her parrots. We hope the birds remain safe. My daughter really loves them.

(IANS, 16 July 2006)

# 20

(A story that touched many hearts. Sobbing and barely able to speak, the widow of Ketheshwaran Loganathan spoke to me about her husband's killing by the LTTE—and how she missed him. Shockingly, a group of Sri Lankan Tamil MPs told the Indian foreign ministry that the Tigers were not to blame for the murder. Politely but firmly, they were asked to shut up.)

## In war torn Sri Lanka, a widow remembers

IT is tough to be a widow. Tougher if the husband is gunned down at your home. Worse, if the frail man had been actually wondering how to cope if his wife died before him. A fortnight after suspected Tamil Tigers killed Ketheshwaran Loganathan, his wife of 28 years is still in shock.

Bhawani Loganathan, 56, breaks down as she recalls the fears Kethesh, as he was popularly known, had voiced barely 10 days before his 12 August murder about his many ailments that included failing hearing, weak eyesight and an irritable bowel syndrome that had never spared him since childhood.

"'How will I manage if you go away before me?' he had asked me one day," said a sobbing Bhawani, speaking over the telephone from her Colombo home. "And I never thought that such a thing would happen, and so soon."

It was about 10 p.m. on 12 August when some men appeared at their Colombo home and called him out. He stepped out warily—and was shot dead.

Bhawani remembers that Saturday night, but recovers quickly and speaks highly of the man she fell in love with about three decades ago in Jaffna and who slowly graduated from a hardcore Tamil militant to eventually become the deputy in the Sri Lankan Peace Secretariat.

"He was a man of courage and he believed in certain values," says Bhawani. "I did fear for him after he joined the Peace Secretariat. I never thought it will happen at home," she adds, referring to the killing blamed on the LTTE. Like in many such incidents, the LTTE has not accepted responsibility.

Kethesh began his political career as an activist of the Left-leaning EPRLF. He was its long-time spokesperson and passionately opposed the LTTE. But he took no part in the India-backed, EPRLF-led administration in Sri Lanka's northeast in 1987–90. He took a fellowship in Norway in the 1990s and then lived in New Delhi for two years. He quit the group in 1994, dabbled in journalism and then took to more scholarly pursuits.

Kethesh and Bhawani had no children. Both were voracious readers, in Tamil and English, and led private lives, never hosting any parties, and going to one only if it was a must. He was 54 when he was killed—two years junior to her.

Early this year he quit a think-tank to join the Sri Lankan government's Peace Secretariat, a move some friends felt was a mistake, since the body plays a key role in Colombo's campaign against the Tigers. But despite the dangers the new job posed, Kethesh politely declined to accept any security from the government that is now locked in a virtual war against the LTTE.

Bhawani, who has two brothers and a sister, recalls fondly the many years she spent in Tamil Nadu as a hospital employee and a state she now plans to visit to scatter Kethesh's ashes in the Hindu holy towns of Rameswaram and Kanyakumari.

"We had money problems but I spent my time treating patients. Nobody in the hospital treated me differently though I was a foreigner. I was treated like one of them. I will go there next month with his ashes."

Life is not easy now. She takes homoeopathy medicines to relax. The telephone receiver is kept off the hook during nights and afternoons so that she can sleep undisturbed. But she has resumed her reading habit and is hopeful of pulling through as a library consultant.

There is one gift Kethesh has left behind that she immensely treasures—a volume of the Hindu epic Bhagavad Gita, authored by Swami Chinmayananda. "He used to read it at night before sleeping. It is with me. It is immortal."

(IANS, 27 August 2006)

# 21

(By the end of 2006, Sri Lanka was in turmoil. The LTTE was belligerent and Colombo was determined to crush the Tigers. India was pressing Sri Lanka to unleash political reforms. Ahead of Rajapaksa's second visit, an aide revealed to me what the president planned to tell the Indian leadership. The story created a mini storm among policy makers in India.)

## Be patient please, Sri Lanka to tell India

IN the face of persistent Indian calls to devolve autonomy to the Tamils, Sri Lankan President Mahinda Rajapaksa arrives here this weekend with a polite request not to rush him into a political settlement.

The president is also expected to tell the Indian political leadership that if and when Colombo agrees to a negotiated settlement, it will not just be with the LTTE but involve other Tamils as well. And such an inclusive process, one that has to satisfy all sections of the ethnic divide in Sri Lanka, will take time, maybe months or even years, and that Colombo should not be pushed into anything.

Highly placed sources told IANS that while Sri Lanka did not see India as just another global player in the ethnic conflict, Colombo was getting tired of being hectored on issues like power sharing and federalism. "India must learn to be patient," one source said, summarizing the thrust of Sri Lankan thinking on devolution of power to the Tamils and other minorities on which Colombo is being pilloried by the international community.

India has repeatedly told Sri Lanka, mostly privately, that while it respects the island nation's territorial integrity, it needs to act fast to come up with a political solution to end a conflict that has taken over 65,000 lives since 1983 and shows no signs of ending. In India's view, the legitimate aspirations of the Tamil community have to be met. A top Indian official warned recently while speaking to IANS that a failure by Sri Lanka on this count could lead to disastrous consequences.

Rajapaksa arrives Saturday for his second trip to India in a year. He will open a conference of mayors in Dehradun in Uttaranchal on Sunday. Later in New Delhi he will meet Prime Minister Manmohan Singh. He returns home on 29 November.

The sources said that India would be told that the Rajapaksa administration's attempt was to move away from the "elitist manipulative" kind of dealings of the past that went in the name of political settlement. "A manipulative mechanism may work immediately but it will never last," the source explained. "And we will not go for a settlement only with the LTTE though it is a powerful military group. Other Tamil groups will be involved. And so will be other communities."

> We cannot have a deal just between a section of the Sinhalese elite, however much they may be supported by Western countries, and a section of the Tamil side. India has to understand this, and India has to support us. Unlike some of the Western countries who may prefer "elitist manipulative" settlements, India needs to see us differently.

The sources said Tamils were getting a "wrong idea" of the present government because of its dependence on Sinhalese nationalist parties such as JVP and JHU. Sections of the Indian establishment also see JVP as some kind of a spoiler, a political entity unwilling to make far-reaching and necessary compromises.

But JVP and JHU have to be taken along, the sources said, because without their involvement, there could be "no southern consensus"—unanimity in the Sinhalese majority southern Sri Lanka—and without which there could be no end to war.

The sources, however, admitted that many innocent Tamils had died in recent fighting in Sri Lanka's northeast, where some 2,500 people have been killed this year, making a mockery of the 2002 Norway-brokered ceasefire agreement.

(IANS, 23 November 2006)

# 22

(Once the European Union outlawed the LTTE as a terrorist group, the Tigers retaliated by asking EU member countries to quit the Sri Lanka Monitoring Mission or SLMM. The departure of Denmark, Sweden and Finland left the Scandinavian SLMM with only members from Norway and Iceland. When the 2002 ceasefire agreement was signed, the SLMM was formed to oversee the truce and rule against violations. The SLMM was stretched to capacity as the war escalated from 2006. This article examines how the truce monitors struggled to keep the peace going in Sri Lanka.)

## Faltering Sri Lankan peace process

THE ethnic differences that later turned into an armed conflict in Sri Lanka, a teardrop nation south of India, came to the surface almost as soon as the British rule ended in 1948. The end of colonialism catapulted to power political parties led by the majority and mainly Buddhist Sinhalese community, leading to tensions with the Tamil minority. Brute Sinhalese domination in governance and in areas such as language, employment and education fuelled complaints of discrimination from the predominantly Hindu Tamils. Amid periodic outbreaks of ethnic violence targeted at Tamils, the Sri Lanka Freedom Party (SLFP) and the United National Party (UNP), which between them ruled the country, failed to make peace with the Tamil moderate leadership, stoking the embers of militancy in the community.

The 1970s and early 1980s saw a mushrooming of Tamil militant groups whose leaders concluded that violence was the only way to combat ethnic discrimination. One such Tamil radical, Velupillai Prabhakaran, shot dead the pro-government Tamil Mayor of Jaffna in the island's north in 1975 and went on to set up the LTTE in 1976. Over the years, besides taking on the state, the LTTE decimated all other Tamil groups, both militant and moderate.

It has today grown to be the world's most feared and most well armed insurgent outfit with tentacles spanning the globe. Its avowed aim is to break away the Tamil-majority northern and eastern wings of Sri Lanka as an independent nation to be called Tamil Eelam. The conflict has thus far killed some 65,000 people, not including nearly 1,200 of the Indian soldiers who fought the LTTE in Sri Lanka's northeast in 1987–90.

Just four years after the Norwegian-brokered 2002 ceasefire agreement between the Sri Lankan government and LTTE raised hopes of a lasting peace, the country has again slid to near anarchy marked by a dramatic and bloody revival of assassinations, suicide bombings, killings, counter-killings, abductions and military operations in which the key victims are innocent civilians, primarily Tamils.

Sri Lanka's new president, Mahinda Rajapaksa, took power in November 2005 on a belligerent agenda. Though he mellowed subsequently, the LTTE—which had continued to kill its rivals even during the ceasefire—stepped up attacks on the military personnel from December 2005. Attacks on Tamil civilians by security forces triggered a panic flight to India from January 2006 that shows no signs of ending. The LTTE's attempted assassination of Sri Lanka's army chief in April dramatically raised tensions.

Since July, ferocious fighting in the northeast has left hundreds dead, many more wounded, and over 200,000 displaced from their homes, making Sri Lanka—with a population of about 20 million—one of the world's leading conflict zones. The truce exists only on paper and the Norwegian-driven peace process is barely alive.

When the ceasefire was signed, the need was felt for someone to oversee the truce. This gave birth to the Sri Lanka Monitoring Mission (SLMM), a Nordic body originally made up of monitors from Norway, Finland, Iceland, Sweden and Denmark. The SLMM, in whose birth India played a quiet but behind-the-scenes role, is the only such grouping functioning outside the mandate of the United Nations. Its aim is to prevent and defuse escalations, advise and assist the two parties in implementing the ceasefire agreement and help bring about normalization in the northeast.

Headquartered in Colombo, the SLMM maintains six District Offices (open around the clock) in the northeast and a Liaison Office in the LTTE-held town of Kilinochchi. The mission also has Points of Contact in the region to interact with the local population. The District Offices run mobile units and until recently did extensive patrolling. The SLMM also has naval patrol units based in Trincomalee and Jaffna. There are also Local Monitoring Committees, each made up of two members, nominated by the government and LTTE with a SLMM representative as chairman.

The committees record and process complaints about truce violations. The monitors enjoy diplomatic privileges, with both the government and LTTE agreeing to provide security to them. Since the 2002 ceasefire, the SLMM has recorded thousands of violations and played a crucial role in preventing violent clashes innumerable times. They were not carrying out an easy job, made more difficult by Tamils opposed to the LTTE accusing the mission of being biased towards the Tamil Tigers.

Things took a turn for the worse for the SLMM after the European Union banned the LTTE as a terrorist group in May 2006. India was the first country to outlaw the Tigers, in 1992, and was followed by Britain, the US and Canada. But after the EU decision, the LTTE refused to accept monitors from Denmark, Finland and Sweden, all of which are EU members, saying they could no longer be neutral. This has left the SLMM struggling with monitors from just Norway and Iceland, sharply reducing its strength from 67 to just 30. This is a blow to Sri Lanka's peace process because the LTTE veto came when the SLMM was contemplating increasing its staff to tackle growing incidents of violence and ceasefire violations.

SLMM officials admit that with fighting now erupting on a large scale all over the north and east of Sri Lanka, monitoring the virtually non-existent ceasefire has become not just difficult but dangerous too. SLMM monitors, who are unarmed, no longer rush to spots of turbulence every time simply because they cannot afford to commit their limited personnel. The high levels of violence have undoubtedly reduced the effectiveness of the Nordic body but they continue to perform a key function. Efforts are on to increase personnel from Norway and Iceland (some who had gone home after serving in Sri Lanka have since returned) to bolster its strength and, if possible, rope in other countries that have not banned the LTTE.

Amid intense international efforts to save Sri Lanka's tottering peace process, it is vital to resurrect the SLMM, whose monitors play the role of independent judges without whose presence whatever is left of the ceasefire will simply wither away.

(*Journal of International Peace Operations*, Washington, November–December 2006.)

# 23

(By the end of 2006, no love was lost between the Sri Lankan government and Norway. One day, Karuna, the former LTTE commander who had teamed up with Colombo, accused Norway's Special Envoy Erik Solheim, of corruption. A bitter Solheim hit back, telephoning me from Africa to say the allegations against him were baseless.)

## Solheim calls Karuna allegations "complete lies"

NORWEGIAN minister Erik Solheim, the architect of Sri Lanka's barely alive 2002 truce, denied as "complete lies" allegations that he had been financed by the Tamil Tigers or that he had given them money.

"These are all lies. Everything is a lie," an indignant Solheim said in a telephonic interview from Burundi.

"It is a lie that I took any money from LTTE. It is a lie that I gave a TV to Prabhakaran. It is a lie that I gave even a cent to (LTTE ideologue Anton) Balasingham. These are lies, these are complete lies," Solheim told IANS.

Solheim's comments were the first public reaction by the Norwegian minister of international development to allegations by Vinayagamurthy Muralitharan alias Karuna, the LTTE's former regional commander who broke away from the Tigers in 2004. Karuna told Sri Lanka's main state-run newspaper *Daily News* that Solheim bought a house in Norway with money provided to him by the LTTE. He also said that Solheim gifted a television to LTTE chief Velupillai Prabhakaran and that he also gave away 16 million kroners ($2.5 million) to Balasingham.

In a statement, the Norwegian foreign ministry said Karuna's statements contained "many incorrect and false claims about Norway and Solheim" and accused the newspaper of spreading lies. Karuna, who was one of the most senior commanders of LTTE and a confidant of Prabhakaran before he walked out of the group with his supporters, later told the *Asian Tribune* website that he stood by what he had said to the *Daily News*. "I think Erik Solheim might not have disclosed the details about the purchase of the TV to the (Norwegian) foreign ministry as it happened especially in Bangkok," he said.

Solheim told IANS: "I am very surprised that Sri Lanka's main government newspaper has published these lies." Asked if Karuna was present when Solheim met the LTTE leader during his missions to Sri Lanka's north, the Norwegian minister replied: "He may have been ... once or twice. I hardly remember. I don't think he was there. He was mostly in Batticaloa. Even if he was, I can't remember."

Solheim scoffed at claims that he advised Prabhakaran how to run the LTTE. "I have of course told Prabhakaran about the importance of human rights and what the international community expects (of LTTE)." Asked if the allegations would affect Norway's role as a peace facilitator in the unending ethnic conflict, Solheim replied: "Both Norway and myself are committed to the peace process as long as both parties (LTTE and Colombo) want us and we have the full support of the international community including India."

Solheim said "the same circles" had earlier accused Oslo of providing military training to the Tigers but Norway did not come out with immediate denials unlike now because "we thought no one would be that stupid to believe all that". Asked if he or Norway had any time provided any aid to the LTTE in any form, Solheim answered: "It is well known that we have provided support to the LTTE Peace Secretariat and also the Sri Lankan government Peace Secretariat. But nothing has been done outside the knowledge of the Sri Lankan government."

Solheim has been a special envoy to Sri Lanka since Norway was asked by Colombo to play the role of a facilitator to help end a conflict that has claimed over 65,000 lives since 1983. He oversaw the signing of a ceasefire agreement between the LTTE and the Sri Lankan government in February 2002. After he became a minister in the Norwegian government, Solheim's colleague Jon Hanssen-Bauer has taken over the role of special envoy although Solheim oversees the developments in the now tattered peace process.

(IANS, 3 December 2006)

# 24

(This was a dream that remained a dream. I was among a handful of journalists who scooped a report by a group of experts who advocated far-reaching political reforms in Sri Lanka. But President Rajapaksa, fearing a storm in the majority Sinhalese community, conveniently buried it.)

## Experts suggest "genuine power sharing" in Sri Lanka

AN experts' panel set up by President Mahinda Rajapaksa has called for wide-ranging "genuine power sharing" to end the ethnic conflict, suggesting among other things a bicameral legislature and two vice presidents from among the minorities. In a 37-page report to be submitted in Colombo, excerpts of which were made available to IANS, the experts have also come up with four ways of deciding the future of the Tamil-majority northeastern province, which the Sri Lankan Supreme Court wants broken up into the north and east.

Another significant suggestion is to create an Autonomous Zonal Council (ANC) and an Indian Tamil Cultural Council (ITCC) to cater to the needs of what in Sri Lanka are known as "Indian Tamils" employed in the country's tea industry. The report was prepared by 11 of the 17 experts. Of the 11, six are from the majority Sinhalese community, four are Tamils and one Muslim. All six dissenting members are Sinhalese.

The experts, who studied several constitutions, including India's, to frame suggestions to act as a viable alternative to Tamil separatism, have admitted that the failure of minorities to have their due share of power has alienated them from the Sri Lankan state.

The report says that as a form of "genuine power sharing" between the different ethnic and religious communities, provincial institutions and local authorities would be set up and all communities shall share power in the central government, "integrating them into the body politic and strengthening national integration". The group has suggested that the country would be called "Republic of Sri Lanka" and described as "one, free, sovereign and independent state", avoiding any contentious tags such as unitary, federal or union of regions or provinces.

Going closest to the right of self-determination the Tamil Tigers seek, the people of the country shall be described in the constitution as being composed of "the constituent people of Sri Lanka".

The right of every constituent people to develop its own language, to develop and promote its culture and to preserve its history and the right to its due share of state power including the right to due representation in institutions of government shall be recognized without in any way weakening the common Sri Lankan identity. This shall not in any way be construed as authorizing or encouraging any action which would dismember or impair, totally or in part, the territorial integrity or political unity of the Republic.

The report covers all areas of governance including constitution, provinces, unit of devolution, judiciary, national security, law and order, relations between Colombo and provinces, local governments, public services, language, land as well as safeguards for provincial powers.

The experts have suggested two directly or indirectly elected vice presidents for Sri Lanka who shall belong to two different ethnic communities distinct from that of the President, who has always been a Sinhalese since the country became independent in 1948. The group has recommended that the strength of the Sri Lankan parliament be limited to 180 MPs, down from the present 225, and a second chamber be elected by provincial assemblies to give the provinces a sense of national belonging.

All legislation, with the exception of Money Bills, may be initiated in the second chamber. The report wants that the cabinet should reflect the pluralistic character of Sri Lanka and be representative of all provinces. For a territorial unit to be devolved, local authority should be, as much as possible, in a geographically contiguous area. However, ethnicity should not be the sole criterion for the establishment of such units.

Among others, it has suggested a single northeastern province with two internally autonomous units to address the concerns of the Muslims and Sinhalese who live in the Tamil-majority region. The group suggests that Sinhala and Tamil shall be the official languages and languages of administration while Sinhala, Tamil and English shall be the national languages of Sri Lanka. It wants Sinhala, Tamil and English to be made compulsory subjects at the school leaving examination over a period of time.

There shall be a National Police Service and a Provincial Police Service, which would work in cooperation. Local bodies should have power to make by-laws so that ethnic communities in the areas are in control of their living environment. It also favours an Indian type "Panchayat" system for villages with modifications. It wants that public service in a devolved system of governance must be organized at the national, provincial and local levels.

The suggestions would be put up before an all-party grouping that is to submit changes in governance to the Sri Lankan President so as to try end a separatist campaign that has claimed more than 65,000 lives in the island since 1983.

(IANS, 7 December 2006)

# 25

(Anton Balasingham was a prisoner of Prabhakaran's politics. He spoke, occasionally, ill of the Tiger chieftain but mostly justified every wrong the LTTE and its boss committed. He also enjoyed a unique relationship with Prabhakaran, and was the LTTE's long-time face for the outside world. He knew how to talk, and he mesmerized many. I wrote this after his death.)

## Balasingham epitomized LTTE's love–hate ties with India

ANTON Stanislaus Balasingham, the diplomatic face of Sri Lanka's Tamil Tigers, was a multifaceted man who enjoyed a unique bond with its chief Velupillai Prabhakaran and one who loved and detested India at the same time.

To those who kept in touch with him until his very last, he came out as a man who passionately believed—like so many Sri Lankan Tamils—that no solution to the dragging conflict would be possible without India's approval.

Yet, he was never wholly enamoured of India and viewed it as a roadblock in the march to an independent state the LTTE seeks to achieve. In the process he saw conspiracies where none existed and imagined shadows of the Indian state where there were none.

It was in keeping with his personality that he made a desperate gamble to resurrect the LTTE's soured ties with India months before he died on Thursday of cancer in London, by making comments many saw as a half-hearted apology for the killing of Rajiv Gandhi, the former prime minister whose hands he warmly shook for the last time in 1987.

Balasingham's forays into India, however, started almost a decade earlier.

A former journalist who embraced Marxism and moved over to Britain, Balasingham first met Prabhakaran in Chennai in 1979 when the latter was a nobody, giving birth to a unique relationship that lasted until Thursday. As one who taught political thought and Marxism to Prabhakaran and others in those formative years, Balasingham gained the reputation of an ideologue and wrote the earliest theoretical publications for the LTTE.

After anti-Tamil violence swept Colombo in 1983, Balasingham plunged into militancy, persuading Prabhakaran—who the previous year had jumped bail and escaped from Tamil Nadu—to move to India and accept military training imparted by New Delhi. Yet, neither Prabhakaran nor Balasingham were ever subservient to India's strategic interests.

For years, as Tamil militancy galloped, sections of the Indian establishment viewed Balasingham with deep suspicion, wondering if it was he—a British citizen married to an Australian—who egged Prabhakaran to always take an intransigent stand. Balasingham's shadow was so heavy that India deported him along with two other Sri Lankan Tamils in 1985, triggering protests in Tamil Nadu. When Prabhakaran later met the then Prime Minister Rajiv Gandhi, he pleaded for Balasingham.

"I do all the thinking and planning in the LTTE," Prabhakaran insisted. "As I am bad in English, Balasingham articulates my views. He only articulates. He does not influence me." Prabhakaran's frankness and Gandhi's role helped Balasingham to return to India.

However, in 1986, Balasingham, Prabhakaran and many others in the militant ranks again found themselves on the wrong side of the law in Tamil Nadu. For a man who led the first LTTE delegation to then Tamil Nadu Chief Minister M.G. Ramachandran to seek funds for the Tigers and one who interacted with Indian officials, Balasingham felt insulted when the police fingerprinted him and took his mug shots.

That was a year after Balasingham survived an attempt, blamed on the Sri Lankan intelligence, to kill him in Chennai where he lived with his wife Adele. It was an implicit recognition by Colombo that this man played a crucial role in LTTE. Balasingham and Prabhakaran met Gandhi on the midnight of 29 July 1987, only hours before the latter flew to Sri Lanka to sign a peace pact that ended up pitting India against the Tigers. Balasingham said then that the LTTE had accepted the India–Sri Lanka pact. Ironically, when Indian troops hunted for Balasingham in Sri Lanka's northeast from October 1987, he escaped to India, lived for a while and then flew out to the West—on a forged passport provided by a contact in the Indian establishment.

After the LTTE and Colombo signed a truce in February 2002, Balasingham described India as the "fatherland" of Sri Lankan Tamils. That remark, however, did not endear him to New Delhi, which had outlawed the LTTE a decade earlier. Balasingham's appeal that India should host the peace talks between LTTE and Sri Lanka and let him take medical treatment in Tamil Nadu was rejected.

In the years since the Norwegian-brokered peace process got under way, Balasingham remained a key player, knowing well that for all the Western countries the LTTE courted, India would matter ultimately.

But poor health (he was a long-time diabetic that caused several complications) slowed him down. There were signs that he was being slowly sidelined. When he died, it was the end of a man who alone in LTTE could take liberties with Prabhakaran, one who wrote his famous annual speeches, and one who was as much loathed outside the LTTE circles as he was admired within.

(IANS, 15 December 2006)

# 26

(I spoke to Mikko Klemetti, a Finland national, when I visited Helsinki accompanying Prime Minister Manmohan Singh. Klemetti had briefly served with the Sri Lanka Monitoring Mission. By the time he returned home he was convinced that the path to peace in Sri Lanka would be long—and bloody.)

## Sri Lanka needs new truce agreement

SRI LANKA needs a new ceasefire agreement to replace the lifeless 2002 Norwegian-sponsored pact and at least 15,000 foreign soldiers in the island's northeast to ensure its implementation, says a former Finnish monitor of the truce.

Mikko Klemetti, formerly of the Finnish Army, also said in an interview that ordinary Sri Lankans, particularly in the troubled northeast of the island, were sick and tired of the conflict between the government and the LTTE and were hungry for peace.

"The Tamils, the Muslims, everyone, they don't want war any more," Klemetti said over the telephone from his home outside the Finnish capital, a month after he quit Sri Lanka after serving as a ceasefire monitor for four months until 1 September 2006.

He was part of the Nordic Sri Lanka Monitoring Mission (SLMM), whose members from Denmark, Finland and Sweden had to leave after the European Union banned the LTTE. All three countries are part of the European Union, and the Tigers refused to accept them after the ban. Only monitors from Norway and Iceland now serve in the SLMM.

Klemetti, 53, was based in the SLMM headquarters in Colombo and the only place in Sri Lanka's northeast he visited was Amparai, which forms the southern most tip of the region the LTTE wants to secede as an independent nation.

Throughout his stay, like his colleagues, Klemetti interacted with hundreds, mostly ordinary, civilians from all ethnic communities. In the process, he got to understand the genesis and complexities of the Tamil struggle closely.

He said while Tamil civilians wanted peace, "they are under heavy, heavy pressure" and could never challenge either the Sri Lankan security forces or the LTTE and also the breakaway Tiger faction led by Karuna.

They cannot do anything. When they are asked for money (by Tamil organizations), they have to give money. I saw many in Amparai who are very poor, who have nothing. Local people struggle for food. It is very, very difficult for ordinary people.

"Even NGOs engaged in relief work," he said, face "lots of problems. There is war all the time. They don't have the freedom of movement."

Klemetti said Tamil and Muslim civilians often complained to the SLMM about armed groups but there was nothing much the monitors could do.

We were only monitoring. We could not do anything. When locals complained, we did not have the freedom to do our work. Our hands were tied. People came to us about young people, both boys and girls, being abducted. They were taken away to camps, by both sides, the LTTE and Karuna. People pleaded: "Please help us, please help us," but we could not do anything except make a report. Of course we would investigate.

Many times we found that the Karuna group, which was not part of the ceasefire, was used by the security forces to do dirty work. They were many, many times behind the abductions. Both (security forces and LTTE) were not telling us 100 per cent truth. The locals could not understand why the war is going on all the time.

Klemetti said that for genuine peace, Sri Lanka needed a new ceasefire agreement (CFA) to replace the one signed by Colombo and the LTTE in 2002.

The CFA is finished. The landscape is empty. It is only on paper. Both parties don't want that paper.

Asked what he thought could be done to improve the situation, Klemetti said that "at least 15,000 peacekeepers would have to be deployed in Sri Lanka's northeast" so that they can force the peace.

They should make a very good demarcation line and say: "This is the Tamil area; this is the Sri Lankan area." And let the people decide after 5–10 years where they want to go. In the meantime, give economic support to both sides.

Norway should try to get something new, maybe a new agreement. Put a lot of pressure on both parties and try to make them talk.

India should once again get involved. They are nearest and biggest country and they should have a bigger and bigger role to resolve the problem.

But a lot of people don't want India. I know about India's past experience. So this is not military (role) I speak about but political. Militarily, India has no chance in Sri Lanka.

Klemetti added that there could never be a military solution to the ethnic conflict. And he described the exit of the SLMM monitors from Denmark, Sweden and Finland as a loss for the people of Sri Lanka. Asked if he would ever return to that country, he answered: "Yes, but not to monitor the ceasefire. That is a paper tiger now."

(*Mainstream*, 22–28 December 2006)

2007

# 27

(This was written after the hanging of Saddam Hussein. I compared George W. Bush with Sonia Gandhi, whose husband Rajiv Gandhi was assassinated by the LTTE. But by the time the war ended in Sri Lanka, the LTTE was accusing Gandhi of orchestrating the military onslaught against the Tigers.)

## Why George Bush cannot match Sonia Gandhi?

GEORGE W. BUSH finally had his revenge as he slept through the judicial murder of Saddam Hussein, who had famously celebrated with gunshots when Papa Bush's term as US president ended without securing the Iraqi strongman's ouster. Once Bush junior decided that all was fair in war, lies about Weapons of Mass Destruction (WMDs) included, Saddam stood no chance. He paid with his throne in 2003 and his neck three years later, hanged to death in the same manner he himself presided over so many executions during the quarter century he ruled Iraq, first as a darling of Washington and then as a resolute foe.

Had Kurds or Shias dragged out Saddam and done him to death, it could have been explained as an act of vengeance by communities whose members he tortured and killed. But even making allowances for the Internet age, they may not have filmed Saddam's execution for the world to see. Only those who humiliated a once proud Arab nation by capturing on movie a petty soldier examining Saddam's dentures could have thought of the ultimate insult.

That Saddam died without any visible expression of fear, refusing to don the death veil even as all his executioners hid their identity by securely covering their faces with black masks), may only end up further tormenting a military whose occupation of Iraq is by all accounts coming to an inglorious end. And the fact that Saddam was put to death hours before Muslims celebrate Eid was the ultimate humiliation of a religious community that is today undergoing an unprecedented sense of persecution, real and perceived.

Far away, in a country that is home to the world's second largest Islamic population but nevertheless overwhelmingly Hindu, there was widespread revulsion over Saddam's killing. It wasn't because the man on the street in India loved Saddam or his ways. But because people felt it was in poor taste to first have a man convicted by a court whose credibility was in doubt—and then film his last moments. How different were Saddam's executioners from those of Al Qaeda?

What has gone unnoticed is the resolve of one individual in India, completely unlike George Bush, to draw a clear line between a personal tragedy, a far more serious one at that, and the affairs of the state as well as the welfare of a people.

Congress party president Sonia Gandhi has acted like a statesman when it comes to Sri Lanka, not letting the assassination of her husband Rajiv Gandhi at the hands of a Tamil suicide bomber cloud her concern for the island's beleaguered Tamil community.

Rajiv Gandhi's grotesque killing in 1991 shattered Sonia, who married him over 20 years earlier, like nothing else. Refusing to be enticed by the office of prime minister offered to her on a platter after his death, she kept away from limelight for years before taking to politics from the very spot where the man she loved was blown up. Even that January 1998, no one dreamt that she would one day lead a moribund Congress to a remarkable electoral win and again say no to the country's top job.

But much before that, one of Sonia Gandhi's finest gestures was to plead for the clemency of a young Indian Tamil woman who was part of the conspiracy that extinguished her husband. She corresponded with Nalini, who had become a mother in prison, and saw to it that her death sentence was commuted. And she did this quietly, without media glare, and never bragged about it.

When the Congress took power in May 2004, many Sri Lankans thought she would go for revenge against the Tamil Tigers for her husband's death. Far from it, Sonia Gandhi has displayed tremendous courage and political maturity to make peace in Tamil Nadu with those who were once and still aligned with the Tigers. No Sri Lankan who has met Sonia Gandhi has left with the impression that she has revenge in mind, although the subject of Rajiv Gandhi's killing, if ever mentioned, draws dark shadows on her face. As the head of India's ruling coalition, she has consistently pleaded for a just settlement of Sri Lanka's ethnic conflict in a manner the Tamils feel justice has been done to them.

It would perhaps be too much to expect Bush to match up to Sonia Gandhi. After all it was he who presided over a crippling UN sanction that killed thousands of innocent Iraqis, children included, for no fault of theirs except that Saddam was their master. Can one who oversaw children die en masse, one who so savagely decimated Iraq, feel remorseful over the revenge killing of Saddam?

(IANS, 1 January 2007)

# 28

(Sri Lanka's civilian suffering was in full flow as the war escalated. Even among the Tamils, women were the worst hit. Tens of thousands of Tamils in the northeast kept moving without respite from one place to another to escape death. A large number escaped to India and the West to start life anew.)

## Misery, epidemic go hand in hand in troubled Sri Lanka

A widow at 20, she trekked through forests nine-month pregnant, gave birth to a daughter in a refugee shelter and almost got drowned with her baby. There is no end to misery in Sri Lanka's blood-soaked northeast, now enveloped by an epidemic that Tamils are calling a second tsunami.

One of the thousands of Tamils displaced by unending fighting between the government forces and Tamil Tigers, Jayanthi epitomizes the enormous suffering the vast majority of civilians are undergoing, more so in the island's east, caught up in a war they never asked for.

According to aid workers and activists who spoke to IANS over telephone from Sri Lanka, Jayanthi lost her husband when an artillery shell fired by the military fell close to her house in Sampur. Devastated and pregnant, she stayed in a camp for a while before trekking with relatives to the Tigers-held Vakarai in August 2006.

She gave birth to daughter Kirthiha that month at a school in Kathiravelli, close to the river Verugal. Both miraculously survived a later military bombing of the school that killed dozens. Jayanthi suffered minor injuries.

On 12 December midnight, she took a boat to go from Vaharai to Valaichenai. But the vessel capsized. Luckily, Jayanthi rescued her baby, lifted it high above her head and waded through neck deep water for over five kilometres before reaching a government exit point from where she reached the eastern town of Batticaloa.

If the military is chiefly to blame for what happened to Jayanthi, who still worries for her parents she has left behind, Tamil boy Kumar, 15, also a refugee in Batticaloa, has a grudge both against the government and the Tamil Tigers.

Kumar lost his eldest brother and seven other members of his extended family also in the military bombing of Sampur. Kumar and his second elder brother Mohan and their injured sister later went to Vakarai, controlled by the LTTE.

Mohan, a talented youngster who aimed to become an engineer, was to sit for his Class 10 examination. According to Kumar, Mohan sought LTTE's permission to take the test in Batticaloa. The LTTE did not let him go. As ill luck would have it, he died in the Kathiravelli school bombing.

A rights activist working among the refugees quoted Kumar as saying:

Mohan would not have died if he had been allowed him to go. Since 25 April I have lived in 12 refugee camps. I have walked miles and miles through thick jungles for days to reach this camp. Most importantly, I have missed nine months of school.

Said another aid worker, speaking from Batticaloa: "Every individual has a tragic story to say. Many are still searching for their missing family members. One refugee camp has 29 pregnant ladies but no medical care."

The Tamil refugee crisis, activists say, is only getting worse. Thousands have been forced out of the multi-ethnic Trincomalee district. Some are being asked to live in tents at a cemetery at Sathurukondan, north of Batticaloa town. The authorities claim the cemetery is not used any more.

If all this wasn't enough, an epidemic of chikungunya, a mosquito-borne viral disease that causes high fever, weakens bones and in extreme cases can kill, has broken out all over Sri Lanka's northeast—and elsewhere in the country. Aid workers and NGOs say the disease, which came from India, was first noticed in October 2006 in the northwestern district of Mannar and quickly spread all over the sprawling region that is at the heart of the Tamil separatist conflict.

In the Tamil majority district of Batticaloa, a vast majority of the 580,000 people and the thousands of refugees are affected. "The Tamils are calling it a second tsunami," said a resident, comparing it with the disaster that killed hundreds of thousands in Indian Ocean countries in December 2004.

The main 700-bed hospital in Batticaloa is overflowing with over 900 patients, with many forced to lie on the floor. Even the staff has been hit hard. Another hospital at Aryampathy, south of Batticaloa town, is also facing a crisis.

Mobile medical teams are on the job, doing what best they can. But a key problem is the high cost of medicines the refugees cannot afford. Worse, Tamil refugees are also beginning to suffer from diarrhoea. This, aid workers say, is mainly because of the half-cooked rice served to them along with staple vegetables like pumpkin, pulses and occasional Soya meat.

The United Nations High Commissioner for Refugees (UNHCR), local NGOs and the World Food Programme (WFP), whose aid is channelled through the government, are the ones mainly working among the refugees. "But this is woefully inadequate," lamented one activist. "Some Tamil children have turned beggars in Batticaloa. How long can this go on? There is real danger of someone or the other turning them into child soldiers. But who is bothered?"

(IANS, 9 January 2007)

# 29

(Once Sri Lanka decided to crush the LTTE, it took recourse to "unconventional steps"—a polite euphemism for extra-judicial methods. Like in the case of the proverbial diamond, Colombo decided to become an LTTE to break the LTTE. Anyone suspected of being linked to the Tigers were abducted in white colour vans. Many of them disappeared—forever.)

## Sri Lanka's abduction industry has top academic in its grip

THE distraught family of Sri Lanka's most high profile kidnap victim is begging the authorities to accept his resignation as vice-chancellor of a university, the key demand of abductors who seized him from under the very nose of the government over a month ago.

In a case that has raised international stink, S. Raveendranath, 55, who headed the Eastern University of Sri Lanka for around three years, sensationally disappeared on December 15 from near a conference hall in a supposedly high security area of Colombo.

Since then, the Tamil man's wife has almost stopped eating and spends her days and nights in agony on bed, their son-in-law and trainee eye surgeon Muthusamy

Malaravan, 36, told IANS over telephone from their Colombo home. "She is crying all the time. The family members are in severe mental trauma." Adding to the worry is Raveendranath's feeble health. He is a diabetic and suffers from hypertension, both of which necessitate regulate doses of medicines. Any slip up can lead to a stroke that can prove fatal.

Malaravan, who has stopped doing surgeries because of the tension he is in, has one humble request to the University Grants Commission (UGC): Please accept my father-in-law's resignation as vice-chancellor so that the kidnappers let him go.

The abductors, widely believed to be the breakaway Tamil Tigers faction headed by Karuna, apparently want Raveendranath, who is from the north of the island, out of the Eastern University, which is located near the eastern town of Batticaloa, in a zone Karuna supporters consider as their own.

The UGC has different ideas. It thinks that if it were to give into the demand of the abductors, its "prestige" will be hit. That "prestige", Malaravan says, is prolonging the agony of an already distressed family—the missing man's wife, two daughters and son-in-law.

In a violence-torn country where kidnappings of Tamils, the rich as well as the not so rich, have become routine, Raveendranath has still attracted a lot of attention in Sri Lanka and abroad as one who joined the Eastern University in 1981 as an assistant lecturer and rose to become the acting vice-chancellor in 2004 before assuming full charge in 2005.

It was in 2004 that Karuna, the once famed regional commander of the LTTE, broke away with his supporters. He has since been locked in a bloody turf war with the dominant LTTE for control of Sri Lanka's multi-ethnic east, apparently with Colombo's backing. "It is more than one month and nobody is telling us where my father-in-law is," said Malaravan. "We have no single clue, nothing. They (police) are blank. Police do meet us, but that is all. And worse, there is no eyewitness to what really happened that day."

UGC has my father-in-law's resignation. They only need to make it public. We are requesting them to do it. We are ready to give 100 per cent firm assurance that my father-in-law will have nothing to do with the university once he is freed. We will not file any case. We pray to god every day.

The family has knocked on every single door in Colombo: President Mahinda Rajapaksa, military officials, foreign embassies, Sri Lankan and global NGOs, the media and also the Colombo-based office of the Karuna group, which is laying the blame for the kidnapping on LTTE.

Raveendranath's problems came in the open when armed men abducted the dean of the arts faculty in September 2005 demanding the vice-chancellor's resignation.

On October 2, he sent his resignation to UGC, and soon the dean was released. According to the family, the UGC asked Raveendranath to work in Colombo. He complied. So he remained the vice-chancellor.

On two later occasions, Raveendranath received telephonic threats: "You are still working. You are not obeying us. You will be in danger." He reported the calls to UGC but his resignation was still not accepted. On 15 December he disappeared, becoming the most high profile of Tamils who have gone missing in Sri Lanka in recent times.

Malaravan details all that his father-in-law has done for the Eastern University and the linkages he has forged with universities around the world, including India. The efforts are visible from the support generated for him in Western academic circles, including the US, Britain, France, Denmark, France, Sweden, Canada and Japan. But he remains missing.

Does the family have hope? "We are still positive but worried," says Malaravan. "UGC must accept his resignation. If everyone works together, I think he can be released. He is a neutral man. Even if there is one phone call saying he is well, we shall be happy. Even that is not there."

(IANS, 18 January 2007)

# 30

(By early 2007 it was clear that the LTTE was using Tamil Nadu to source and to ship war material to Sri Lanka. It was also evident from the seizures in Tamil Nadu that the Tigers were preparing for a long war. Tamil Nadu became vitally important for the LTTE after Sri Lanka began to decimate Tamil Tiger ships involved in long-distance arms smuggling.)

## War material seizure signal LTTE bracing for guerrilla war

SRI LANKA'S Tamil Tigers may be preparing for a sustained guerrilla war if the growing seizures of war materials in India are any indication. In the last three months, authorities in Tamil Nadu have taken into their possession equipment and vast quantities of materials that can be used to make bombs meant for the LTTE. Officials monitoring the seizures say it is now clear that smuggling of the materials must have been going on for at least a year and that a large quantity may have slipped past the Indian coastline.

The latest find took place in Chennai on 24 January 2007 when five Sri Lankan Tamil and three Indian men were taken into custody with two tonnes of iron ball bearings, following a strong lead from the Indian security establishment. A day later three more tonnes were seized and another Indian was arrested. All the stuff had been bought in Mumbai. "It is clear the LTTE's reliance on Tamil Nadu is slowly increasing," an official told IANS, referring to the state separated from Sri Lanka by a strip of sea and which for years served as a crucial rear base for Tamil militants.

In January 2006, the Sri Lankan Navy intercepted a boat that had sailed from Tamil Nadu with 60,000 detonators and five Indian fishermen. The cargo had been bought in Hyderabad and had reached Tamil Nadu from Kerala. After a long gap, in November 2006, a lathe machine, which can be used to make shells for bombs, was found in the seabed near the Indian coast.

Later that month, 30 boxes of gelex boosters, which can help increase the velocity of bomb shrapnel, were recovered in a van that met with an accident 45 km from Madurai in Tamil Nadu. The cargo was destined for Sri Lanka. Again, fishermen from Rameswaram found three live rockets in their fishing nets.

Indian officials think the LTTE network in Tamil Nadu, carefully laid out over the years, has been activated to procure materials to be used in explosives, the prime need in any long drawn guerrilla war. But they add that it would be a mistake to link up these activities with Tamil Nadu's ruling DMK party, pointing out that LTTE supporters have been busy for at least a year. The DMK took power only in May 2006.

"At least in one case one of the suspects who was arrested admitted he had dispatched four to five consignments," one official said. "He said he was in it for money." Another official pointed out that it looked as if LTTE supporters were consciously buying bomb materials in other states in India and bringing them to Tamil Nadu to be taken to Sri Lanka.

Tamil Nadu's coastline is over 1,000 km long. Although there is heightened vigilance in the coastal districts, it is virtually impossible to provide round the clock surveillance, that too with some 400 "landing points" for boats. The smuggling of war materials from India coincides with escalating violence in Sri Lanka's northeast where the military has seized several areas from the Tamil Tigers in recent months, forcing the Tigers to retreat.

Analysts here believe that the LTTE, which is highly unlikely to shake hands with Colombo, will eventually opt for guerrilla war, to bog the Sri Lankan security forces down once they get thinly spread out.

Officials say the increasing dependence on Tamil Nadu could reflect one of two things: that some other supply line has been cut off or that the LTTE has decided to use its finances judiciously by going for purchases in a place close to the war theatre. Although the LTTE is outlawed in India, many in Tamil Nadu, including those in influential positions, still sympathize with its fight for an independent state. But the mass sympathy the cause once evoked has abated.

(IANS, 30 January 2007)

# 31

(The assumption that the LTTE cannot be defeated militarily was widely shared in the international community. In retrospect, this has been proved to be wrong. But statements such as this one by the US envoy to Sri Lanka lulled the LTTE into complacency and made it believe that it can never be overcome militarily.)

## LTTE cannot be defeated militarily, US tells Sri Lanka

DESCRIBING the situation in Sri Lanka as "serious", the US envoy to the island nation has warned against attempts to underestimate the Tamil Tigers and asserted that they cannot be defeated militarily. Ambassador Robert Blake also said in a telephonic interview from Colombo that his country "respectfully disagreed" with those in Sri Lanka who feel a military solution was possible to end the dragging Tamil separatist campaign.

The ambassador, who took charge in September 2006, made it clear that only devolution of powers that satisfy the "legitimate aspirations" of the Tamil minority could be the basis for any negotiations between the Sri Lankan government and the LTTE. Blake's comments to IANS came as thousands of Tamil civilians began fleeing northern Sri Lanka amid fears of full-scale war and a declaration by the LTTE that it was resuming its "freedom struggle".

"The situation is serious but there is light at the end of the tunnel," said the envoy, whose country is a key and most outspoken member of the international community that oversees Sri Lanka's now virtually dead peace process. He said a majority in the southern part of Sri Lanka, populated mainly by the dominant Sinhalese community, felt that "a military solution is possible. We respectfully disagree. The LTTE cannot be defeated militarily without a parallel political strategy to address the grievances of the Tamil community..."

> I don't think a military solution is possible without a parallel political strategy. The LTTE has significant capability to attack, using terrorist means. We should not underestimate that. I think there would be costs (to pay) to a military strategy. The most important thing in our view is to come up with a credible (political) process.

Blake, however, suggested that while he thought that Sri Lanka remained committed to peace despite the military pursuing a military strategy, the LTTE's credentials vis-à-vis a negotiated settlement were doubtful. "The government is committed to peace. Every time I speak to (President Mahinda Rajapaksa) and senior members of the government, they assure me they are committed to a peaceful settlement. I have no reasons to doubt that."

> The military believes in a military solution but the policy of the government is to pursue (a negotiated settlement). At this point of time, without a proposal, there is nothing to negotiate over. As for the LTTE, I cannot say if they are committed to peace. Their record of 20 years shows they have never seriously pursued the peace option. The government will have to soon give them a chance to see if they are ready to negotiate in good faith.

The internationally backed Norwegian-sponsored ceasefire agreement (CFA) signed by Sri Lanka and the LTTE entered its sixth year on 22 February with all signs pointing to a war again in the island. According to peace monitors, some 4,000 Sri Lankans, mainly Tamil civilians, have been killed in fighting and tit-for-tat attacks and more than 200,000 people, again mostly Tamils, displaced from their homes in the past 15 months. Thousands of Tamils have fled to India while abductions have become routine in parts of Sri Lanka.

"Since last year, the human rights situation has also deteriorated," Blake said. "There is therefore an urgent need to end the fighting and resume talks (for) a negotiated settlement." He said the US believed that a body representing almost all political parties and tasked to come up with power sharing proposals provided an important opportunity to achieve peace.

We very much hope the proposals that emerge will be credible and meet the legitimate aspirations of the Tamil people in particular but also of the other communities. This could be the basis for the talks between the government and the LTTE ... The most important thing is the government has an opportunity. It must come up with a credible solution. They have the votes in parliament. There is very strong evidence that (the main opposition United National Party) will support a credible solution. That would be a major, major step forward.

The ambassador pointed out that there had been "very significant consequences" for the failure of the LTTE to settle for peace since the last round of talks in Geneva that ended in a fiasco. "We think there is a strong incentive for both sides to go back to the table." But irrespective of what happens, he said "we cannot imagine a situation" when the US would support an LTTE state, which for all practical purposes now exists in parts of Sri Lanka's north and where Colombo's writ does not run. "The US takes a very hard line regarding the LTTE."

Asked if India needed to play a more pro-active role, Blake said he disagreed with the surmise of the question.

India is already playing a very active role and is a major if not the pre-eminent player in Sri Lanka. The US cooperates very closely with our Indian friends on the situation in Sri Lanka. I don't see any difference in our analysis of the situation or what needs to be done. We will continue our cooperation with India.

(IANS, 25 February 2007)

# 32

(Once war resumed in 2006, the LTTE made great use of Tamil Nadu to ferry war material to Sri Lanka. Indian security agencies promptly went after LTTE activists and supporters in Tamil Nadu and succeeded in preventing tonnes and tonnes of arms, explosives and related stuff from being smuggled out.)

## India concerned over LTTE explosives smuggling

MASSIVE smuggling of explosive material from India to Sri Lanka by the Tamil Tigers has raised serious concerns in India, with one official warning that the problem may be bigger than previously thought of. Indian security agencies have in recent months seized, mainly from Tamil Nadu and off its winding coastline, a huge quantity as well as variety of stuff that can be used to make lethal explosives. They have also arrested several suspects.

The seizures have sparked some alarm in Tamil Nadu, whose Chief Minister M. Karunanidhi has declared he would not tolerate any illegal activity even as he sympathized with the suffering of the island's Tamil community. But Indian home ministry officials say that Tamil Nadu needs to do much more to ensure that those covertly assisting the LTTE in smuggling out explosive substances from the state are put out of business.

"We feel the magnitude of the problem is bigger than what it was thought to be," a senior official told IANS. "It is clear more than one network is operating in Tamil Nadu. Just how many, we don't know. It is disturbing."

Tamil Nadu is separated from Sri Lanka by a strip of sea and has been home to Tamil militants in the past. A previous Karunanidhi government was sacked by New Delhi in 1991 following reports of widespread LTTE presence in the state. LTTE activities in the state virtually ended in the wake of a crackdown that followed the May 1991 assassination of former Prime Minister Rajiv Gandhi near Chennai. They picked up from the latter part of the 1990s but never reached the levels of the 1980s.

The latest bout of smuggling appears to have coincided with a dramatic surge in violence in Sri Lanka from December 2005, soon after President Mahinda Rajapaksa took power and the LTTE vowed to renew its separatist campaign.

The Sri Lankan navy seized some 60,000 detonators from the sea on its way from Tamil Nadu in January 2006. In November, a large quantity of boosters to produce explosives was found in Tamil Nadu's Sivaganga district from a van that met with a road accident. The consignment was headed to Sri Lanka. Since then, the Indian Navy, Coast Guard, police and other security agencies have seized or recovered huge volumes of explosive material, bought mainly from other Indian states but routed to Sri Lanka from Tamil Nadu.

"Everything is in tonnes," said a Tamil Nadu police officer. "The material is being bought from places like Andhra Pradesh and Maharashtra while Tamil Nadu is used as a transit point." The most notable of the finds were arms and ammunition, including a 7 kg suicide belt from an explosives-packet boat off the Tamil Nadu coast in February 2007. The boat has since been destroyed.

Home Ministry officials admit that for every tonne of material seized, much more may have gone past the Tamil Nadu coast. "Those arrested say they have clear-cut instructions from the top (LTTE leadership) to avoid any skirmish with Indian security forces," said one source.

Another officer said it was clear the Tigers' dependence on Tamil Nadu had soared parallel to its mounting difficulties in the Western countries, many of which have outlawed LTTE as a terrorist outfit. "The LTTE has the support of a hardcore base in Tamil Nadu. They may be small in number but they are dedicated to the LTTE cause," the officer said. "With violence rising (in Sri Lanka), Tamil Nadu's importance has naturally gone up."

(IANS, 27 February 2007)

# 33

(This is the tragic story of a Tamil woman who lost her husband while fleeing to India with one of her children. Tamil civilians underwent enormous suffering because of a war they never asked for.)

## Husband dead, Tamil woman wants to return to Sri Lanka

A Sri Lankan Tamil woman who sailed to India in search of a new life is now pining to return home, unable to bear the drowning of her husband when he tried to swim to Tamil Nadu's coast to seek help for their ailing daughter after a boatman dumped them on a remote sand dune.

Daisy Paulin, 33, has not stopped crying since reaching Tamil Nadu after an Indian Navy helicopter spotted her, her four-year-old child and some other Tamil refugees on a sand dune south of Rameswaram, leading to their rescue.

By then, however, Daisy's life had turned upside down. Her husband Chandran Thavakumar, three years younger, had met a watery grave after sneaking out of the sand dune close to midnight, moved by the pain of their daughter who was constantly vomiting and suffering from diarrhoea.

Daisy would later say that she would have stopped her husband from undertaking the dangerous voyage if only she had not gone off to sleep on the sand dune, some 18 hours after the boatman left the group there saying it was Rameswaram, their destination in Tamil Nadu.

It was not. It was one of several huge sand dunes that dot the sea south of Rameswaram where fishermen often rest. This was early on the morning of 16 February about 10 hours after they set out from Mannar in Sri Lanka's northwest. Soon after the family of Thavakumar, which had left behind two other children aged 9 and 7 with his parents, landed on the sand dune, the daughter, who was with them, began to wail for food and water.

But the biscuits and water they had were exhausted. In desperation, the parents gave the hungry daughter water from the sea to drink. She started vomiting. Very soon diarrhoea set in. Unfortunately, some Indian fishing boats that sailed past did not come to their rescue. A crackdown was on in Tamil Nadu to check smuggling of explosives to Sri Lanka, and the fishermen opted to stay away from trouble.

"Fearing something would happen to the child, Thavakumar asked the wife if he could swim across to Rameswaram for help," said M. Sakkariyas, a Sri Lankan who works with an NGO looking after refugee welfare in Tamil Nadu. "Daisy was not very happy with the idea and she told him not to go. But at 11 p.m., without telling her, he set out with another man, Anton," Sakkariyas, 61, told IANS over telephone from Chennai.

"According to Anton, both swam past two sand dunes. There were eight or nine along the way to Rameswaram. But Thavakumar was unable to proceed. Anton helped him, more or less carried him some distance."

Anton eventually left Thavakumar on a sand dune and reached Rameswaram. Nothing further was heard from Thavakumar until his body was washed ashore. By the time the distraught Daisy, her daughter and the others were rescued at around 3 p.m. on 17 February they had spent a harrowing 36 hours stranded without food or water.

The child recovered. But Daisy, one of the thousands of Tamils fleeing to India to escape the violence in Sri Lanka, is unable to overcome her grief.

Her dead husband had been a welder by profession and had been earning just enough to keep the family going in the northern Sri Lankan district of Vavuniya since returning from Saudi Arabia some time ago.

Sakkariyas quoted Daisy as saying that her husband returned home promptly by 6 p.m. and never slept outside fearing the military or Tamil militants might take him away. Daisy always worried for him. Eventually they decided to shift to India, without realizing what fate awaited them.

Said Sakkariyas:

I saw Daisy thrice at a refugee camp at Rameshwaram. She would cry each time she began to speak. She kept saying: "He went away without telling me, he went away without telling me." When I saw her, I almost broke down. She presented a pathetic sight. She cannot even walk. She is desperate to go back to Sri Lanka to rejoin her other two children. We have applied for a passport for her. Once it comes and a ticket follows, we will send her to Colombo.

Although a Hindu, Thavakumar was buried at Arichamunai, close to Danushkodi on the Tamil Nadu coast, Sakkariyas said. "Daisy keeps asking again and again. 'Our family's sole wage earner is gone. Who will look after us now'"?

(IANS, 11 March 2007)

# 34

(It was a bilateral pact that President J.R. Jayewardene signed with Indian Prime Minister Rajiv Gandhi probably because he had no choice. But it failed. The 20th anniversary of the India–Sri Lanka accord of 1987 passed off quietly. This article examines why.)

## A historic accord few remember today

IT was hailed as India's biggest diplomatic coup when it was signed amid violent street protests. Twenty years and thousands of deaths later, the India–Sri Lanka accord of 1987, which sought to restore peace to the island, has become history—almost.

It was on 29 July 1987 that then Indian Prime Minister Rajiv Gandhi flew to Colombo to sign the agreement with President J.R. Jayewardene in a bid to end a raging Tamil separatist drive. That was not the only thing the accord sought to achieve.

For the first time in Sri Lanka's troubled history, the country was formally re-cognized as a multi-religious, multi-ethnic and multi-lingual society. It also brought about the only major act of constitutional reforms, devolving powers to minorities in the form of provincial councils with judicial, civil and police services. It made Tamil an official language of the country, declared the island's northeast as "areas of historical habitation of the Tamil speaking people" and had provisions to end state-sponsored colonization of Tamil areas.

Starting from the evening of 29 July, thousands of Indian troops began to be deployed in the war-torn northeast, heralding a sudden peace the country had not known for years. But after putting down a small part of its weaponry, the LTTE refused to disarm itself, citing security reasons, and went on a killing spree of its rivals and others.

Sections of the Jayewardene government unhappy with the pact and also India's role were intent on tripping the Tigers. In the complex tragedy that followed, the Indian troops took on the LTTE in Jaffna from 10 October 1987.

The fighting dragged on for well over two years. By the time the soldiers returned home, both Gandhi and Jayewardene were out of office. An India-backed provincial government in the northeast had collapsed. And the Tigers ended up controlling Jaffna and large parts of the northeast.

But many blood-soaked years later, the LTTE and the Sri Lankan government are still fighting, India remains an interested but distant party to the goings on, and there is no light at the end of what looks a dark and unending tunnel.

Amid growing international concerns over Sri Lanka, does the accord still have some relevance? "Though the agreement is a dead letter, though neither government wants to give any life to it, there are some fundamental principles advocated in it that still remain a source of inspiration," said S. Sahadevan, a South Asia expert at Jawaharlal Nehru University in New Delhi. "It can be the starting point for a discourse on devolution of powers. However, legally and politically, the importance of the accord is somewhat lost now."

P. Rajanayagam, editor of *Tamil Times* of Britain, told IANS:

The accord provided for a reasonable and comprehensive institutional architecture for the settlement of the ethnic conflict. The accord substantially addressed almost all the grievances of the Tamil people that had remained unresolved for decades. It presented a historic opportunity to once and for all resolve the ethnic conflict but was squandered away... The rejection of the accord, not allowing it to be implemented and taking up arms against India are acts of criminal folly and an utter betrayal of the Tamil people.

V. Suryanarayana, another Sri Lanka expert who is based in Chennai, said the accord collapsed because it was never seriously implemented. "The tragedy today is that the Sri Lankan government is not willing to give even what was in the accord."

The fighting between the LTTE and Indians not only led to the death of nearly 1,200 Indian soldiers and hundreds of Tamils, combatants and non-combatants, but also disrupted the historically warm ties between India and the Tamil community. So why is the accord's 20th anniversary passing so quietly?

Explained Sahadevan: "Both the governments have buried the agreement. Not just Sri Lanka, India also does not remember it. When you don't remember, how do you expect the other party which never liked it to remember?"

(IANS, 28 July 2007)

# 35

(The LTTE's ballooning growth is a fascinating story. In its formative years it relied on cycles to reach its victims. Many bloody years later, its obsession with military technology led it to use smuggled light aircraft to drum up a nascent air wing. But LTTE planes could not alter the course of the war.)

## On to Tamil Eelam: From bicycle to aircraft

WAY back in 1983, Velupillai Prabhakaran, on the alert, rode a bicycle through Jaffna to oversee a spot near the university his colleagues had picked to ambush Sri Lankan troops. Few people knew him then, and fewer had heard of the Tamil Tigers. A quarter century later, the same man, now a legend, has made history by using Tamil ingenuity to transform two light aircraft into stealthy bombers to target the air base of his enemy right in the heart of Sri Lanka.

From the humble bicycle then to the breathless display of air power in 2007, this is the extraordinary achievement of a man who has presided over a sharp and intelligent growth of the LTTE, taking it from a band of barely 40 men in 1983 to become the world's first insurgent group to carry out an aerial attack without any external state support.

A simple device, the cycle proved an ideal transport for Tamil militants in the 1970s and 1980s. Young men would come riding, looking like any other cyclist, fire at their targets and coolly pedal away. A frustrated administration decided to ban the use of cycles in Jaffna, forcing a Jaffna magazine to ask: "What will the terrorists do next? Take to tricycles? Will tricycles be banned too eventually?"

Using anything and everything that could advance the cause of Tamil Eelam was something Prabhakaran learnt and began implementing a long time ago. During the years he was underground but largely unknown, he opted to use chilli powder to keep policemen at bay if nothing else was available. Weapons bought second hand and stolen or snatched from security forces followed. There was of course no stopping of his dreams.

In 1982, while residing in Madurai town, Prabhakaran confided to Tamil Nadu politician P. Nedumaran: "How I wish I would be able to see at least 100 LTTE armed members walk in a marching column one day!" Just a decade later, he was presiding over Jaffna peninsula at the head of a huge LTTE army, having ousted Indian troops from Sri Lanka's northeast with a blend of guerrilla tactics and cunning diplomacy.

In that tumultuous decade, Prabhakaran provided the Tigers an identity as a fighting force and presided over the slow, steady and secret build up of a group that grew and grew, whatever the consequences, whatever the price. He was not worried about the methods, and he certainly did not mind doing away with real or perceived foes.

What came in the beginning were a secret code, a constitution, and simple rules of discipline (not always adhered to). Then came the bigger dreams—uniforms for his men, more weapons, more modern weapons, deadlier weapons, sanctuaries, training manuals, training grounds. These too turned into reality over time.

By then, cycles were no more the mainstay of the guerrillas, whose leaders, Prabhakaran included, had long grown out of their teens. They were no more just another militant group. They were the first among equals, and path breakers in technology that could kill. Motorcycles, tractors and jeeps were added to the LTTE arsenal. Deep underground bunkers were dug.

Boats, speedboats, larger vessels and even bigger ships joined the Tamil Tiger assets, making it the first insurgent group in this part of the world to have a naval wing. The Tigers also brought down fighter jets. And Prabhakaran had a huge crop of suicide bombers—the most dangerous of weapons of all in his inventory.

The LTTE, however, lacked one thing: planes. But it did not lack innovative capacity. If the Tigers used huge, improvised catapults to overwhelm the Jaffna Fort, they never stopped trying to build something that could fly. Anyone who knew the Tiger mindset was sure the planes would make their appearance one day.

That they did, initially to sprinkle flowers on cemeteries of LTTE fighters in 1998. Nine years later, as the country slept, they flew to Colombo to bomb Sri Lankan air force jets. 26 March 2007 may just be the beginning of a new war front in a country that battles men and women who adamantly refuse to give up.

(IANS, 27 March 2007)

# 36

(Once Rajiv Gandhi was assassinated, India took a hands-off approach to Sri Lanka. Later, it covertly got involved in the Norway-brokered peace process. As Eelam War IV raged, India tilted towards Sri Lanka, first quietly and later vocally.)

## Amid war, India's emerging Sri Lanka tilt

AFTER witnessing the steady demise of a peace process it quietly helped put in place, India is caught between a belligerent Sri Lankan regime and the Tamil Tigers. Now it seems to be slowly tilting towards Colombo. Despite some vocal bad blood vis-à-vis Colombo, New Delhi appears to be throwing its weight behind Sri Lanka in the war against the LTTE even while overtly maintaining equidistance.

Some of the visible changes come amid Sri Lanka's determination to pursue a political and military approach that is not totally to India's liking but which New Delhi is painfully realizing it can do nothing about. The Indian policy movements also come at a time when the international community is learning the limitations of outside forces forcing a settlement that will help bring genuine peace to Sri Lanka.

In recent days, National Security Advisor M.K. Narayanan has gone public asking Sri Lanka not to shop for weapons in China or Pakistan—comments that raised many eyebrows—while ruling out sale of "offensive weapons" from India. Simultaneously, he made it clear—in New Delhi and then in Chennai, both after meetings with Tamil Nadu Chief Minister M. Karunanidhi—that the LTTE was a terrorist group and that its sea and nascent air wings posed a threat to India.

Also last week, Sri Lanka's Defence Secretary Gotabaya Rajapaksa, who oversees the war against the LTTE and is a brother of President Mahinda Rajapaksa, flew to India from Turkey and met officials of the security and military set-ups, giving his assessment of the situation and outlining Colombo's military needs.

Even as his brother was here, President Rajapaksa—who has nursed a sense of hurt since late 2005 over the treatment New Delhi gave him during his first foreign trip after taking office—told an interviewer that Sri Lanka was only prepared to listen to India, not the West. His comments came amid speculation that India was covertly assisting Sri Lanka with vital military hardware.

Sri Lanka has in recent years followed a strategy aimed at increasing India's economic stakes in the island so that any security threats to Colombo would also be deemed a threat to New Delhi. While India has gone for limited sale of arms to Sri Lanka besides sharing intelligence and providing naval and air defence cooperation, it has not fulfilled the many other military requirements of Colombo.

This has forced Sri Lanka to turn to Pakistan and China among other countries, knowing well that India would be unhappy. This puts pressure on New Delhi— either continue with a "no-offensive-weapons-for-sale" policy or go in for covert assistance.

Adding to the haze is the LTTE's uncompromising attitude. The overall assessment remains that the Tigers are not India friendly and only want to use New Delhi to further their interests. At the same time, President Rajapaksa has gone back on assurances given to Indian Prime Minister Manmohan Singh in Havana last year to keep the northeastern province united to satisfy a very basic Tamil demand. A reasonable devolution package for the Tamils is also nowhere in sight.

And while Indian officials say their repeated expressions of concerns have reduced civilian deaths caused by Sri Lankan air and artillery attacks, Tamil rights activists say that killings and kidnappings of Tamils of all hues have become rampant. In the present circumstances, India is in no position to broker any deal between Sri Lanka and LTTE. Its influence is limited vis-à-vis both the Colombo regime and the Sinhalese society, which lacks a bipartisan approach to the conflict.

And contrary to widespread belief, India also has no tangible influence over the LTTE, which is working, despite many setbacks, towards reversing the military tide one day.

Tamil sources say the one major difference between the 1980s and now is that India was then seen as a major power that could one day militarily intervene in Sri Lanka to set things right. It did just that, paid a heavy price and withdrew bleeding. Now it has stated repeatedly that there will be no further military intervention in Sri Lanka.

(IANS, 7 June 2007)

# 37

(I wrote this commentary after police tossed out some 500 Tamils from lodges in Colombo and packed them off to Vavuniya and Batticaloa towns as part of a crackdown. My argument was that ordinary Tamils should not be made to pay the price for the follies of a group that acted in their name but without their permission.)

## How to tell Tamils they don't belong to Sri Lanka?

ANY government in any country can err. But some errors can turn out to be political blunders. Sri Lanka's startling move to throw out Tamils from numerous lodges in the capital Colombo falls in that category.

For too long it has been claimed by Sri Lanka's ruling elite that there cannot be a concept of "Tamil homeland" because more Tamils now live outside of the war zone that is the northeastern province, which was once overwhelmingly Tamil. Government leaders would point this out to outsiders gleefully.

On Thursday, the Sri Lankan police's high-handed action seemed to prove that the "Tamil homeland" does exist and it does constitute precisely that region the LTTE wants to secede. Citing security reasons, some 500 Tamils staying in the many small lodges in Colombo's predominantly Tamil areas were ordered to pack up their bags—never mind why they were in the city—and get into buses that took them to Vavuniya in Sri Lanka's north and Batticaloa in the east. Vavuniya and Batticaloa are among the major towns in the island's northeast, which the Tamils describe as the "Tamil homeland".

In one stroke, Colombo appeared to prove right the LTTE argument that Sri Lanka is made up of two nations—the Sinhala nation and Tamil nation—and that these two nations can never co-exist. No wonder, then, the mass expulsion ignited widespread condemnation, from within and outside Sri Lanka. Mercifully, the Supreme Court ordered a halt to it.

But the damage has been done—in the minds of ordinary Tamils at least.

The police argue there may be LTTE agents—even potential suicide bombers—among the Tamils in the lodges. That may well be true. But what is the guarantee that LTTE sleeper agents don't live elsewhere in Colombo, pretending to be normal law-abiding residents? So will all Tamils be made to quit Colombo—as a precaution against terror attacks?

In the 1980s, as Tamil militancy took root in Jaffna, the authorities decided to ban cycling because Tamil guerrillas were using them to bump off unsuspecting security personnel and pedal away. *Saturday Review*, the now-defunct outspoken Jaffna weekly, had asked: What will happen if the militants take to tricycles, will they too be banned? And it went on: Should sex be banned because some cheat their spouses?

Those of us who have lived in Colombo for short and longer durations know that a deep though unfortunate Tamil–Sinhala divide very much exists. Indian families who employ Tamils as domestic help intervene occasionally when these men and women get picked up from buses and streets on suspicion of being linked to Tigers and at times end up spending a night or two in police custody. Tamil Hindu women are known to take off their "bindi" when they step on to the streets so that it doesn't mark them out as Tamils.

I have travelled many times in three-wheeled autos in Colombo whose Tamil drivers would promptly switch off Tamil radios when they are near police or military checkpoints. And they would whisper: "If they ask who you are, don't say you are a Tamil. Say you are an Indian, from Delhi."

A Sri Lankan army major who "raided" the Colombo house of Indian journalist Nirupama Subramanian asked her, after viewing a photograph of her standing by a LTTE signboard in Batticaloa: "So you have been to Tamil Eelam?" "Sorry Major," she replied, "we call it Batticaloa."

Sri Lanka is no doubt fighting a very difficult war, and against a very determined and sophisticated enemy. But throwing out Tamils from Colombo lodges, even if the number is only 500, reflects poorly on a society and a government who are expected to prove wrong the LTTE ideology. On Thursday, however, as they were forced out of Colombo, many of the Tamils may have asked if they were citizens of Sri Lanka or Tamil Eelam.

(IANS, 8 June 2007)

# 38

(It is rare for LTTE guerrillas to get arrested—and then talk. A group of LTTE Sea Tigers taken into custody by the Coast Guard off the Indian shores was no exception. They clammed up after giving elementary details about themselves. However, as the interrogation continued, one of them bared his heart to officers from the Tamil Nadu Police Q Branch. What follows is based on the young man's conversation. It provides a rare insight into the making and thinking of LTTE fighters.)

## Action above ideology for Black Sea Tigers

MOST accounts of LTTE guerrillas are based on impressions others have of them. LTTE fighters may speak if reporters bump into them on the battlefield. But that is very rare.

In February and April of 2007, around 10 Tigers were arrested off Tamil Nadu and are now in prison. Indian officials who interacted with them were impressed by their commitment to the Tamil Eelam cause, however utopian it might seem to others. They also came out as men who knew what they were fighting for and why—and as humans with normal feelings of hurt, pride and agony. Their remarks give valuable insight into the LTTE.

One of the two Black Sea Tigers—members of the LTTE naval wing's suicide squad—was arrested in February. He tried to commit suicide by biting a cyanide pill when the Indian Coast Guard confronted them. Other LTTE cadres stopped him just in time. The Tigers were to say later that suicides were not being encouraged now because of a serious shortage of experienced fighters. Replacing a battle-hardened and tested guerrilla would be very difficult.

Their first encounter with the Indian Coast Guard, which patrols the sea dividing India and Sri Lanka, was an unpleasant one. The Coast Guard personnel thrashed the

LTTE members for entering Indian waters. An elderly man among the LTTE crew who was a cook was forced to sit on the hot deck. One officer thrust a pistol into the mouth of one guerrilla while another addressed them derisively.

One LTTE prisoner said later that they could have shot down the entire lot of Coast Guard personnel. "But our leadership has instructed us that we should not do anything that harms Indian interests," he said. In an apparent reference to the 1991 assassination of Rajiv Gandhi, he added: "We have done this once, we don't want to do it again."

The Tigers did not regret the assassination of Gandhi but admitted it had caused them enormous problems. They dubbed Gandhi a "Hindi kaaran" (Hindi-speaking person) and Indian troops sent to Sri Lanka in 1987–90 also as "Hindi speakers".

The Black Sea Tigers looked a tough lot and every inch capable leaders. They were always alert while in Indian custody. Their eyes never rested in one place, scanning each and every Indian in the interrogation room.

One Sea Tiger explained how tough the LTTE training was. In no time following his enlistment, both his arms had deep gashes, caused by the concertina wire he had to crawl under repeatedly. He also became an adept swimmer and got trained as a frogman too, enabling him to stay under water for a long time. When his trainers were impressed, he became a Black Sea Tiger.

The Tigers were contemptuous of the Tamil Nadu policemen guarding them—and told the startled officers that the men needed better training! One prisoner pointed out flaws in the way the policemen held their guns, the way they stood, and the way they chatted on mobiles and with one another when they were to focus all attention on their prisoners.

One of the Black Sea Tigers related he was once sent on a suicide mission. But it failed because the mechanism to trigger the explosives did not go off. The man tried again and again to activate it but eventually returned to shore. Asked what happened to the person who designed the explosive laden boat, he replied: "He was torn to pieces!" (LTTE does not accept failures.)

Indian officials queried them about the LTTE ideology. One of the prisoners, a school dropout with an unhappy childhood, replied: "We don't believe in theory, we believe in action."

The Sea Tigers maintained that the LTTE military wing was very effective. They added that all cadres were devoted to Velupillai Prabhakaran and believed that an independent Tamil Eelam was the only answer to Tamil problems in Sri Lanka. "The Sinhalese will never accept us as equals. We can never live with them."

What if Prabhakaran were to die one day? One prisoner answered without blinking: "In that case the only way out would be to commit suicide en masse. There will be no other option."

http://ipcs.org/article/maldives/action-above-ideology-for-black-sea-tigers-2311.html (June 2007)

# 39

## Use dignified language, Bhagwati tells Sri Lanka

A former Indian chief justice who presides over an international panel overseeing probes into rights abuses in Sri Lanka has taken strong exception to a harsh attack on him by a top official in Colombo.

P.N. Bhagwati said that Sri Lankan Attorney General C.R. de Silva made "very indiscreet observations" while criticizing reports put out by the International Independent Group of Eminent Persons (IIGEP), which the Indian heads.

De Silva "should not have made the very indiscreet observations," Bhagwati told IANS. Bhagwati, 84, who headed India's Supreme Court in 1985–86, said:

> He has every right to make his own submission or even to give a different opinion. As a judge, I have always welcomed dissent because dissent helps to discover the truth. But such criticism should be in proper language, respectful language. If it extends to abuse, it is wrong.

President Mahinda Rajapaksa set up IIGEP in February to oversee the investigations carried out by the Presidential Commission of Inquiry, which came up in November 2006 to look into several high-profile human rights violations. In June 2007, the IIGEP, which also has eminent jurists from other countries, said the Presidential

**100**    The Tiger Vanquished

Commission had not made noticeable progress in investigating rights abuses and that its independence, timeliness and witness protection did not meet international standards. It also sought an international human rights monitoring mechanism to be set up in Sri Lanka or be invited to the war-torn country.

In response, de Silva alleged that Bhagwati's remarks were based on ignorance, were not in good faith and that it would have been far more prudent if Bhagwati had personally observed the proceedings of the Presidential Commission.

Speaking in the Indian capital, Bhagwati found fault with de Silva's language. "I don't mind the attorney general criticising IIGEP, after all I represent the committee. It is not a personal thing. If he thinks we are wrong, he should say so in proper, dignified language." Asked if he would talk personally to the attorney general, Bhagwati replied: "Why should I descend to this? I have all the support of my colleagues in IIGEP. We have the support of the (Sri Lankan) president. We are independent persons, what does it matter to us? I have an international reputation."

Soon after he was offered the job of heading a body of jurists from various countries to oversee investigations into growing human rights violations in the island nation, Bhagwati had told IANS in November 2006 that he would throw it off if there was interference in his work.

Bhagwati maintained now that he had not studied the rights situation in Sri Lanka thoroughly. "I have not really studied the situation, yet. It is just the beginning. The Presidential Commission of Inquiry has just started work." But he made it clear that the job of international jurists, including him, was only to see if the investigations were being done properly and not to do any probing themselves. "Ours is a supervisory body."

Bhagwati explained that he had gone to Sri Lanka "twice or thrice, but every time only to organize the things" related to IIGEP whose members, he said, were people of "high standing, independent and fair-minded".

(IANS, 30 June 2007)

# 40

(Among all the things the LTTE did, its suicide attacks made the maximum international impact. It showed repeatedly that the LTTE could target anyone, anywhere. It also earned for the Tigers the opprobrium of being terrorists—a tag they hated. July 2007 marked 20 years of the birth of LTTE suicide cult.)

## Two decades later, LTTE suicide bombers live on

TWENTY years after a young man drove a truck packed with explosives into a military camp on this day, Sri Lanka's Tamil Tigers remain passionately wedded to the cult of suicide bombings. It all began on 5 July 1987 when a guerrilla, known as "Captain Miller", was videoed smiling at the wheels of a truck full of explosives that later smashed into a building at Nelliady in Jaffna, killing scores of soldiers. The suicide bomber also perished.

It was the first attack of its kind. For three years, even as Indian troops were deployed in the island and quit with a bloody nose, the LTTE did not repeat the feat. But a deadly and secretive unit called "Black Tigers" was born—with "Captain Miller" as the idol.

From 1990, the LTTE has carried out close to 200 suicide attacks, the largest by any insurgent group in the world. Excluding those operations the LTTE did not claim, at least 273 Black Tigers have died in the attacks, 74 of them women.

Many of these took place in the sea and were credited to "Black Sea Tigers", who would ram fast-moving explosives packed boats into Sri Lankan naval vessels to send the sailors to watery graves. The LTTE never claimed responsibility for some of the deadliest suicide missions, including the blood-curling assassinations of former Indian Prime Minister Rajiv Gandhi in 1991 and Sri Lankan President Ranasinghe Premadasa in 1993.

As the Tigers carried out one suicide attack after another, they almost turned assassinations into a fine art. But eventually, it was these suicide missions that forced the world to take hard line vis-à-vis the Tigers. The suicide cult in the LTTE was, however, born even before the Black Tigers came into being. LTTE cadres always carried cyanide vials they were expected to bite so as not to fall in enemy hands. Now, more and more LTTE cadres infiltrating into military-held Jaffna in Sri Lanka's north are armed not with cyanide but "suicide jackets"—that have explosives in them and are detonated by a battery-operated switch, of the kind used to blow up Premadasa and Gandhi. The intention is not to die a lonely death by biting the cyanide pill if necessary, but to kill as many of the enemy as possible.

A long time ago, LTTE chief Velupillai Prabhakaran explained that by carrying out suicide attacks, "we can terrorise the enemy and demonstrate that though small, we have the potential to inflict heavy damage on them". He called the Black Tigers a voluntary group from which people are picked "whenever there is a specific operation". But he declined to divulge how Black Tigers were trained, saying it was a secret.

An Indian official who follows the LTTE closely told IANS that although the world has dramatically changed—in contrast to the times when countries continued to deal with the LTTE despite the killings of Premadasa and Gandhi—the Tigers were unlikely to give up suicide missions. "This is the most important weapon they have." He added: "Unlike other groups, the LTTE chooses targets carefully, targets whose death would bring major strategic gains for it."

Another officer agreed and felt the Tigers might increasingly concentrate on military targets. It was one such audacious attack, although a failure, on Sri Lanka's army chief in April 2006 that dramatically escalated the present conflict in the island nation.

Two of the LTTE cadres the Indian Coast Guard arrested off Tamil Nadu in February this year were Black Sea Tigers. Although the LTTE conducts far less suicide attacks now, the men and women trained to die by exploding themselves for the cause are still a potent weapon against a militarily superior state.

There is nothing to indicate that the LTTE has any intention of giving up this arsenal in return for diplomatic recognition, even in a post-9/11 world that has no appetite for terror technology of any kind, anywhere. If anything, the LTTE may only be increasing the number of suicide bombers, to make up for a serious shortfall in manpower. "This is a quantum change in strategy," said a Sri Lanka watcher in New Delhi.

(IANS, 5 July 2007)

# 41

(Indian military officials frequently ask why Sri Lanka never built, despite promises, a memorial to honour Indian soldiers who died fighting the LTTE. Here, the man who led the Indian troops in Sri Lanka wants to know why India never raised a memorial for its own men.)

## "Why no memorial for the IPKF in India?"

INDIANS may be upset that Sri Lanka has not set up a memorial to Indian soldiers who died fighting the Tamil Tigers two decades ago. But the man who led the troops asks: why is there no monument for them in India?

Recalling the difficult period when the Indian troops fought the LTTE in Sri Lanka's northeast in 1987–90, Lt. Gen. (retired) A.S. Kalkat says Colombo's indifference pains the families of the dead soldiers. "Our soldiers and their families do feel hurt that they (Sri Lankans) could not provide a memorial. And the soldiers died for their sovereignty," Gen. Kalkat told IANS on the 20th anniversary of the India–Sri Lanka agreement signed in July 1987.

"But what about India? I feel sad that there is no memorial in India to honour those brave soldiers who fought under the Indian flag in Sri Lanka. More so when we have impressive and massive memorials for the two World Wars when Indian soldiers died under the Union Jack," the retired general said at his New Delhi house.

Indian troops deployed in Sri Lanka's northeast under the accord ended up fighting the Tigers for well over two years, losing nearly 1,200 men, before they returned home in March 1990. Many hundreds were wounded and maimed.

Kalkat, who continues to keep in touch with Sri Lankan developments but has avoided visiting Colombo, said the Indian Peace Keeping Force (IPKF) broke up the LTTE "as a fully functional organization" in the fighting that erupted on

10 October 1987 and ended only in 1990. This is the reason, he asserted, that LTTE leader Velupillai Prabhakaran made a dramatic U-turn and shook hands in 1989 with the government of Ranasinghe Premadasa, otherwise seen by Tamils as a Sinhalese hardliner. "That is why they embraced the Sri Lankan state," he said. "Can you ever believe Prabhakaran embracing the Sri Lankan military? Because he had lost out! He was seeing the political demise of LTTE in sight. The embrace was for his survival."

Prabhakaran's decision to go for talks with the Premadasa government made the latter demand the withdrawal of Indian soldiers from the island, embarrassing India and leading ultimately to the Tigers taking control of large parts of the northeast.

So was the Indian intervention in Sri Lanka worth the human and financial cost? "Whether it was worth it or not should be seen in the light of the geographical political canvass," said Kalkat.

The pity is the success of the IPKF was not allowed to be consolidated because (the V.P. Singh government that took power in December 1989) stood for the IPKF pullout and (Premadasa was) totally opposed to the 1987 agreement and the devolution of powers (to Tamils in Sri Lanka).

Kalkat called Premadasa, who was assassinated by the LTTE in May 1993, a "hostile President", one "who did not want a Tamil province in the northeast".

Obviously what was worrying Premadasa was that a Tamil chief minister in the northeast must not get stabilized and firmly established. Then he could not have undone the Tamil administration. In the hurry, he ordered his officers to start providing weapons and ammunition to the LTTE, which (by then) had been reduced to a marginal role.

Kalkat says that by the time it was all over, the Indian military had earned a very good understanding of the ethnic conflict, which continues to bleed the country.

What does Kalkat think of the LTTE? "LTTE is no doubt one of the most professional and formidable and dedicated militant forces," said the man who oversaw the Indian military capture of Jaffna in late 1987 and then commanded the IPKF from January 1988 until March 1990. "After all they were the original inventors of improvised explosive devices and human bombs. Much later it has come in vogue in the Middle East and Kashmir and the rest of the world," he added, hastening to add that he considered the LTTE and the Tamils two distinct entities.

Will Prabhakaran ever make peace? "I do not think Prabhakaran will ever settle for less (than Tamil Eelam). I always felt that. He has talked himself to a point of no retraction. Now even if he wants to step back, he cannot do it."

(IANS, 29 July 2007)

# 42

(The year 2007 marked the 20th anniversary of the India–Sri Lanka agreement signed by Rajiv Gandhi and J.R. Jayewardene. When it was signed, it was seen, mainly in India, as a diplomatic triumph. The reception in Sri Lanka was subdued. The accord failed to bring peace to Sri Lanka, but it led to certain constitutional changes to provide autonomy to the minorities.)

## India–Sri Lanka accord: Does it still flicker?

TWENTY long years after it was signed, the Indo-Sri Lanka Peace Accord of 29 July 1987 seems like a hazy affair, a dream gone by, one that probably never happened, considering the fact that an ethnic conflict it sought to end still rages on, with no apparent solution in sight.

It is significant that neither the Indian nor the Sri Lankan government did anything to mark the anniversary of the agreement that two decades ago was widely viewed as New Delhi's biggest diplomatic coup and of immense strategic value.

The pact followed months of intense diplomatic discussions between New Delhi and Colombo, mostly behind the scenes, after India concluded that the separatist violence in the island nation had to halt, for the sake of everyone, and a parallel political process was required to satisfy the Tamil community's legitimate political aspirations. And it had also become evident to Indian policy makers, after repeatedly trying but failing to push Colombo and the Tamil sides to make peace, that this would happen only if New Delhi played a pro-active, even interventionist, role in the process.

The 1987 agreement sought to address most of the concerns plaguing the Indian and Sri Lankan governments besides the Tamil community. But the bloody and complex aftermath that followed ended up pushing it to the margins of history in a manner few anticipated.

Although neither India nor Sri Lanka has officially renounced the accord, its failure to resolve the ethnic conflict underlines the complexities that continue to grip the strife-torn country, disappointing the various international actors now in the fray. The most significant highlight of the agreement was that it brought about, for the first time, devolution of powers to the minorities in the shape of provincial councils with civil, police and judicial powers, courtesy the 13th amendment to the Sri Lankan Constitution and the Provincial Councils Act enacted by that country's parliament.

The Accord acknowledged in a formal sense that Sri Lanka was a multiethnic, multi-lingual and multi-religious plural society (Sections 1.2 and 1.5), recognized that each ethnic group had a distinct cultural and linguistic identity that had to be carefully nurtured (Section 1.3), and agreed that the northern and eastern provinces (the war theatre) were "areas of historical habitation of Tamil speaking peoples" (Section 1.4). It also led to the mergre of the northern and eastern provinces, again for the first time, into one administrative unit with an elected Provincial Council, one Governor, one Chief Minister and a Board of Ministers (Sections 2.1 and 2.2).

The agreement also sought to help the thousands displaced by the conflict (mainly Tamils) to return to areas in the northeast where they once lived (Section 2.4). At the same time, there was to be a cessation of hostilities within 48 hours after the signing of the accord and a surrender of all arms held by Tamil militants within 72 hours along with the confinement of Sri Lanka's army and other security personnel in their barracks as they were on 25 May 1987 (Section 2.9). Sri Lanka agreed to abide by the provisions of the Accord (Section 2.12) and India pledged to guarantee and under-write the resolutions (Section 2.14). New Delhi also promised not to allow its territory to be used by Tamil militants (Section 2.16, a) and consented to provide military assistance to Sri Lanka if asked for (Section 2.16, c). An annexure to the Agreement dealt mainly with issues of strategic interest affecting India as well as Sri Lanka.

Looking back, the Indo-Sri Lanka accord could have been the best deal at that time for the beleaguered Tamil community, providing a foundation that could have been cemented over months and years if everyone had genuinely respected it. It is also clear in retrospect that the Accord came about suddenly, almost like a bolt from the blue, taking by surprise even those who had no quarrel with peace. The abruptness meant that no serious analysis was probably done to determine in advance if there could be spoilers and what should be India's response in such an eventuality.

India's then external affairs minister, P.V. Narasimha Rao, was the most senior figure in the Rajiv Gandhi government who felt that the Accord should be signed by the LTTE and Colombo. He was, however, overruled. Over the years, the LTTE has taken most of the blame for the failure of the Accord, a development that led to a military showdown between the Tigers and the Indian military causing misery to innocents. There is no doubt that the LTTE wanted the pact to fail. It was in no mood to give up its armed campaign for a separate Tamil state for the sake of India. The LTTE chief, Velupillai Prabhakaran, was frank—and audacious—enough to tell an Indian journalist he had known for years, P.S. Suryanarayana, that he would scuttle the pact in such a manner that no one would be able to pin him down.

Nevertheless, it would be too simplistic to point the accusing finger only at the LTTE. Sections of the Sri Lankan state that could not reconcile to India's military intervention also played a significant role that led to the agreement's failure. Sri Lankan Prime Minister, Ranasinghe Premadasa—who later became the President—shook hands with the LTTE and ordered the Indian troops to go home. This contributed in a major way to undermining the peace pact. The lack of political consensus in India, a situation that got aggravated once Indian troops began to die on Sri Lankan soil in large numbers, added to the mess.

Once the last of Indian troops had returned home in March 1990, soon after Prime Minister Rajiv Gandhi was voted out, New Delhi more or less lost any interest in the agreement.

Gandhi may still have had a desire to resurrect the Accord if he had returned to power but that never happened. After a LTTE suicide bomber assassinated Gandhi in May 1991, the loss of sympathy in India for the Tamil cause made matters worse. The killing left an indelible mark on the psyche of the people of India, which meted out a collective punishment to the Tamils of Sri Lanka in the form of a non-solution to the ethnic problem. More and more Sri Lankan Tamils of all hues think today that their community may have been spared the suffering of the past 20 years if only the 1987 Agreement had not been allowed to fail and if only Gandhi's assassination had not compounded an already bad situation.

In any case, the Indian establishment has not been able to forget the bitter truth that Colombo teamed up with the LTTE to trip the Indian military, which had taken on the Tigers so as to help preserve Sri Lanka's territorial integrity. The military help Sri Lanka provided to the LTTE created a feeling of betrayal in the Indian psyche that refuses to go away.

Even when Gandhi and J.R. Jayewardene—the two signatories to the Accord—were in power, the agreement could never be implemented the way it was meant to be. The LTTE never gave up all its weaponry, arguing that it would be suicidal to disarm unless Colombo was truly ready to embrace the Tamil minority. As the Tigers asserted later, they never accepted the pact in the first place, and it is now widely accepted that the LTTE remains firmly committed to its goal of setting up an independent Tamil state, come what may.

The fact is the Tigers were not ready to make up with anyone in 1987—Colombo or the other Tamil groups. And once the Indian Army went after the LTTE, the suffering of the civilian population robbed the Accord of its sheen. The Sri Lankan state itself turned into a spoiler once Premadasa replaced Jayewardene as President.

While elections took place to pick a Northeastern Provincial Council, their fairness was in doubt in Sri Lanka's Northern Province. The experiment, however, could still have made a mark if Colombo had been sincerely committed to the devolution of powers. But Premadasa was determined not to let the Northeastern Provincial administration succeed, and this suited the LTTE too. Boxed in by Colombo and the LTTE, the Tamil provincial administration quickly collapsed. Once that happened, the 1987 pact lost all meaning.

The 1987 Agreement marked the first major international effort to bring peace to Sri Lanka. Its failure holds several lessons to anyone, including international actors, now desirous of playing peacemakers in the ethnic conflict.

When the 1987 agreement was drafted, the underlying assumption in New Delhi was that the Tamil side (LTTE included) was willing to shake hands with the Sri Lankan state, and that the latter too was ready to bury the past. Two decades of bloodletting has proved this wrong. The "Tamil-speaking peoples"—which is how the Accord defined the inhabitants of Sri Lanka's northeast—have ceased to be the one single entity they once were. The fissures that developed slowly between the Tamils and the Tamil-speaking Muslims have led to a political divorce between their representatives. The LTTE's massacre of Muslims in the east and the ouster of Muslims from the north and the later birth of radical thinking among eastern Muslims have contributed to the sorry state of affairs.

The 2004 split in the LTTE and subsequent actions by the breakaway faction that target the "northern (Jaffna) Tamils" have also produced a new and completely unexpected factor in the dynamics of the northeast that nobody had bargained for. Even without this, the Sri Lankan Supreme Court edict bifurcating the north and east as two independent entities—a controversial ruling that would effectively take away Tamil control over the island's multi-racial eastern wing—means that the "northeast" as defined by the 1987 Accord is dead for all practical purposes.

Most important, even international actors now active in Sri Lanka have come to one painful realization—no peace is possible in the island nation as long as the two main actors in the battlefield do not want to make peace. The LTTE remains adamantly wedded to the cause of breaking up Sri Lanka. The present dispensation in Colombo, meanwhile, is supremely confident that it can bring about a military solution to the ethnic conflict by crushing the LTTE. Despite suffering serious setbacks, the latter however, feels it can overcome the military challenge as it has done in the past.

It is highly doubtful if either Colombo or the Tigers would ever like to act by the dictates of the 1987 Accord again. Politically, the agreement is dead and gone. That the 2002 Norwegian-sponsored and internationally backed Ceasefire Agreement too has suffered a similar fate should cause no major surprise. Both have revealed the limitations of outside powers to influence the course of events in Sri Lanka. However, both agreements, and in particular the 1987 Indo-Sri Lanka pact, can act as foundations to build a peaceful Sri Lanka if and when an opportune time comes.

http://ipcs.org/pdf_file/issue/1226731325IPCS
-IssueBrief-No50.pdf (August 2007)


# 43


(By the time the LTTE was crushed, Sri Lanka and Britain were at loggerheads. Britain was seen to be interfering in Sri Lanka's internal affairs in a manner detrimental to Colombo's interests. A top Sri Lankan official says that Britain was keen to see the exit of President Rajapaksa.)


## Britain favours "regime change" in Sri Lanka

BRITAIN is looking for a "regime change" in Sri Lanka because it favours the opposition United National Party (UNP) over the present ruling party, the head of the island's peace secretariat has said. "They would be delighted if there was a regime change," Rajiva Wijesinha, secretary general of the Secretariat for Coordinating the Peace Process (SCOPP), said while hitting out at sections of Western human rights and other interest groups.

Speaking to IANS in New Delhi, Wijesinha was particularly critical of the Europeans and singled out Britain. He praised the US approach towards Sri Lanka and at the same time urged India to do more to end his country's nearly 25-year-long ethnic conflict. "At one stage they (Britain) would have liked to replace the Norwegians," the peace facilitators, said Wijesinha, 52, a politician-cum-academic who took charge of SCOPP in June, succeeding Sri Lankan Foreign Secretary Palitha Kohona.

Wijesinha said Britain had taken the lead in undermining Sri Lankan Defence Secretary Gotabaya Rajapaksa, a brother of President Mahinda Rajapaksa. The younger Rajapaksa heads the country's war machine against the Tamil Tigers.

"One of the main problems they have is they still hanker after the UNP," he added, referring to Britain, which in recent times has displayed active interest in trying to defuse ethnic tensions in Sri Lanka. "They would be delighted if there was a regime change... People think it is on the cards now." Asked if he really meant that Britain was working towards toppling President Rajapaksa, he answered: "They would prefer it... They don't like the status quo now."

Wijesinha has in recent times taken an aggressive stand against Western human rights groups that have flayed Sri Lankan authorities for a variety of rights violations including killings, disappearances, arrests and mass displacement of civilians. "What I see is a concerted campaign to attack the Sri Lankan government on the human rights issue, with a particular thrust to impose an external authoritative mechanism."

Referring to specific reports from the International Commission of Jurists (ICJ), Gareth Evans of the International Crisis Group and also the Human Rights Watch, Wijesinha asked: "My point is, what is the reason for all this?" He said some Western rights groups—as opposed to Sri Lanka's University Teachers for Human Rights "for which have the highest regard"—were acting in concert with the UNP and the LTTE.

Wijesinha added that the LTTE, which has suffered military reverses in the eastern province, would like to undermine the government on the issue of rights abuses. "This is where there is a congruence in (their) positions." The peace official said that most Sri Lankans wanted India to be more closely associated with the co-chairs group of countries overseeing the island's now battered peace process—the US, Japan, Norway and the European Union.

"India should do more," he said while pointing out "fatal flaws" in the 1987 India–Sri Lanka pact that sought to end the ethnic conflict. "Successive Sri Lankan governments have rightly understood that any solution should be in consultation with India."

(IANS, 30 August 2007)

# 44

(Tamilchelvan's killing did prove to be a massive blow to the LTTE—but not to S
Lanka. The fear that, with his death, Colombo may have no one to talk to among th
Tigers proved incorrect for the simple reason that Sri Lanka was no more intereste
in any kind of negotiations with a group it concluded was not interested in peace

## Tamilchelvan's killing a disaster to LTTE—and Sri Lanka

SRI LANKA'S dramatic killing of S.P. Tamilchelvan, who many diplomats saw
the "friendly face" of the Tamil Tigers, is a huge blow to the rebels and is bound
cause more bloodshed in the island.

Although he joined the LTTE as a fighter while in his teens, it was his growin
importance as a negotiator in peace talks that fetched Tamilchelvan a larger than li
image. Western diplomats and Indian officials who spoke to IANS warned that h
death could complicate an already complex situation in Sri Lanka, stifling even th
marginal hopes of restarting negotiations between the LTTE and Colombo.

The LTTE had been trying to groom Tamilchelvan to fill the shoes of Antc
Balasingham, the long-time negotiator of the Tigers, when Sri Lanka's air force bombe
a LTTE camp in the rebel-held Kilinochchi while he was closeted with his milita
colleagues. Five LTTE military leaders also died in the strike. Both Balasingham, wh
died of cancer in December 2006, and Tamilchelvan were considered extremely clo
to Prabhakaran. And though Tamilchelvan did not have the kind of command ov
English Balasingham enjoyed, he more than made it up with his friendly attitude
diplomats and others who came calling on the LTTE.

"Tamilchelvan's killing wipes out the institutional memory of the peace tall
(of recent years)," a diplomat in Sri Lanka said. "Who are the Sri Lankans going

talk to now? This is the real problem." Added another diplomat: "It is a huge blow to negotiations. With Balasingham dead, Tamilchelvan would have played a key role in any future negotiations."

Some Indian officials warned that this could trigger a tit-for-tat response from the LTTE. "This is going to spiral everything," said one official. "The LTTE will argue that while it is targeting the Sri Lankan military people, the Sri Lankans have killed a key political personality."

The death is sure to hit the morale of the LTTE, which is still celebrating last week's crippling attack on the Sri Lankan Air Force base in Anuradhapura that wiped out military helicopters and planes worth millions of dollars. A Tamil source said: "The LTTE will miss him. He has been with Prabhakaran for 25 years. He has enjoyed his trust."

Hailing from a poor family in Chavakachcheri in Jaffna, Tamilchelvan—like many young Tamil men of his era—drifted to militancy and later teamed up with LTTE founder leader Velupillai Prabhakaran. As a guerrilla, he took part in many battles and graduated to become "an excellent shot", said a Sri Lankan Tamil who has known Tamilchelvan intimately. "He could hit any target from a distance."

But a battle wound brought about a change in his profile, and the man who could fight to kill was anointed the head of the LTTE's political wing. That designation coupled with his intimacy with Prabhakaran earned him pride of place in the LTTE negotiation teams post the 2002 truce although he remained under the shadow of the elder Balasingham for a long time. He was the senior most leader of the LTTE most visitors to the Tiger region met. Even those who got to meet Prabhakaran had to go past him.

Tamilchelvan considered himself devoted to Prabhakaran. He married within the LTTE. The couple had two daughters. As the violence escalated in Sri Lanka from December 2005, Tamilchelvan had a tough time defending the LTTE even as more and more countries turned against the group.

Tamilchelvan was always confident of the success of the LTTE's cause. He said more than once to those close to him: "I shall not die until I see the birth of Tamil Eelam." That was not to be.

(IANS, 2 November 2007)

# 45

(When Eelam War IV began in 2006, it seemed uncertain to most people what direction it will take. By the time 2007 ended, it was clear that Sri Lanka was gaining, and irrevocably so. Once the LTTE lost its eastern regional commander Karuna, Prabhakaran should have seen it happening.)

## Sri Lanka gained upper hand over LTTE in 2007

SRI LANKA'S failure to unveil a political package to end years of war and its military successes against the Tamil Tigers marked the highlights of one of the world's longest running conflicts in 2007.

After decades of seesaw fighting, Colombo took a visible upper hand vis-à-vis the LTTE, driving it away from the country's eastern province and crippling its shipping network. The LTTE and its chief Velupillai Prabhakaran suffered a serious blow when its political wing leader S.P. Tamilchelvan was killed in a Sri Lanka Air Force attack on 2 November.

But the LTTE sprang its nascent air wing on Sri Lanka with military precision on more occasions than one, stunning everyone and injecting a new dimension to a horrific conflict that began a quarter century ago.

With many countries supporting its war effort openly or not so openly, Colombo displayed no great urgency in opting for a power-sharing package for minorities that would effectively negate Tamil calls for separation. A path-breaking and seemingly sound devolution formula a group of experts came up with in December 2006 suggesting federalism to placate restive minorities got shot down by the government and Sinhalese nationalist groups.

By the end of 2007, there was no firm indication—only hopes—that the All Party Representative Committee (APRC) would prepare a new document acceptable to everyone in a country badly divided on ethnic and political lines.

Sri Lanka took an aggressive approach towards charges of human rights abuses, going to the extent of branding UN Under Secretary John Holmes a "terrorist". But it was embarrassed when a Tamil Tiger breakaway leader it had backed, Karuna, was arrested in Britain after sneaking into the country on a false passport provided by Colombo. Karuna has been widely accused of conscripting children into his group in the east, an allegation also made against the Tigers.

The international community was mostly despairing on Sri Lanka, whose top leaders declared that they had no use for the 2002 Norway-brokered truce or for homilies from the West on human rights.

On 30 December Defence Secretary Gotabaya Rajapaksa trumpeted that Prabhakaran may have been killed in an air force bombing on a bunker in the country's rebel-held north on 26 May. The same day, army chief, Gen. Sarath Fonseka, thundered that Prabhakaran may not be able to survive for more than six months.

The internationally backed peace process collapsed in 2007. India remained an active though not a successful player vis-à-vis Sri Lanka, where violence since President Mahinda Rajapaksa took power in late 2005 has left thousands dead. As the year ended, Sri Lankan troops were knocking on the doors of the Tiger territory in the country's north in an attempt to take the war to the very heart of Prabhakaran's fiefdom.

Throughout the year, tens of thousands of civilians suffered enormously due to fighting between the LTTE and the military. Rights activists say kidnappings and killings by groups backed by the state are rampant. Ahilan Kadirgamar of the Sri Lanka Democracy Forum told IANS:

> The military establishment is gearing up to use a purely military approach. The LTTE is also committed to escalating the war. Tamil civilians bear the brunt of the conflict. Minorities fear the resurgence of Sinhala Buddhist nationalism... Sri Lanka could well be in another protracted cycle of war and the year ahead looks very bleak.

(IANS, 31 December 2007)

2008

# 46

(The Tigers never change their stripes. So it was proved when LTTE agents in Tamil Nadu were arrested on charges of trying to abduct a Sri Lankan politician who lived in India. After Gandhi's killing, the LTTE decided it would interfere no more in India's internal affairs. But Indian security agencies never lowered their guard.)

## LTTE man's arrest for abduction plan first since 1991

THE arrest of a Tamil Tiger operative on charges of planning the abduction from India of a prominent Sri Lankan Tamil politician is the first time the rebels have gone this far since the 1991 killing of former prime minister Rajiv Gandhi.

According to Indian Home Ministry sources, the Intelligence Bureau played a key role in the arrest on Wednesday night of Thambiturai Parameswaran alias Surli alias Nathan from Madipakkam, a thickly populated Chennai suburb near an IT corridor that is home to many Sri Lankan Tamils.

Nathan, who entered India illegally by sea in February 2007, has been described as a member of the intelligence wing of the LTTE. He had been tasked with the responsibility of planning the kidnapping of Annamali Varadaraja Perumal, the former chief minister of Sri Lanka's northeastern province who has lived in and around the Indian capital for years under Indian protection.

A native of Jaffna, Nathan had bought a van in Chennai that he plied as a taxi to give himself a respectable cover. He had over a period of time moved close to two relatives in the area of Perumal, as he is widely known, and also Douglas Devananda, Sri Lanka's rabidly anti-LTTE Tamil cabinet minister.

Devananda, who has escaped several assassination attempts blamed on the LTTE, is a frequent visitor to India. Following Nathan's arrest, the Tamil Nadu Police took into custody seven other Sri Lankan Tamil men who were identified only as Reagan, Anand, Kesavan, Paris, Akilan, Sudarsanan and Aravindan. All seven apparently acted as Nathan's sub-agents, collecting information that was passed on to the LTTE in Sri Lanka.

According to home ministry sources, the likely kidnapping of Perumal could have taken place when his eldest daughter was to get married in February 2008 in Rajasthan, where he had lived under protection in Ajmer city before moving closer to the Indian capital. Nathan had reportedly offered his taxi to a relative of Perumal he had befriended so as to drive him to Rajasthan—and thus get close to the intended victim.

Although other LTTE operatives have been arrested in Tamil Nadu in recent times, this is the first time since the 1991 assassination of Rajiv Gandhi that anyone from the group's intelligence wing has planned an action that would have meant harming a target sheltered by the Indian state.

The police and home ministry sources are not revealing operational details that led to the arrest of Nathan, who may have been under watch for some time. Like other LTTE militants netted in Tamil Nadu, Nathan was said to be smuggling goods the Tigers need in their war against the Sri Lankan military. Seized from him were the taxi, ball bearings, plastic granules, two wheelers and cash.

Nathan and the others have been charged under the Foreigners Act and the Unlawful Activities (Prevention) Act as well as Section 120B of the Indian Penal Code (conspiracy).

Although he is far moved from active politics, Perumal takes a keen interest in Sri Lankan developments, attending meetings and TV shows and also interacting with diplomats and academics. He is a senior member of the Eelam People's Revolutionary Liberation Front (EPRLF) faction that is bitterly opposed to the LTTE.

This is not the first time the LTTE has tried to harm Perumal after he quit Sri Lanka in March 1990, just before the Indian troops left the country, and then took refuge in India after spending some time in Mauritius. According to Home Ministry sources, one of the accused in the Gandhi case, Shankar Koneswaran, was also asked by the LTTE to zero in on Perumal.

But Koneswaran got arrested after Gandhi's killing when he got off a train at Madurai while travelling from Chennai to the Tamil Nadu coast Vedaranyam. When he was caught, he had with him the telephone numbers of two key LTTE men who played a major role in the Gandhi assassination.

Since then, Permual has more or less lived a seemingly secure life in India.

(IANS, 18 January 2008)

# 47

(This proved to be one of my most controversial stories. It was the first time anyone revealed India's covert involvement in the Norway-brokered peace process. No story I did on Sri Lanka evoked more queries than this one. I have elaborated the story in this book.)

## India's covert role in Sri Lanka's ceasefire

NOW that Sri Lanka has jettisoned the Ceasefire Agreement (CFA) with the Tamil Tigers, one of India's best kept secrets can be revealed: it was New Delhi that quietly authored the process that led to the Norway-brokered pact.

The dominant thinking in India and Sri Lanka, and even elsewhere, is that New Delhi has been a distant watcher to the goings on in the war-hit island barring its interactions with Colombo and countries like Norway as part of a "hands off" policy sparked off by former Prime Minister Rajiv Gandhi's 1991 assassination.

While it is true that India took a detached view of the ethnic conflict in the aftermath of Gandhi's killing, things changed shortly after Atal Bihari Vajpayee took office in 1998 at the head of a non-Congress coalition.

By 1999, the Indian state had concluded after years of study that there could never be a military winner in Sri Lanka: neither the government nor the LTTE would reign supreme although at that stage the rebels appeared to hold an upper hand. The Indian government then took the view that it was time for a major peace push in Sri Lanka.

Supervised by National Security Advisor Brajesh Mishra, the Indian establishment got into the act of ushering in peace in Sri Lanka, with just one rider: everything would be done away from media glare. Only a few would be in the know of what was being planned.

Then Sri Lankan President Chandrika Kumaratunga was waging a "war for peace" against the LTTE that steadily lost steam as the Tigers hit back with a military precision that stunned the world.

The stalemate was a continuation of what had happened earlier. The Indian military intervention in 1987–90 had run aground; the fighting between 1990 and 1994, mostly during Ranasinghe Premadasa's presidency, led to no decisive result; and the war during Kumaratunga's presidency was going the same way.

The Indian establishment, however, felt that Kumaratunga was incapable of making peace. What Sri Lanka needed, so went the reading, was a leader who was ready to shake hands with the LTTE with a long-term vision to bring peace to the country.

It may have been a coincidence, but political convulsions quickly rocked Colombo, destabilising Kumaratunga's government and sparking an election in 2000 and a second election the next year. The Indian establishment felt there was a need to bring in an international player to facilitate peace in Sri Lanka, a party both Colombo and the LTTE could do business with as they appeared incapable of talking to one another.

Kumaratunga's first choice was France, but this the LTTE rejected. India by then had zeroed in on Norway. Norwegian diplomats began visiting New Delhi. No publicity was given to these brainstorming trips.

Norway was picked for mainly three reasons: it was physically far removed from South Asia; it had no territorial ambitions; and it had a proven record in peace building. Kumaratunga and the LTTE eventually settled on Norway as the peace facilitator. The war, however, continued to rage.

Norway's chosen Special Envoy Erik Solheim travelled to Kilinochchi, the LTTE-controlled northern part of Sri Lanka, in November 2000 and met the group's top leader, Velupillai Prabhakaran, for the first time. The next month, the LTTE offered a ceasefire and extended it, month by month, for four months. After that the Tigers again took the offensive. In July 2001, the LTTE virtually overran Sri Lanka's international airport at Katunayake, dealing a shattering blow from which Colombo never recovered.

The second of the two elections followed, and Ranil Wickremesinghe, the opposition leader, became prime minister in December 2001. Events galloped at a rapid pace, in both New Delhi and Colombo, but all under wraps.

Overseen by New Delhi, a truce document began to be drafted. Norway was deeply involved in the exercise, roping in some of its veteran diplomats. Eventually, this translated into the CFA. India also told Norwegian diplomats to let the LTTE know about the Indian involvement in the entire effort.

On 21 February 2002, LTTE chief Velupillai Prabhakaran signed the CFA. Wickremesinghe put his signature a day later. Since India never publicised its role in the developments, many Indians argued that New Delhi was letting Sri Lanka slip into Western hands!

By then, India had also mooted the idea of a Sri Lanka Monitoring Mission (SLMM), the first such international peace monitoring body outside the UN aegis. India wanted Nordic countries—Norway, Iceland, Sweden, Denmark and Finland—to make up the SLMM to oversee the ceasefire.

The arrangement between India and Norway was that the latter would keep New Delhi informed about its peace diplomacy. At some point of time, irritations did crop up in this deal but these were quickly sorted out.

The CFA was a watershed in Sri Lanka's blood-soaked history but within months things began to go wrong.

Norway came under attack from large sections in Sri Lanka. Solheim bore the brunt of the criticism, at times too personal, though he was only the best-known face of an international exercise that had India's solid backing and he himself had no axe to grind.

In May 2004, Vajpayee gave way to Prime Minister Manmohan Singh, who headed a Congress-led coalition government. J.N. Dixit, a former Indian envoy to Colombo during the turbulent 1980s, was named the new national security advisor.

The nuts and bolts of India's involvement in Sri Lanka's peace process was till then known only to a few in New Delhi. Dixit's eyes opened up when Wickremesinghe, who by then had lost power, flew to New Delhi and gave a detailed briefing about India's deep and covert role in the entire process.

It was the first time Dixit realized that India had for years pursued a pro-active policy towards Sri Lanka but quietly—in complete contrast to the public perception that New Delhi had lost interest in the ethnic conflict. Dixit was to learn quickly that this was also the case vis-à-vis Nepal and Bangladesh. Unfortunately, Dixit died in office in 2005, and with him died many secrets.

India's active participation in the later much-maligned peace process in Sri Lanka is as deep as was its role in the military training of Tamil militants two decades ago. Officially India denies that it ever trained Tamils in warfare. In the case of the peace process, even many in India are not fully aware of the story.

This was evident in some of the statements made in India when Colombo axed the CFA. This has also been evident in repeated statements from many quarters in Sri Lanka urging India to step in and throw out "imperialist" Norway and the West!

In Norway, one diplomat recently made a public comment about India's entanglement with the peace process without, however, spilling out any details. Vidar Helgesen, who was assistant foreign minister of Norway during the inception of the peace process and is now secretary general of the Stockholm-based International Institute for Democracy and Electoral Assistance, said:

> I may reasonably say that the Norwegian contribution in structuring the CFA ... was, indeed, crucial. However, we could not have achieved any success without the active role played by India at every step of the negotiations. Nothing could be attempted without Indian support at every step, including the CFA.

(IANS, 17 February 2008)

# 48

(Although the Janatha Vimukti Peramuna (JVP) has traditionally been anti-India, Indian security agencies helped one of its top leaders to flee Sri Lanka in the late 1980s. After a brief lull, the group returned to its familiar anti-India rhetoric.)

## India meddling in Sri Lanka affairs, says JVP

A leader of Sri Lanka's third largest political party asserts that India is again interfering in the country's affairs by forcing Colombo to devolve powers to minorities. Vijitha Herath of the Sinhala-Marxist Janatha Vimukti Peramuna (JVP) also said in an interview that India's backing for a power sharing formula amounted to giving ideological backing to the Tamil Tigers.

"Indian ideas on devolution are indirect support to the LTTE ideology," Herath told IANS in New Delhi shortly before returning home. Herath, who is secretary of the JVP's international affairs department, came to India to attend a meeting of the All India Forward Bloc party at Jabalpur in Madhya Pradesh.

He praised his country's military for waging war against the LTTE. He was furious over what he said were repeated appeals by India and the West to Sri Lanka to go for a political solution to the ethnic conflict that has left some 70,000 people dead since 1983.

Herath, 39, argued that the LTTE needed to be defeated militarily before any political solution could be thought of. He argued that India could help Colombo militarily but it had no right to hector the country over a political solution.

After referring to the training of Tamil militants in the 1980s in India and the later Indian military intervention in Sri Lanka, the JVP leader said: "Now also the Indian government is trying to interfere in our internal matters. India wants Sri Lanka to give powers over land and police to provincial assemblies that were set up in line with the India–Sri Lanka accord of 1987. This is interference."

"If the Indian suggestion is implemented, the chief minister of the provincial council in the (war-hit) northeast may try to use the police force to create a separate state. Some Indian officers, but not all, are trying to mislead politicians in Delhi on this subject," he added, without taking names.

The JVP is a well-knit Sinhalese nationalist party with Marxist moorings that has carried out two armed insurrections in the 1970s and 1980s that left thousands dead. It is now the third largest party in the 225-seat parliament, with 37 MPs. Though it supported Mahinda Rajapaksa when he became president in 2005, it is now in the opposition.

Asked about evidence that India meddled in Sri Lankan affairs, Herath said:

There are logical reasons to assume this. And as an experienced political party, we can understand this… There is a hidden hand. Not only India, no country has a right to interfere in our problem. We don't have a problem if they have a dialogue with Sri Lanka as a neighbouring country. India must support us to defeat the LTTE militarily and ideologically. That's India's duty.

Does it mean that without outside support the LTTE cannot be defeated? "If India and other countries support Sri Lanka, the LTTE can be defeated easily. Otherwise it will still be possible but it will become somewhat difficult."

Asked about the JVP's threats to call for a boycott of Indian goods if New Delhi continued to press for devolution of powers, he said his party would not take such a step. "But we want to stress the idea of a boycott. It is something we learnt from Mahatma Gandhi."

(IANS, 14 March 2008)

# 49

(Many well-meaning people thought they could help brighten up the picture in Sri Lanka. It never happened that way. Tamil-speaking Sri Sri Ravi Shankar, who commands a large following in that country, travelled to the north to meet the LTTE. They did not pay heed to him. I was among the people Ravi Shankar spoke to before making the visit.)

## I want to bring peace to Sri Lanka: Sri Sri Ravi Shankar

INDIAN spiritual guru Sri Sri Ravi Shankar is keen to play the peacemaker in war-torn Sri Lanka. Claiming that he enjoys the trust of both the Sri Lankan government and the Tamil Tigers, Ravi Shankar says he does not need any invitation to act to try ending one of the world's longest running armed conflicts.

"If someone's house is burning, you don't expect an invitation from them! A sensitive person will simply jump in," the spiritual guru told IANS over email from Norway. "Since 'Vasudhaiva Kutumbakam' (the world is one family) is in our veins and blood, we can't but act," he added. "I think it is quite normal for anyone with a sense of belongingness to just act."

The Tamil-speaking Ravi Shankar was asked if he wished to play a role to help end the Sri Lankan conflict and whether he enjoyed the trust of Colombo and the LTTE. "Of course, yes! I guess they realise that we have no ulterior motives other than to bring peace to one and all."

Ravi Shankar's comments came following the conclusion in Oslo last week of a peace conference organized by his Art of Living Foundation that brought together a variety of players from Sri Lanka, India and Norway. Cabinet ministers, opposition leaders and Buddhist monks came from Sri Lanka. The most high profile Tamil representative was Vaiko, the Marumalarchi Dravida Munnettra Kazhagam (MDMK) leader from India, who pleaded for the Tamil cause in Sri Lanka. Norway's Special Envoy to Sri Lanka, Jon Hanssen-Bauer, and members of the European Parliament also took part.

Ravi Shankar, 51, is the founder of Art of Living, which enjoys millions of followers worldwide. He has visited Sri Lanka thrice, the last time in September 2006 when he went to the LTTE-held Kilinochchi district.

Members of the Sri Lankan establishment as well as the Tamil National Alliance, which is sympathetic to the LTTE, have interacted with him in India.

Ravi Shankar said the Oslo conference went off very well. "Though there were heated arguments and accusations, no one walked out (usually in such instances they walk out)! There was a strong commitment for peace and understanding."

But can a spiritual leader succeed where international actors have failed? Answer:

There may be big powers in the world, but they cannot unite the hearts and minds of people. Mahatma Gandhi was a deeply spiritual person. Only because of that he could engineer the freedom movement.

I have always dreamed the impossible and it has become possible. If conflicts could be resolved in Kosovo, in Ireland, in Baku (where Art of Living played an important role) and if Mahatma Gandhi could bring freedom to India, (the ability to end) the conflict in Sri Lanka through dialogue should not be dismissed. I don't mind going to the end of the world if it helps to bring peace and lessen the suffering of the people.

(IANS, 18 April 2008)

# 50

(India's decision to build a mammoth power project in Sri Lanka's east evoked strong reactions from the Tamil community. They feared that the project would permanently displace them. The project is to come up on a large swathe of land the military seized from the LTTE, and turned into a High Security Zone after civilians fled in thousands.)

## India's Sri Lanka power project runs into Tamil storm

AN Indian project that seeks to provide electricity to Sri Lanka's war-hit east has run into rough weather amid allegations that it will displace Tamils who have lived in the area for generations. Indian arguments that the coal-based plant is meant to benefit locals in Trincomalee are having no effect on rights activists and the thousands who fled the region after fighting between the Tamil Tigers and the military.

India's National Thermal Power Corporation (NTPC), the sixth largest thermal power generator in the world, will build a 500-MW thermal plant in Sampur, a large and populous fishing village overlooking Trincomalee port. "The project will pave the way for affordable electricity to the people of the region and take India–Sri Lanka ties to a new level," NTPC Chairman and Managing Director Ram Sharan Sharma told IANS.

Involving a $500-million investment, a joint venture company of the NTPC and the Ceylon Electricity Board will implement the project spread over 500 acres of land. A jetty is also to come up in Sampur. It will be one of the largest infrastructure investments in Sri Lanka.

But these statistics have no relevance for those who lived in Sampur until last year when the military seized it from the LTTE after heavy fighting that left at least 350 civilians dead and hundreds injured and depopulated the area.

The authorities have declared Sampur a High Security Zone, making it out of bounds for civilians, most of whom now live in refugee camps in the neighbouring district of Batticaloa. "We are desperate to get back to Sampur, to our homes, but it seems this will remain a dream," a Tamil inmate of a refugee camp who did not want to be identified by name told IANS over telephone from Batticaloa.

A Tamil rights activist, who too did not want to be identified for fear of reprisals, was blunt in saying the Indian decision to pick Sampur for the power project had added to the people's misery. "I have interacted with Indian diplomats (in Colombo) and am certain they are very sensitive to the human rights and humanitarian issues. But if India is involved in this, it will be a grave disappointment, even a terrible scandal," the activist argued, speaking on the telephone.

The issue has united almost all sections of Tamils—those who back the LTTE and those who don't.

"The NTPC project will affect a large number of people," said K. Thurairetnasingham, a Tamil National Alliance (TNA) MP from Trincomalee, speaking from Sri Lanka. The TNA is allied to the LTTE. "We have conveyed our feelings to Indian diplomats. Our people cannot accept this," he added. "This is where our forefathers lived. It is the only land in a largely dry area with water resources suitable for cultivation."

"We are not saying we don't want the project. But why build it in an area that will force Tamils to give up for ever their ancestral land?"

Added a Tamil political leader in Colombo who opposes the LTTE: "This is a good way to ease Tamils out of Trincomalee; it is a process that has gone on for decades so that Trincomalee will become fully Sinhalese one day."

In a bid to keep away Tamils from Sampur, activists say that the displaced residents are under pressure to resettle in two places, including at Raalkuli, near the river Mahaveli that overflows during monsoon. "The government is sending village headmen to get the signatures of the displaced, suggesting that if they don't take this, they will get nothing. This is blackmail."

An NTPC official said the project was to originally come up at Nilaveli, also in Trincomalee. But that area was dropped after the locals protested. "The new site (Sampur) was chosen in consultation with Sri Lankan authorities. If people are going to object to every area, where can the project come up? People should realise that this project will provide them jobs," the official said. Another NTPC official, however, said he was not aware of objections to the Sampur site.

A Tamil source said India originally wanted the project at Nilaveli. But it went with Sri Lanka and chose Sampur after Colombo reportedly threatened to hand the project over to China. Argued a Tamil rights activist: "Already people can see that their homes in Sampur are being bulldozed. This would not happen if the affected people were Sinhalese." Said another activist in Colombo: "India is getting involved in a highly controversial project. The rights of the people are not being respected."

(IANS, 10 May 2008)

# 51

(As the world pressed Sri Lanka to talk to the LTTE, one of its most outspoken diplomats—he has since returned to journalism and academics—explained why Colombo would not negotiate with the Tigers until the latter are disarmed. This interview is significant because much of what Dayan Jayatilleka said proved prophetic.)

## Sri Lanka cannot negotiate with LTTE, says diplomat

A negotiated end to Sri Lanka's dragging conflict is still possible but not before the Tamil Tigers are "verifiably demilitarized and democratized", says one of its most high-profile diplomats. Dayan Jayatilleka also said in an interview that the conflict would only end when Velupillai Prabhakaran, the elusive and feared leader of the LTTE, gets "demilitarized one way or another".

Jayatilleka, who enjoys a close rapport with President Mahinda Rajapaksa, was asked if there was any room for a possible negotiated settlement to end a war that has claimed over 70,000 lives since 1983 and still rages. "Yes, but not with the Tigers, and certainly not with Prabhakaran," the 51-year-old said over email from Geneva where he is Sri Lanka's permanent representative to the UN and other international organizations based in Switzerland.

Referring in some detail to the 1991 assassination of former Indian prime minister Rajiv Gandhi by an LTTE suicide bomber, Jayatilleka said of Prabhakaran: "With him there can be no peace. A peaceful, negotiated settlement is possible only if it recognizes that any solution has to be within a single, united Sri Lanka, and the Tigers are verifiably demilitarized and democratized."

Jayatilleka is a political analyst and academic who served briefly as a minister in the provincial government in Sri Lanka's northeast when Indian troops were deployed there in 1987–90. He was posted in Geneva in June 2007 as fighting escalated between the military and the LTTE and Sri Lanka came under intense attack over rampant human rights violations.

Asked how the war in Sri Lanka will end, Jayatilleka asserted:

> It will all end the way it all ended in Angola after decades of conflict when (rebel leader) Jonas Savimbi was killed by the Angolan armed forces. It will all end the way it did in Chechnya when the Russian army got Djokar Dudayev, defeated the Chechen separatist militia in fierce combined arms warfare... Angola and Chechnya are peaceful and prosperous now. It cannot end while Prabhakaran has not been demilitarized one way or another.

Claiming that Sri Lanka's "human rights record, our record of civilian casualties, compares favourably with that of the West in theatres where its armed forces" operate, he said the West's use of human rights as an instrument was "most disturbing". "The issue of Kosovo (and the de facto separate status of Iraqi Kurdistan) reveals that the West is not averse to the splintering of existing states and the carving out of new ones."

Jayatilleka added: "The West does not seem to believe in a brotherhood of legitimate states which are besieged by terrorism. For the West, terrorism is a problem only if the anti-state movement in question claims to be Islamic or Leftist."

In contrast, most Asian countries back Sri Lanka on the issue of human rights, he said, because "they are not possessed of colonial or neo-colonial habits of centuries", because they believe in "non-interference in the internal affairs of others", and also because they "know what it is to experience the threat of secession and terrorism".

Jayatilleka accused the University Teachers for Human Rights-Jaffna (UTHR-J), a respected rights group, of "becoming part of the West's civil society pets... It has joined several other Tamil dissident groupings in showing extreme distress at the thought of military defeat of the LTTE.

"These elements just do not want the Sri Lankan state to win... They must comprehend that Tiger fascism cannot be defeated by unarmed Tamil expatriate dissidents... It can only be defeated by the guns, men and women of the Sri Lankan armed forces and their Tamil partners."

(IANS, 1 June 2008)

# 52

(President Chandrika Kumaratunga once told an Indian journalist that the LTTE controlled a third of Sri Lanka's land territory and two-third of its winding coast. This was de facto Tamil Eelam. By mid-2008 the LTTE territory had dramatically shrunk.)

## In Sri Lanka, LTTE territory shrinks and shrinks

AMID continuously shrinking Tamil Tiger territory, the Norwegian-sponsored peace process is on hold in Sri Lanka with no signs of resuming any time now. Less than three years after it took on Colombo with aggressive war mongering, the LTTE is desperate for fighters, say Tamil activists and diplomatic sources.

According to Tamil sources in the island's troubled northeast, the LTTE is appealing to Tamil families to contribute at least one member each, irrespective of age and gender, to take on the advancing military. The LTTE now controls about 4,000 sq km—or just six per cent of Sri Lanka's land territory. And the population under its control is said to be about 250,000—a mere 1.25 per cent of the country's total.

This is a far cry from 2005 when it controlled a vast area in Sri Lanka's north and east. However, soon after President Mahinda Rajapaksa took power in November that year, the LTTE took the offensive, stoking a war that rages to this day.

Military officials say that the LTTE's ability to counter-attack in a major way has been seriously eroded over the past year. The loss of the east has meant that the LTTE has lost valuable training ground and a region where it recruited cadres to wage war.

While Sri Lankan leaders admit that it will be impossible to crush the LTTE as long as a sense of Tamil nationalism exists, the LTTE appears to be on the retreat in the north. But those who have known the LTTE warn that it will not give up, come what may.

Western diplomats say that Norwegian facilitation will remain on hold as long as fighting rages. There is unlikely to be any advancement in the peace process in the near future. Although Norwegian diplomats do not travel any more to LTTE areas, they are in touch with the Tigers through other means. Norway is also in close touch with India, which everyone agrees matters the most in Sri Lanka.

Most diplomats feel that neither Colombo nor the LTTE desire talks. Colombo certainly thinks it is winning the war. And although the pro-LTTE media makes noises about the need for a dialogue, there is no guarantee the LTTE wants that.

In any case, calls for peace talks are dismissed in Colombo as a disguised pro-LTTE stand. The state refuses to listen to hectoring on human rights. Western activists are told that they cannot cross a line. If they do, reaction is swift.

Sri Lanka knows it needs to keep India on its side. For the first time in a long time, the Indian state does not seem to be making any bones about being neutral in Sri Lanka. Despite pro-LTTE noises in Tamil Nadu, India refuses to publicly criticize anything it feels is going wrong on the Sri Lankan war front. The refugee flow into India is manageable. New Delhi is also relentlessly pursuing the LTTE in Tamil Nadu and elsewhere so that it does not source war materials from India. This is music to Colombo's ears.

In Sri Lanka, the two most key anti-LTTE Tamil leaders, former Tiger commander Karuna and his deputy and Eastern Province Chief Minister Pillayan, appear to have made up. Residents in the east say that Karuna will be in charge of party affairs while Pillayan will handle only affairs related to the provincial government.

Karuna's men are reportedly looking for 300 ex-LTTE cadres they believe are hiding in Colombo. It is trying to hunt them down in the Tamil areas of the capital with the help of the security forces. At the same time, Sri Lanka seems to be in no hurry to unveil a political package that would be acceptable even to Tamil moderates.

It is amidst this complex scenario that Indian Prime Minister Manmohan Singh met an array of Sri Lankan political forces in Colombo on Friday, ahead of the SAARC summit. Those he met included Tamil groups opposed to and sympathetic to the LTTE. To everyone he had one message: India would like democratic forces to prevail in Sri Lanka's northeast.

(IANS, 5 August 2008)

# 53

(Sri Lanka Defence Secretary Gotabaya Rajapaksa, who the LTTE tried to kill in 2006, has always been clear: the LTTE had to be destroyed to bring peace. He unveiled his mindset in one of the interviews he gave me. Rajapaksa had told me early on how he would militarily throttle the LTTE.)

## We have failed to convince the world: Sri Lanka defence secretary

THE spearhead of Sri Lanka's war against the Tamil Tigers has made light of India's criticism that Tamils were not with Colombo, saying the government had failed to convince the world about its sincerity to resolve the ethnic conflict.

Defence Secretary Gotabaya Rajapaksa added that Sri Lanka would never talk to the LTTE because it would be a wasted effort. Rajapaksa, brother and confidant of President Mahinda Rajapaksa, was asked to comment on India's National Security Advisor M.K. Narayanan's comments on Tuesday that even if Sri Lanka won the battle against the LTTE it would not win the war because "they haven't got the Tamil population on their side".

Narayanan also told *The Straits Times* that India had been urging Sri Lanka to get the Tamils on their side by devolving more power to minorities. "What the Sri Lankans are not factoring in is the great deal of sullenness in the Tamil man."

Rajapaksa told IANS over the phone from Colombo:

The only area where we have failed is to show our genuineness, to convince the outsiders, about our sincerity in resolving the problem. In action we have proved it. Unfortunately, we are not good at propaganda. If Tamils indeed are not with us, then it is our weakness.

There is nothing negative to what Narayanan has said. In my opinion, he has only put in different words what our president has been saying, that we need to defeat terrorism but the (ethnic) problem needs to be resolved (politically).

There is nothing bad against Sri Lanka in what Narayanan has said. It is significant that he has said that the military is winning. And he has never said that we should talk to the LTTE. These are very positive things. On the whole it is the inability of the president and the government to show the sincerity to the Tamils and to the outside world. We have to improve that... It will take time... As for Narayanan, I understand him very well. I know his vision.

Rajapaksa, who narrowly escaped an assassination attempt blamed on the LTTE in 2006, has been widely blamed for the growing climate of intolerance bordering on violence in Sri Lanka as well as rights abuses in the conduct of the war.

He, however, maintained that Colombo—which has captured the multi-ethnic eastern province from the LTTE and is now trying to seize the Tamil-majority north—would never talk to the Tigers. Pointing out that all previous negotiations with the LTTE had failed to resolve the problem, he said: "It is very clear it is useless talking to the LTTE because it is not genuine or sincere (vis-à-vis a negotiated solution). Ultimately, there will have to be a political solution, a permanent solution. And my solution is political."

Thousands have been killed in renewed fighting between the military and the LTTE since 2005-end. Though Colombo has vowed to prevail over the LTTE, Sri Lankan leaders admit that Tamil nationalism can't be wished away without a genuine power sharing deal.

Rajapaksa admitted that in the past 25–30 years promises were made to the Tamil community that were not kept by Colombo. He referred to the provincial elections in the east in May that led to a former LTTE guerrilla, Pillayan, becoming the chief minister of the province.

He said President Rajapaksa was determined to replicate what had been achieved in the east in the country's north, parts of which are held by the LTTE and where heavy fighting is now raging.

Asked if seizing the LTTE-controlled north would be as easy as in the east, he said:

The LTTE are not in the Mullaitivu jungles because they wanted it but because they were pushed into it. They would have preferred Jaffna peninsula or Trincomalee. That would have been advantageous because those are built-up areas... But they were chased away from Jaffna, chased away from Trincomalee. However it will take more troops in the Sri Lankan north because it is a large area. Ultimately, we all have to learn to be Sri Lankans. The day we are able to think as Sri Lankans first, and later as Tamils, Sinhalese, Muslims and Burghers, that is the day we will win. That will be the winning point.

(IANS, 13 August 2008)

# 54

(As the LTTE faced the crunch, an unexpected development took place. Relations between Norway, the peace facilitator, and a frustrated LTTE soured. Western diplomats told me what really happened.)

## Norway–LTTE ties sour over theft of NGO vehicles

NORWAY'S decision not to hail a truce the Tamil Tigers declared before the SAARC summit of August 2008 seems to have fuelled a crisis that has for the first time soured ties between the rebels and Oslo, the peace facilitator in Sri Lanka.

Norway, seen by many in Sri Lanka as sympathetic to the Tigers, has been acutely embarrassed after the LTTE commandeered heavy vehicles belonging to the Norwegian People's Aid (NPA), an Oslo-based NGO, in the rebel-held Kilinochchi district.

The NPA, which has worked in Tamil areas since a Norway-backed ceasefire was signed by the LTTE and Colombo in 2002, has been accused of not reporting the theft to the defence ministry. The NPA says it discovered on 24 July that the vehicles had been taken away from a compound in Kilinochchi "in the preceding days" and that it reported the matter to the nation building and infrastructure development ministry.

The vehicles were being used to clear mines in the north as part of a programme that has been suspended since January. The ministry oversees the mine-clearing project. Colombo says the LTTE will use the vehicles now for its war efforts. The military, which is trying to capture the rebel-held north, has vowed to destroy the vehicles.

According to informed sources who spoke to IANS on the condition of anonymity, the NPA and Norway have both complained to the LTTE. But there is no sign the Tigers plan to return the vehicles, which include two Ashok Leyland trucks, a Tata pick up vehicle, a Tata 407 mini truck and a Tata water tanker. Also in the lot are an excavator earth moving vehicle, a tractor with water browser trailer, a Toyota Land Cruiser jeep and a Mitsubishi Canter twin cab vehicle.

The LTTE has not reacted publicly on the issue, and diplomats are now linking its action, which is bound to affect its standing in the West, to the unilateral truce it announced in July 2008—and what happened later.

Unknown to most people, Norway worked behind the scenes advising the LTTE not to carry out any attack when the South Asian Association for Regional Cooperation (SAARC) summit takes place in Colombo on 2–3 August.

Accordingly, on 22 July the LTTE declared a ceasefire, from 26 July to 4 August, apparently in the hope that it would lead to at least a temporary halt in fighting. That did not happen. Sri Lanka derisively dismissed the LTTE gesture and vowed to keep up its military onslaught. The Tigers felt badly let down.

The LTTE was more furious that the international community, Norway in particular, did not hail its gesture even if privately they thought it was a good move. Norway, which had not expected the ceasefire declaration, tried to reason with the LTTE that as a peace facilitator it could not afford to take a stand on any issue that may seem partial to either of the parties in the conflict. This hasn't cut much ice with the LTTE, which argues that the international community is repeatedly leaning on it while going soft on Sri Lanka.

The theft of NPA vehicles, discovered on 24 July (two days after the LTTE ceasefire became known), has upset Norway, which feels that its stature in Sri Lanka has been compromised as a result. Some sources say that the NPA—and also Norway—may not now want the vehicles back.

Norway has explained its stand on the vehicles to Sri Lankan leaders and briefed other countries linked to the now dead peace process, India included. But the facilitator remains frustrated that its diplomats are barred by Colombo, along with other diplomats, from going to LTTE areas in the island's north for talks with Tiger leaders who matter in war and peace.

(IANS, 21 August 2008)

# 55

(The increasing losses in the battlefield made the LTTE turn viciously anti-India. This was reflected in the sentiments expressed by pro-LTTE politicians and media who came to believe, erroneously, that Sri Lanka would not go this far but for India's overt as well as covert, blessings.)

## India under attack in pro-LTTE media

INDIA has come under attack from a media sympathetic to the Tamil Tigers since a dramatic guerrilla air raid on a Sri Lankan military base left two Indian engineers wounded. The revelation about the presence of the Indian radar experts at the base at Vavuniya, 254 km north of Colombo, shocked many even in India, which has repeatedly advocated a negotiated settlement to the quarter-century-old ethnic conflict.

Sections of the Sri Lankan Tamil media known to be sympathetic to the LTTE are livid.

Tamil newspaper *Sudar Oli*, which is believed to reflect the thinking in the LTTE, said in a stinging editorial that the presence of the Indians in a military base had "exposed" New Delhi. "It has been proved once again that India makes its moves to suit its geographical, political and economic interests," it said on Sunday. "Now it has come to light that India had supplied not only weapons but also troops (to Sri Lanka) to fight the war while preaching a political solution."

The LTTE carried out a stunning pre-dawn suicide attack on the military base on 9 September and claimed to have destroyed its radar installations, the communication and engineering facilities as well as anti-aircraft weapons and ammunition depot. It said all its 10 Black Tigers, or suicide commandos, including five females, were killed in the meticulously planned raid. It claimed to have killed 20 military personnel.

The wounded Indians, who Indian sources said were radar operators, were quickly flown to Colombo. New Delhi has admitted to providing radars to Sri Lanka to detect low-flying light wing LTTE aircraft.

Another Sri Lankan Tamil newspaper, *Uthayan*, has also lashed out at India, accusing it of duplicity. In an editorial, it echoed criticism by pro-LTTE politicians in Tamil Nadu that Prime Minister Manmohan Singh's call for negotiations to end the Sri Lankan conflict was not borne out by "this brazen and material manpower support" to Colombo.

The LTTE has not commented on the presence of the Indians in Sri Lankan military bases. But it has in recent times been very critical of New Delhi's support to Colombo. India says it is opposed to any break-up of Sri Lanka but that Colombo must work towards a credible power-sharing deal with the Tamil minority.

India's National Security Advisor M.K. Narayanan recently stated that Colombo may be able to win the battle against the LTTE, but it cannot win the war because it does not have the Tamils on its side.

The pro-LTTE media and Indian Tamil politicians sympathetic to the Tigers, however, blame Narayanan for India's de facto military support to Sri Lanka while publicly declaring that it will not provide offensive weapons.

India's relations with the LTTE have undergone dramatic changes since 1983 when anti-Tamil riots in Colombo led to New Delhi's overt and covert intervention in the island nation. From a country that provided sanctuary to the LTTE in the 1980s, India became the first to outlaw the Tigers after the outfit was blamed for the 1991 suicide killing of former Prime Minister Rajiv Gandhi.

(IANS, 16 September 2008)

# 56

(As the Tamil Tigers began to sink, pro-LTTE politicians in Tamil Nadu became restive. But they failed to realize that whatever they do, New Delhi would not be deterred from backing Colombo. The politicians also never realized that the mass of people in Tamil Nadu had lost all sympathy for the Tigers a long time ago.)

## Tamil Nadu ferment stuns Rajapaksa but war will go on

THE sudden tumult in Tamil Nadu seeking an immediate truce in Sri Lanka has hit President Mahinda Rajapaksa where it hurts him most. But he is most unlikely to go for a ceasefire with the Tamil Tigers, regardless of what India may desire.

Until Tamil Nadu's DMK and its allies dramatically told the Congress-led central government to pressure Colombo to cease its military campaign against the LTTE by 29 October 2008, Sri Lanka believed it was on the victory lap, with no roadblock seemingly in sight.

Despite a creaking economy, what favoured Rajapaksa was that large sections in the majority Sinhalese community shared his view that the costly conflict against the LTTE was about to end, on Colombo's terms. The present war is thus the President's political lifeline. This is why his government contemptuously dismissed the LTTE's unilateral announcement of a ceasefire ahead of the SAARC summit in Colombo on 1–3 August.

Only the naïve can expect him to take a U-turn now when he thinks, rightly or wrongly, that his moment of glory is around the corner. The military's ability to clear the eastern province of the LTTE and kill some of its key leaders besides putting the guerrillas on the defensive in the north made many to gloat in Colombo that success was finally in sight.

That is when Tamil Nadu erupted, taking Rajapaksa and his advisors by surprise. In the process, India–Sri Lanka ties are under strain again. Anti-India sentiments are on the rise among the Sinhalese who until the other day were happy with New Delhi's military and diplomatic support.

But it will be a fallacy to believe that Rajapaksa's ire is caused solely by the unrest in Tamil Nadu. And it will be equally wrong to assume that Prime Minister Manmohan Singh needed the Tamil Nadu protests to wake him up to the grave and complex situation in Sri Lanka.

While Sri Lanka wants deeper economic and even strategic ties with India, this wavelength gets disturbed every time India does or says what Colombo thinks is interference in its affairs.

Much before Tamil Nadu's politicians roared this month, New Delhi had been telling Colombo repeatedly but quietly that there can be no military end to the conflict; there has to be a broader devolution process; bombings of civilian areas should stop; and the thousands displaced by fighting needed to be helped to rebuild their homes.

All these points have been reiterated this month——but loudly.

Contrary to public knowledge, Manmohan Singh has discussed Sri Lanka with select policy makers several times in recent years. But the one time he met the pro-LTTE Tamil National Alliance MPs in New Delhi, Rajapaksa was furious and asked editors in Colombo to "hammer" Manmohan Singh. But Manmohan Singh has persisted. This August, in his close-door talks with some key political players in Colombo, he posed a pointed query: Will Sri Lanka agree to a genuine power sharing minus the LTTE?

This makes many in Sri Lanka to feel that India may be trying to quietly keep alive the Tigers à la 1987 when it forced Colombo to halt a successful push into Jaffna, leading eventually to the India–Sri Lanka accord. But 2008 is not the 1980s. The LTTE is today outlawed in various countries, including India. And in this age of war on terror, no one can be seen to be on the side of a violently insurgent group.

However, there is one common thread to the 1980s and now: LTTE's determination to carve out an independent state and its confidence—which its critics say is misplaced—that the goal can be achieved yet. The LTTE is telling the population in the area it controls that it needs only two more months to turn the tables on Colombo. It is also furiously enlisting Tamils, including the young, to fight on. As for Sri Lanka, Defence Secretary Gotabaya Rajapaksa, who presides over the war machine, has declared that no purpose will be served by a ceasefire.

As long as both Colombo and the Tigers do not agree to sincerely embrace peace, there can be no lasting truce to a conflict that has foxed even Norway, veterans in conflict resolution. Can Tamil Nadu succeed where Oslo failed?

(IANS, 21 October 2008)

# 57

(The protests in Tamil Nadu prodded India to send a large consignment of relief material to people displaced by war in Sri Lanka. I revealed the quantity of goods India was planning to ferry with the help from the ICRC.)

## India to send 2,000 tonnes of relief goods to Sri Lanka

IN what is a sharp departure from what it did in 1987, India will soon ship 2,000 tonnes of relief material to Sri Lanka for tens of thousands of people displaced by war. This time, however, the delivery will be done through the International Red Cross.

The Tamil Nadu government will put together individual family packs containing food and non-food items including clothes and hygiene products in a bid to ease hardships to civilians forced to flee their homes due to fighting between the military and the Tamil Tigers.

New Delhi is coordinating with the Tamil Nadu authorities and to help facilitate and transport the material to Colombo, where the Indian high commission will receive it. The International Committee of the Red Cross (ICRC) will then take charge and do the distribution to those in need of food and shelter.

This will be the biggest Indian humanitarian intervention in Sri Lanka after the 2004 tsunami. It will also be the most significant relief effort since India undertook a controversial and unilateral sea and air borne operation to deliver food to the civilian population in Jaffna in June 1987.

Like in 1987, the present situation in Sri Lanka's north, where the military is trying to seize areas the LTTE holds, has led to protests in Tamil Nadu and caused concern in the Indian capital.

"Yes, we have been approached by the government of India about (providing) assistance in Sri Lanka, chiefly in Wanni," Francois Stamm, head of the ICRC Regional Delegation in New Delhi, told IANS. Wanni is the name of a large area that includes the districts of Kilinochchi and Mullaitivu districts where the LTTE is now resisting an advancing army. "To my knowledge, this is the first time India has approached ICRC for such a purpose," Stamm said. "We are very glad."

Until now, New Delhi had kept a distance from the ICRC, whose main task in India is to oversee the welfare of prisoners in Jammu and Kashmir. Stamm said the ICRC was now discussing details of the logistics with the Indian foreign ministry. "There is clear intent by India to provide assistance and to do it through the ICRC."

Stamm, who took up his assignment in New Delhi only in 2008, described the situation in Sri Lanka's north as "dire" and said people had been displaced and houses destroyed due to fighting.

We are not targeting any specific ethnic group. We have people (in Sri Lanka) to assess the needs (of the population). We want to make sure that the end users are the intended beneficiaries and there is no diversion. We have the means to do it. We will see how quickly, how efficiently we can distribute this.

Since Indian troops deployed in Sri Lanka's northeast returned home in March 1990 after losing nearly 1,200 men in fighting against the LTTE, New Delhi largely kept away from the ethnic conflict—for a long time. Once again, India has begun playing a pro-active but largely diplomatic and political role in Sri Lankan affairs.

(IANS, 6 November 2008)

2009

# 58

*(The capture of Kilinochchi from the LTTE at the dawn of 2009 marked a turning point in the Tamil Tiger history. Once a small quaint town, Kilinochchi became a symbol of LTTE's defiance after it became its political hub, playing host to foreign diplomats and visitors.)*

## Kilinochchi's fall a major setback to LTTE

TEN years after they captured the northern Sri Lankan town of Kilinochchi in a blitzkrieg that stunned the world, the Tamil Tigers have finally lost it to a military determined to crush the rebels. The fall of Kilinochchi after months of fighting is a huge blow to the LTTE.

Kilinochchi is a small but strategically located town that served as the political hub of the once sprawling LTTE territory in the north and east of the island. It was where LTTE leaders met diplomats and met government representatives during congenial times. It is where LTTE chief Velupillai Prabhakaran, once the emperor of all that he purveyed, spoke to the media in 2002, just two months after signing a Norway-brokered ceasefire agreement with Colombo.

Most important, Kilinochchi town sat on a winding highway known as A9 that linked Jaffna in the northern tip to the rest of Sri Lanka. Once A9 fell to the Tigers, the government had no option but to keep feeding supplies to the military in Jaffna by sea and air, making the war extremely costly.

Kilinochchi was thus a constant sore thumb for Colombo, where Mahinda Rajapaksa came to power in November 2005, ironically due to a blunder by the LTTE that asked the Tamils to boycott the presidential polls. The fiat spiked the prospects of the other contender, Ranil Wickremesinghe, who as prime minister signed the 2002 truce with the LTTE.

The LTTE argument was simple. Wickremesinghe may have signed the peace pact but his aim was to create an international safety net for Sri Lanka. He was compared to a python that would quietly devour the Tamils one day, even if the world saw him as man of peace. The Sinhalese nationalist Rajapaksa was called a cobra—an identifiable enemy. The surmise was that with a Rajapaksa ruling Sri Lanka, it would be easy for the LTTE to re-ignite the Tamil–Sinhalese war.

The LTTE did precisely that, from about the end of 2005, with disastrous consequences, leading first to the loss of the entire eastern province in 2007 and now to the fall of Kilinochchi.

As the Rajapaksa regime celebrates the victory in Kilinochchi, which has come at the cost of tremendous suffering for the civilian population in the northeast, the question being asked is: What will the LTTE do now?

As it has done in similar circumstances in the past, the LTTE will follow a twin path. The bulk of its fighters, the leadership included, will take shelter in the more impenetrable Mullaitivu, the last district in the Tamil majority north still under Tiger control. This is where Prabhakaran was based when he spearheaded the earlier bitter war against the Indians. This is where the group has built seemingly secure underground bunkers that have served the LTTE chief and his lieutenants well until now.

At the same time, when things become relatively quiet, the LTTE would want to unleash hit and run attacks against the military. So Colombo is most unlikely to ease pressure on the Tigers. This means that Sri Lanka is unlikely to see peace in the short run, Kilinochchi or no Kilinochchi.

Informed sources say that the LTTE has recently managed to smuggle in a new load of arms and ammunition into northern Sri Lanka. If that is true, one can expect more fireworks from the LTTE. Since neither Colombo nor the Tigers appears eager for genuine peace talks, it will be safe to conclude that there is no light at the end of the tunnel of war.

(IANS, 3 January 2009)

# 59

(As the Tigers got cornered, one of Prabhakaran's former colleagues insisted that the LTTE boss would never be able to flee Sri Lanka. Karuna argued that an escape from Sri Lanka would lead to Prabhakaran's political death. So he would have to remain in Sri Lanka and fight—and die. Karuna was proved right.)

## Prabhakaran cannot escape from Sri Lanka, says former aide

THE Tamil Tigers' cornered chief Velupillai Prabhakaran cannot escape from Sri Lanka, and even if he were to do so it would amount to his "political death", according to a former confidant. Vinayagamurthy Muralitharan alias Karuna, who revolted and broke away from the LTTE in March 2004, also said that the Tigers would soon be confined to the jungles of Mullaitivu district.

Even that would not guarantee them a secure future because the Tamil population was no more supportive of the Tamil Tigers, Karuna told IANS in a telephonic interview from Sri Lanka. Karuna's comments came a day after Sri Lankan troops pushed their way into Mullaitivu town, the last major stronghold of the LTTE, which has steadily retreated from all its bases unable to face a determined military advance.

Karuna, 42, was once a bodyguard of Prabhakaran and then served as the LTTE's commander for the eastern region of Sri Lanka. He was considered a Prabhakaran loyalist and took part in the talks between the LTTE and Colombo during the Norway-sponsored peace process that started in 2002.

The rapid shrinking of LTTE territory in Sri Lanka has fuelled speculation that Prabhakaran, 54, may have escaped from the country or may be thinking on those lines. Karuna insisted that escaping would not be easy—any more.

"Prabhakaran cannot escape from Sri Lanka. He cannot go to India because of the problems there. He is wanted for the (1991) killing of (former Prime Minister)

Rajiv Gandhi. Going to Southeast Asia is also not going to be easy. But even if he flees Sri Lanka, it will amount to his political death because he won't be able to return to Sri Lanka," said Karuna.

Karuna said the LTTE was now left with only 30 sq km of land area and 20 km along the coastal belt, all in Mullaitivu district. "The army is advancing from both sides. They (Tigers) have been severely damaged militarily. The only major place they still control is Puthikkudiyirippu," a small town located on the A35 highway that links Paranthan and Mullaitivu.

"But they cannot control even that for too long," he went on.

In two or three weeks even the areas now under LTTE control will be captured by the military. After that they will be left only with the jungles. They will then go back to small scale hit and run guerrilla war.

Fighting from the jungles will not be easy. We did it (when I was in the LTTE) against the Indian troops in (Sri Lanka's) northeast because we had tremendous support from the people. Ordinary people gave us food and medicines when Indian troops had us cornered in Mullaitivu. All that has changed. Even people in Jaffna and the east have mostly turned against the LTTE. In the Wanni (region), there is a lot of discontent over what the LTTE has done for so many years.

In such circumstances it will be impossible, not just difficult, to sustain even a guerrilla war. Yes, one can survive in the jungles but that too will be difficult in the long run without people's support. Also, now the Sri Lankan forces have very modern technology that can help them locate where the LTTE is, even in the forests.

Karuna blamed Prabhakaran for the LTTE's present mess.

There were many opportunities when the Tigers could have come to an honourable political settlement. But Prabhakaran followed a totalitarian policy. He would not listen (to us).

When the peace process was on, I tried to reason with him, tried to persuade him to go for some sort of a settlement. But he was too proud of his strength. Our (2004) defection changed everything. When Prabhakaran fought the Indian troops, he was young. That is not the case now. Knowing him, I know he will be mentally distraught today.

(IANS, 26 January 2009)

# 60

(It was clear as 2009 dawned that the LTTE was dying. Tamils who had watched it grow without any fascination for its politics were not unhappy. Some of them complained that the Tigers, in the name of "liberating" the Tamils, had bruised the community like no one ever before.)

## After 25 years, cornered LTTE faces deathly crisis

OVER a quarter century after Tamil militancy erupted in Sri Lanka, the once formidable Tamil Tigers are in dire straits, vanquished but not crushed by a rampaging military. Less than seven years ago, the LTTE and its founder leader Velupillai Prabhakaran looked like the masters of Sri Lanka's northeast after virtually bringing Colombo to its knees.

Today, in a dramatic reversal of fortunes, the Sri Lankan military has brought the very same region under its control barring a small stretch in the northeastern district of Mullaitivu. This is where Prabhakaran, 54 and father of three, is now holed up, apparently in deep underground bunkers chiselled long ago out of hard rocks, still guarded by committed men and women ready to die for him.

But although the LTTE has declared it will fight on, there is hardly anyone outside the group who believes that its dream of carving out an independent state for Sri Lanka's Tamil minority can ever become a reality. Tamil activists who too once shared the dream are blaming it all on Prabhakaran, a school dropout who shaped a ragtag LTTE of the 1970s into the world's most feared insurgent group.

"From when we all took to the gun for the Tamil cause, we are today not in zero but in minus," said Dharmalingam Sidharthan, a former Prabhakaran associate who broke away from him a long time ago. "The Tigers have finished off the Tamil cause," the former MP told IANS over telephone from Colombo.

All this happened because Prabhakaran wanted to be the sole spokesman of the Tamil people and so did away with even Tamils who disagreed with him. After years and years of bloodshed, (Tamil) people are fed up. This is the beginning of the end for the LTTE, he said.

Even if they (Tigers) survive, they can never recapture the territory they have lost.

Agreed human rights activist Rajan Hoole: "Today the Tamils are in a bigger mess than in 1983 (when militancy began). At least we didn't have anarchy then, one could live in the northeast. Life is insecure now. The hijacking of the Tamil struggle by the LTTE was a disaster."

The LTTE was just one of five militant groups in the early 1980s. But as militancy ballooned after 1983, partly with India's covert support, the LTTE decimated other Tamil groups. It grew from strength to strength, taking on the Indian Army in Sri Lanka's northeast in 1987–90.

As the Tigers later set up a de facto Tamil state in the northeast, while at the same time fighting the military, they assassinated former Indian Prime Minister Rajiv Gandhi in 1991 and Sri Lankan President Ranasinghe Premadasa only two years later.

By then the LTTE had mastered suicide attacks. Prabhakaran became a "wanted" man in India, which in 1992 outlawed the group it once harboured. The LTTE is now banned in some 30 countries including the US.

The Norway-backed 2002 ceasefire agreement brought glory to the Tigers. But its refusal to come to any settlement added to the unravelling of the peace process by 2005–06. By then the LTTE had suffered a crippling split in the eastern province.

Tamil and other sources say that the LTTE now controls just 300 sq km of land in Mullaitivu district, a third of which are impregnable forests. It also has a presence in nearby jungles. The LTTE is still estimated to have some 2,000 guerrillas, half of whom can be called "hardcore".

Sri Lankan sources say they would have seized even the area now with the LTTE but for the presence of a large number of Tamil civilians, the greatest sufferers in the seemingly unending war. While a much smaller LTTE took on the Indian troops about 20 years ago, long-term survival in the present scenario could be much more difficult, say Tamil sources.

Colombo's aim is to cut off all supplies to the cornered Tigers by occupying areas around the forests and choking the winding coast. Without food, medicines and new shipments of arms and ammunition, it is believed, the LTTE will have to give up.

But LTTE supporters assert they will never wave the white flag. At the same time, Sri Lanka has no desire for any further peace talks. A repeat of the guerrilla war of the 1980s seems unlikely. Amid the chaos, all eyes are again on Prabhakaran, the Jaffna man who started it all.

(IANS, 28 January 2009)

# 61

(This is an account of the viciousness of the war in the weeks preceding the LTTE's destruction—as seen by a Tamil civilian who managed to escape out of the northeast. Like most civilians, the man did not want his name and location revealed.)

## Tamil man recounts tales of horror in Sri Lanka war

TAMIL civilians trying to flee Sri Lanka's war were blown up and some bled to death on the streets due to shelling by the military, an elderly Tamil man said, recalling the horrifying scenes he saw before escaping from the Tamil Tiger zone in the country's north.

Thousands of panic stricken men, women and children were also desperate to quit the badly shrunk LTTE territory but were not sure how they would be received by the government, the man said in a telephonic interview from a town near Colombo.

The man spoke in English and Tamil to IANS on the condition that he should not be identified either by his name or profession because it could cause him "serious problems". He declared that he was not an LTTE supporter but believed "in the justness of the original Tamil cause".

In his early 50s, the man said that the incident he witnessed took place in Udayarkattu, an area designated a "safe zone" by the government. It is in Mullaitivu district, where the last of the Tamil Tiger guerrillas are holding out against the steadily advancing Sri Lankan troops.

Backing the versions given out by international aid agencies and rights groups, the man said that it was on the morning of 26 January that large numbers of Tamils moved to the "safe zone"—only to die. "Around noon shells began to suddenly rain on the people who had thought they were in a safe area," he said. "Men, women and children ran here and there. I saw even a disabled man run for his life. But no one was sure which place was really safe. Panic took over."

People screamed in pain and terror. I saw badly mauled bodies on the street. One woman of 40 had lost both her legs. One man had a hand blown off. There was blood everywhere. Body parts were everywhere. Many had been wounded and cried in agony. They were sprawled on the road. But we could not do anything. There was no vehicle to transport them. People bled in the open. Believe it or not, it remained like that for hours. There was a church in the vicinity. Many ran there. The priests there gave out tea and biscuits.

It was only in the evening that some of the wounded were moved to a hospital using bullock carts, tractors and even bicycles. Some people simply carried the wounded in their arms. The hospital was no good. First, there was hardly any vacant place. The wounded lay on the floor. There were hardly any medicines. Even doctors and nurses were scarce. People kept crying in pain. We could do nothing, absolutely nothing.

The man said that at least 20 people died on 26 January and that similar shelling took place for three days. "There were LTTE offices in the area but they did not get hit. It is the ordinary people who got hit." The man said there was anger and resentment against the government among the civilians over the shelling and bombing of "safe zones".

"The people trusted the government and went to the safe zone. But the government betrayed their trust," he said.

It is not that people want to be in LTTE area. But they hear that people crossing over to government territory are being kept in virtual prisons. They do not want that. If some neutral body were to promise them safety and freedom, thousands would leave the Wanni.

He added, describing that part of Sri Lanka's north the LTTE still controls.

Sri Lanka says the Tigers are holding back as "human shield" the civilian population that Colombo and aids group say could total between 100,000 and 250,000. The LTTE denies this. Sri Lankan troops have made dramatic advances into LTTE territory in recent months. The Tigers now control only a small part of Mullaitivu. Sri Lankan leaders say the war will not end until the LTTE is crushed.

The man said that most people now in Mullaitivu had retreated with the Tigers from others areas and led a terrible life.

Most live in tents made of old bags and clothes. Many are in school buildings, others in the open, under trees. They cook in open spaces. For toilets, they go to the forests. They are sick and tired of the war. They want it to end. As for the LTTE, it is too busy taking care of itself to take care of the people.

(IANS, 5 February 2009)

# 62

(When the Sri Lankan military carried on its website pictures of Tamil Nadu politicians with the LTTE chief, I revealed what kind of similar pictures and videos Indian security agencies seized over a period of time and what they said about the intimate ties between the LTTE and Tamil Nadu politicians.)

## Vaiko has been an undisguised supporter of the LTTE

SRI LANKA'S decision to make public videos and photographs showing Vaiko with Velupillai Prabhakaran is bewildering since the Tamil Nadu politician's association with the Tamil Tigers chief has never been a secret. Nor is it unknown that Vaiko defied the laws of both India and Sri Lanka to make a clandestine visit by sea to the Tamil Tiger lair in the island's north in 1989 when he was an MP and when Indian troops were battling the rebels.

Vaiko was then in the DMK, and his secret journey, undertaken without the knowledge of the party as well as its leader M. Karunanidhi, strained his ties with the latter. Eventually, Vaiko—then known as V. Gopalasamy—left the DMK and went on to form the MDMK that he now heads.

Vaiko is an undisguised supporter of the LTTE. The association began, like with many in Tamil Nadu, a long time before the LTTE was outlawed in India for assassinating former Indian Prime Minister Rajiv Gandhi at an election rally near Chennai in May 1991.

When the police in Tamil Nadu and the Central Bureau of Investigation (CBI) cracked down on the LTTE after Gandhi's killing, they uncovered 464 videos produced by the Tigers besides a mountain of photographs. One of the videos was exclusively devoted to Vaiko's trip to Sri Lanka during which he met Prabhakaran and many LTTE leaders in camps even as Indian troops hunted for the Tamil Tiger chief.

In that video, Prabhakaran tells an amused Vaiko how the LTTE intelligence chief acquired the *nom de guerre* Pottu Amman. In his discussions, Vaiko refers to Prabhakaran as "thalaivar" (leader) while the LTTE chief addresses the Indian as "anne" (brother). Among the others Vaiko met in LTTE camps were Gopalasamy Mahendrarajah alias Mahattaya, the once number two in the LTTE, and his associate Yogi.

Details of Vaiko's trip are known in India. Some of the LTTE cadres who provided security to the Indian politician in Sri Lanka now lead quiet lives in the West. Indian investigators, for reasons both political and diplomatic, refrained from publicizing any of the meticulously preserved photographs, videos and LTTE documents they seized, some dating back to the 1970s.

When the Gandhi killing was being investigated, detectives found a diary belonging to Sivarasan, the "one-eyed Jack" who witnessed the assassination from close quarters and who reported directly to Pottu Amman. One noting in the diary puzzled the police. It read in Tamil: "V Ko".

Detectives initially feared that "V Ko" might be "Vaiko" in short and it could signify that the politician was perhaps secretly meeting Sivarasan, who was from the LTTE intelligence. However, a police officer soon realized that the code stood for "Valluvar Kottam", a place in Chennai where Sivarasan had been meeting his contacts.

The reality is that Vaiko, like most Indians, was blissfully unaware of the LTTE's plot to kill Gandhi. But he did tell a friend shortly after the death of Gandhi that he feared he might be arrested. From the huge pile of photographs and videos seized in Tamil Nadu, the CBI used only 10–12 videos to build up its case that the LTTE had indeed killed Gandhi.

The photographs and videos made public by Colombo also show Tamil Nadu politician P. Nedumaran with LTTE leaders. Formerly the head of the Congress in Tamil Nadu, he is clearly Prabhakaran's oldest ally in India. Unlike Vaiko, Nedumaran is low profile and does not any more take part in electoral politics.

When Prabhakaran was given bail by a court in Chennai (then Madras) in 1982 after his dramatic arrest in the city following a shootout, the then unknown rebel lived with Nedumaran in Tamil Nadu's Madurai town for around six months.

Nedumaran threatened to sail to Sri Lanka in 1983 in a boat but had to return to shore after the vessel began to leak. In 1985, he paid a clandestine visit to the LTTE lair in Sri Lanka's north, spending days there. He wrote a book on his journey and followed it up with a slim biography of Prabhakaran, both in Tamil.

(IANS, 3 March 2009)

# 63

(Although this story did not say definitively that the LTTE military spokesman was no more, it did hint that. I was wrong, and I apologize. But my sources, which I trust, maintain that Ilanthirayan was very much in LTTE custody before he was pronounced dead in a battle. Some day his true story will emerge.)

## Has LTTE executed its military spokesman?

SRI LANKA'S Tamil Tigers may have killed their high-profile military spokesman on charges of being a "traitor" when they began suffering heavily early this year, Tamil sources say. Speculation that Irasiah Ilanthirayan alias Marshall has been executed has been doing the rounds of Tamil circles for around a month. The sources now say that he could have been done away within January.

The LTTE has not commented on the whereabouts of Ilanthirayan or his fate. There have been no references to him for some months in the media sympathetic to the LTTE.

Ilanthirayan, who was adept in English and Tamil, was based in the LTTE territory in Sri Lanka's north when Colombo started a major offensive from late 2008, forcing the Tigers to cede land they had held for long years. According to the Tamil activists who spoke to IANS from Sri Lanka, Ilanthirayan was accused of being linked to the Sri Lankan intelligence and of plotting against the LTTE. The LTTE intelligence wing would have carried out his execution, the sources say.

In the ultra-secretive LTTE, Ilanthirayan emerged as a valuable media source from August 2006 as fighting escalated between the military and the Tamil Tigers in Sri Lanka's eastern province. Proactive by nature, he interacted with journalists in Sri Lanka and abroad, at times making friendly and informal telephone calls too. Ilanthirayan also kept in touch with MPs from the pro-LTTE Tamil National Alliance (TNA). None of the MPs have heard from him for months.

Although he was supposed to deal only with military matters, he took questions from journalists on other issues as well. He could be contacted on telephone as well as email.

It was Ilanthirayan who announced the appointment of B. Nadesan as the LTTE's political head in November 2007 after incumbent S.P. Tamilchelvan died in a stunning Sri Lankan air raid. His last major public statement was made in May 2008 when he claimed the death of 30 Sri Lankan soldiers and the capture of weapons from the military following heavy fighting in Mannar.

If reports about Ilanthirayan's execution are true, then he must be the most high profile LTTE personality to be purged violently within, following a string of killings in the wake of the split in the Tigers in March–April 2004.

Since its formation in 1976, the LTTE has killed a large number of Tamils it has accused of betraying its cause. In August 1993, the LTTE arrested its then number two, known as Mahattaya, and many of his supporters on charges of being Indian spies. He was executed in December 1994.

Paranoid about infiltration into its ranks, the LTTE does not take kindly to unauthorized contacts by its members with outsiders. Even those allowed to interact with the outside world are closely monitored. Any act, seen as treachery by the LTTE, is neither forgotten nor forgiven.

(IANS, 13 March 2009)

# 64

(As the war neared its end, no single individual outside of Sri Lanka became such a hated figure in LTTE circles as Sonia Gandhi, the Congress party chief and the head of India's ruling coalition. Only the LTTE's aversion to logic could have made it believe that a woman widowed by Prabhakaran would come to his rescue.)

## LTTE media targets Sonia over war debacle

CONGRESS president Sonia Gandhi has come under vicious attack in Tamil Tiger media over India's failure to end the war in Sri Lanka, worrying the Indian security establishment. In media controlled or influenced by the LTTE and also in pro-LTTE street protests, fingers are being pointed at New Delhi for the stinging military reverses the Tigers have suffered.

In this scenario, Gandhi is seen as the villain because of whom India has started publicly calling the LTTE terrorists—for the first time in years and in a language mirroring Colombo's. Gandhi is also held responsible for what the Tiger media say is India's covert backing to Sri Lanka's war that has come close to crushing the LTTE, which assassinated her husband and former Prime Minister Rajiv Gandhi in 1991.

Along with Sonia Gandhi, her ally and Tamil Nadu Chief Minister M. Karunanidhi is also a target of the LTTE media.

The Puthinam Tamil website, which is reportedly linked to the LTTE political wing, has carried a long commentary faulting India and Gandhi for the killings and suffering of the Tamils. "This is India's war, Sri Lanka is but a puppet," said the commentary. It added that India would not allow the war to end even if Sri Lanka wanted to.

It alleged that Gandhi "will not sleep in peace till the last nail is hammered on (LTTE leader Velupillai) Prabhakaran's coffin". It concluded: "Not Sri Lanka, India is the enemy of Tamils."

Nitharsanam, a Tamil website identified with the LTTE intelligence, has a caricature of Gandhi, portraying her as a bloodthirsty goddess—implying she is culpable for the bloodshed in Sri Lanka.

LTTE media has also asked its supporters to focus their energy on India so as to bring pressure on it to make Colombo end the military offensive that has now left the Tigers with a small chunk of land in just one district: Mullaitivu.

The Congress party is frequently dubbed "Sonia Congress" in their media. Prime Minister Manmohan Singh and other key figures in New Delhi do not figure in this frenzy, implying that Gandhi is singularly responsible for the Tigers' predicament.

All this is in contrast to the manner in which Gandhi's elevation as the power behind the Indian government was viewed by the LTTE soon after a Congress-led government took office in May 2004.

At that time, a confidant of Prabhakaran had voiced admiration for Gandhi. Fears that she might avenge her husband's killing virtually disappeared in Tiger thinking as she made friends with parties like DMK and the vocally pro-LTTE PMK in Tamil Nadu.

The Gandhi family's interest in the welfare of Nalini, an Indian woman accused in the Rajiv Gandhi assassination case, also conveyed an impression that the Congress president might have forgiven the LTTE for what it did to her husband. At the same time, India appeared to pursue a hands-off approach vis-à-vis Sri Lanka.

That perception quickly changed as Sri Lanka launched a military offensive against the LTTE from mid-2006, inflicting one major loss after another on the Tigers. As the war progressed, India made repeated appeals for a political solution to the ethnic conflict but refused to pressure Colombo to halt the war. LTTE supporters say this was a ploy to covertly aid Colombo with military hardware and equally valuable intelligence.

The concentrated attack on the Indian government and Sonia Gandhi equals the vehemence shown against President Mahinda Rajapaksa and his aides who oversee the war against the LTTE.

(IANS, 9 April 2009)

# 65

(This was a commentary on the politics of Tamil Nadu, whose political leaders could do nothing concrete for Sri Lanka's Tamil community because many were biased towards the LTTE.)

## Playing politics with Tamil lives in Sri Lanka

SRI LANKA's beleaguered Tamil community deserved better from Tamil Nadu. As the West gets hyper to know what it can do to end the killings of innocent civilians in the conflict and assist their flight from the war zone, election-bound Tamil Nadu is obsessed with street protests.

A political class leading a state of 70 million Tamils, more than three times the population of Sri Lanka, seems to be crippled, unable to think beyond the mundane denunciations and name calling.

The once formidable Tamil Tigers, who for long enjoyed sanctuary in Tamil Nadu, are now left with a just sandy coastal strip in Mullaitivu district. Colombo has vowed to crush the LTTE and net, dead or alive, its elusive leader Velupillai Prabhakaran, who has had long-standing links with many political players in Tamil Nadu.

Beyond blaming the government of Prime Minister Manmohan Singh and Congress president Sonia Gandhi for the LTTE's predicament, none of these players has done anything to minimize the Tamil suffering.

While New Delhi has set up a hospital to treat the civilian wounded and ferried large quantities of relief material, Tamil Nadu's politicians have been busy giving emotive speeches and threatening to break up Sri Lanka.

The latest has come from AIADMK leader Jayalalitha who, after being opposed to the LTTE for years, has now pledged to send the Indian Army to Sri Lanka to do a Bangladesh—if she gets to rule the country. When she was chief minister, Jayalalitha had in December 2005 refused to meet Mahinda Rajapaksa when he came to India on his first visit abroad as Sri Lanka's newly elected president. The last minute "no" embarrassed the Indian external affairs ministry, which scrambled to arrange a face-saving trip for the president to Kerala.

That was when Prabhakaran called the shots in Sri Lanka's northeast. It was also when Rajapaksa was settling down and toying with the idea of meeting some Tamil Nadu leaders, including those rabidly pro-LTTE, to see if they could contribute to peace in Sri Lanka.

On a later occasion, the president publicly urged Tamil Nadu's top political leaders to visit Sri Lanka and persuade the LTTE to give up violence. Not one leading political leader in Tamil Nadu has gone to Sri Lanka to understand the complexities of the conflict rather than view everything from the LTTE's narrow prism. Yet a few have quietly visited the LTTE zone to meet Tamils. Imagine if a Pakistani politician were to make a similar clandestine trip to India and meet members of, say, the Muslim community!

Contrary to what many may think, no political player from Tamil Nadu has had any real influence over Prabhakaran with probably one single exception—P. Nedumaran, the LTTE chief's oldest and most loyal ally in India.

But it is doubtful if Prabhakaran would have lent an ear even to Nedumaran if he had urged him to drop the cause of Tamil Eelam. Nedumaran has been a consistent supporter of Prabhakaran since he first met the rebel way back in the early 1980s and he is open about it. But at least the two main parties in Tamil Nadu should have intervened when Tamils began killing Tamils in Sri Lanka a long time ago, resulting in fratricidal clashes that ultimately weakened the LTTE.

Had they done it, it is possible the LTTE may not have landed in the terrible mess it is in today. Instead, the Tamil Nadu leadership quietly oversaw a quarter century of bloodshed without making any meaningful contributions towards a political settlement and for the ordinary Tamil people's betterment.

Even in this dark hour, there is duplicity.

A politician who now threatens to create Tamil Eelam earlier jailed another over a pro-Eelam speech. A political party accusing the Congress of betraying the Tamils was one of its key allies for four and a half years. And a political veteran lauds Prabhakaran one day, backtracks the next day.

To the Tamil folk in Sri Lanka, will any of this make any sense?

(IANS, 4 May 2009)

# 66

(I wrote this just before Prabhakaran got killed—after coming to know that the LTTE may be talking to the US in a desperate bid to save itself. People who had once said that their children would fight on for Tamil Eelam if they themselves died, proved to be men of clay.)

## Is LTTE in secret, indirect talks with US to surrender?

SRI LANKA's embattled Tamil Tigers may be engaged in secret though indirect talks with the United States for a face-saving formula to save its militarily cornered leadership.

It has been known that the LTTE has reached out to the new US administration, courtesy Norway, one factor why an upset Colombo stripped Oslo of its role as the peace facilitator. IANS has learnt from reliable sources that Norway—the former peace facilitator between Sri Lanka and the LTTE—is in regular touch with Tamil Tiger representatives outside the island nation.

S. Pathmanathan, the newly appointed LTTE's head of International Relations department, is in touch with some Western diplomats to find out if the military onslaught in Sri Lanka can somehow be halted.

Unimpeachable diplomatic sources have confirmed to IANS the LTTE's moves, but say they are not sure if Pathmanathan, widely known by his alias KP, is acting on his own or on the direction of the rebel leadership. Said one source knowledgeable about the development: "If we get information they are ready to surrender, it might be possible to arrange that. But time is very short. It is very late in the game."

The aim of the LTTE representatives engaged in the exercise is to see whether an agreement can still be worked that would lead to a honourable exit of LTTE leader Velupillai Prabhakaran from the scene. The LTTE has concluded that the only country that has the power to influence such an outcome is the US. But since the LTTE is designated a terrorist group in the US, it cannot have direct contacts with Washington. Hence it is using Western intermediaries to convey its thinking to the US.

The LTTE is only expected to accelerate its diplomatic contacts in view of the danger faced by Prabhakaran, whose escape routes have been blocked, and due to developments in India where the Congress party, which has no sympathy for the Tigers, has returned to power with greater numbers after a parliamentary election in which Sri Lanka was a campaign theme, particularly in Tamil Nadu.

The LTTE is citing the civilian deaths and suffering in the last strip of territory in northern Sri Lanka still with the Tigers to impress upon the international community to act—and act fast.

On 13 May President Barack Obama urged Sri Lanka to stop "indiscriminate shelling" that kill innocents and give access to the civilians still in the conflict zone. He also asked the LTTE to surrender its arms.

On Saturday, Pathmanathan—who is trying to get into the shoes of the late Anton Balasingham, the long-time international face of the LTTE—said in significant comments that the Tigers were ready to heed the call by Obama and that "at this juncture we are ready to (do) anything necessary to save the Tamil people".

Equally significantly, the statement shed all pretensions of viewing Sri Lanka as a foe. It sought cooperation from Colombo and said "our people are now at the mercy of the international community"—words the LTTE have rarely ever used.

"Both the Sri Lankan government and us, we together have to find a solution and a way to resolve the crisis," it said. "We are ready to cooperate and work towards peace as Obama has insisted. We heed the call by the US president and are prepared to take measures that will spare the (lives) of our people." And instead of harping on an independent Tamil Eelam, Pathmanathan, a confidant of Prabhakaran, re-iterated the LTTE's commitment to an internationally mediated solution to the conflict.

Pathmanathan, who has been based outside Sri Lanka for years, came out with another SOS on Friday: "The Tamils of this world are begging the international community to shed its cloak of indifference and save the hapless Tamil civilians on the brink of extinction. We appeal to your kindness and values."

Pathmanathan's comments come at a time when the LTTE, which only six months ago was mocking at President Mahinda Rajapaksa, has been crippled militarily. Its leaders, Prabhakaran included, are on the run, unable to stand up to the military offensive.

(IANS, 17 May 2009)

# 67

(I wrote this obituary in April, knowing that Prabhakaran was, most probably, about to be killed. It moved on the IANS wire on 18 May 2009. As I wrote the obituary, I realized I had been pursuing the story for over a quarter century!)

## Prabhakaran: From catapult killer to ruthless insurgent

HIS first victims were squirrels and birds, and his first weapon a humble catapult. From such beginnings, Velupillai Prabhakaran—who died ignominiously on Monday—grew to be the world's most shadowy and ruthless insurgent who at one time lorded over vast areas in Sri Lanka's northeast.

The over 35 years Prabhakaran spent underground building the once unknown Liberation Tigers of Tamil Eelam (LTTE) into an awesome war and terror machine transformed the Indian Ocean island from an idyllic tourist haven into a bleeding state.

His unforgiving campaign for an independent Tamil Eelam state, to be carved out of the Tamil-majority northeastern province, left nearly 90,000 dead, gave birth to a cult of suicide bombings that shook the world, and cast a long shadow on nearby India.

By the time destiny caught up with Prabhakaran on 18 May 2009, he had acquired legendary notoriety. To critics he was a megalomaniac, one who had turned assassinations into a fine art. To his admirers he was a doughty fighter, unlike Tamil leaders of an earlier era.

Driven by a worldview that Tamils could not live within Sri Lanka because the Sinhalese would never treat them as equals, Prabhakaran decreed that anyone deemed an impediment in his path needed to be done away with. And he did that with a vengeance that was numbingly brutal, producing dread and even awe.

He had leaders of two countries killed. One was former Indian premier Rajiv Gandhi, who was assassinated when a woman strapped with explosives blew up in May 1991 while pretending to touch his feet. The other was Sri Lanka's president Ranasinghe Premadasa, torn apart at a 1993 May Day rally by a young male who had infiltrated his house a long time ago.

But none of the attributes of blood and gore that made him so ruthless was evident when he took birth in a simple middle class home in Jaffna, the Tamil heartland, on 26 November 1954. That was when ethnic unrest was starting to engulf Sri Lanka, involving the largely Buddhist Sinhalese majority and the mainly Hindu Tamil minority.

Born to a disciplinarian father, who a Sri Lankan government employee, and a devout mother, Prabhakaran was the youngest of two daughters and two sons, the natural darling of the family.

His early idols were two Indian independence heroes, including Subhas Chandra Bose, who chose gun over Mahatma Gandhi's non-violence. Prabhakaran dropped out of school due to the pull of a nascent Tamil militancy. He fled his home for good in 1972 after a vicious police crackdown.

Prabhakaran's first major act of violence was the gunning down of Jaffna's Tamil mayor in 1975. The LTTE took birth the next year but remained largely unknown till it issued its first press statement in 1978. Those were dark days for the young Prabhakaran. With the police looking for him and lacking enough hideouts, he would sail stealthily to India's Tamil Nadu state. Money was a problem there too. There were nights when he went hungry.

In a dramatic event, the import of which was then lost, the unknown Prabhakaran was arrested—for the first and last time—in Madras (now Chennai) in May 1982 after trying to kill a rival. But with help from Indian politicians, he got bail and escaped to Sri Lanka to resume his bloody innings.

It was Prabhakaran's ambush of an army patrol in Jaffna in July 1983 that killed 13 soldiers and sparked off terrible anti-Tamil violence, leading to a full-blown insurgency. Once New Delhi began clandestinely training and arming Tamil militant groups, including the LTTE, Prabhakaran shifted to Tamil Nadu and lived there for over three years while the LTTE grew and grew.

From the safety of India, Prabhakaran ordered murderous attacks in Sri Lanka. Even as he fell in love with a Jaffna University student and fathered three children, he set up a clandestine network to feed the LTTE weapons and ammunition from around the world.

Prabhakaran quit India in January 1987. When India and Sri Lanka signed a pact later that year to end Tamil separatism, he appeared to go with it but then audaciously took on the Indian Army deployed in Sri Lanka's northeast.

Prabhakaran killed at will—be they Muslims, perceived foes among Tamils, Sri Lankan leaders or Sinhalese civilians. His suicide bombers were an elite force, whose members had their last supper with him before setting out on their missions.

Even in his bunkers, Prabhakaran was a doting father, cutting cakes on his children's birthdays. He loved good food, ice cream in particular. He had a fetish for cleanliness, was paranoid about his security, and exercised regularly. He was soft spoken. He expected complete loyalty from his band of men and women. Dissenters got no mercy.

As the body count mounted in Sri Lanka, he became uncompromising vis-à-vis his goal of Tamil Eelam. He ruled Jaffna for five years until 1995. By the late 1990s, the LTTE had large parts of the island's north and east under his control.

The LTTE had by then grown into a mammoth, fearsome entity, with the trappings of a de facto state. LTTE offices spawned in numerous countries. Unable to meet its military challenge, Sri Lanka requested Norway to broker peace, leading to a truce in 2002.

But lack of mutual trust and a crippling split in the LTTE in 2004 shattered the peace. In late 2005, Prabhakaran asked Tamils to boycott the presidential polls, leading to the narrow victory of Mahinda Rajapaksa. He believed that a Sinhalese hardliner in office would help rally the Tamils.

It turned out to be his biggest blunder—after Gandhi's 1991 killing.

LTTE provocations led to war in 2006. By 2007, Colombo brought the entire eastern province under its control for the first time in several years. By 2008, better-equipped and trained Sri Lankan troops began capturing territory in the north and began killing Prabhakaran's close lieutenants.

Kilinochchi, which was Prabhakaran's de facto capital, fell in January 2009. Just four months later, the man himself lay dead while trying to flee from pursuing soldiers, dropping the curtains on one of the world's longest and bloodiest insurgencies.

(IANS, 18 May 2009)

# 68

(Former Prabhakaran loyalist Karuna described to me the final moments of the LTTE chief—and the dead man's ego that prevented him from coming to a settlement when an honourable peace deal would have been possible.)

## Prabhakaran was with 18 men when he was killed: Karuna

TAMIL Tigers chief Velupillai Prabhakaran was with 18 of his most loyal bodyguards when he was trapped and killed by the Sri Lankan military, one of his former rebel associates told IANS. Vinayagamurthy Muralitharan alias Karuna, whose 2004 revolt played a vital role in the weakening of the LTTE, also said the Tigers would never rise again.

Among the handful of people who identified the body of Prabhakaran was Karuna, a long-time confidant of the LTTE chief who sensationally revolted with thousands in March 2004 seriously weakening the group.

According to Karuna, now the minister for national integration and reconciliation in President Mahinda Rajapaksa's cabinet, it did not take him any time to confirm that the man lying dead on a stretcher was none other than Prabhakaran, once his mentor and leader. "He had thinned somewhat (from when I saw him last)," Karuna said over telephone, speaking in Tamil. "Otherwise he was much the same. The face, the eyes... it was Prabhakaran."

Karuna said the soldiers who killed Prabhakaran were surprised after sighting him because some of them had thought the man had killed himself earlier. "They did not expect to see him at all."

The fighting with Prabhakaran and his men erupted at 4 a.m. Monday and was over within 90 minutes, leaving the man who had terrorized the country for over a quarter century dead near a lagoon in Mullaitivu district.

Karuna, who is also an MP and vice president of the ruling Sri Lanka Freedom Party (SLFP), confirmed that the upper portion of Prabhakaran's head was blown off. By then, the military had already killed his son Charles Anthony as well as all his top associates.

A politician today, Karuna dismissed speculation that sections of the surrendered LTTE cadres or its supporters abroad would be able to revive another group à la the Tigers. "It is not possible," Karuna said with an air of authority. "There are no circumstances, no conditions for such a thing to happen. People are fed up with all this violence. There are absolutely no chances of another LTTE coming up."

Karuna, a native of Batticaloa, joined the LTTE in 1983 and went on to become the commander of the entire eastern province. For years he was seen as a Prabhakaran loyalist. He was a member of the LTTE delegation that held talks with the Sri Lankan government between 2002–03 and was on the side of Prabhakaran when he addressed the media in April 2002.

Karuna blamed Prabhakaran for his death, saying if he had been a better strategist he should have dispersed his forces and senior leaders once the Sri Lankan military went on the offensive from late last year. "But he did not do that. It shows he was foolish. He must have perhaps thought that somehow the international community would be able to enforce a ceasefire due to the plight of civilians and he would survive?"

"Indeed, if he had been a good leader, he would not have insisted on an independent state for so long. He should have known it would never happen. If only he had transformed his military victories into political victories, the Tamils would be holding their heads high today. That did not happen."

Karuna said he had advised both Prabhakaran and the then LTTE political wing leader S.P. Tamilchelvan, who was killed in 2007, to understand the global changes and reform the LTTE. But they did not pay heed. "The problem is some of those close to Prabhakaran had boosted his ego. They made him think he was infallible, that he could never be defeated. He was misled," Karuna said, recalling the times when he was in the LTTE.

The way forward for the Tamils, Karuna said, was democracy.

"That's the only way. Imagine if we had a good parliamentary bloc, we could have done wonders for the Tamils, even in this dark hour. The TNA is useless," he said, referring to the pro-LTTE Tamil National Alliance, the largest Tamil grouping in the 225-seat Sri Lankan parliament.

Karuna said the Tamil community was at a crossroad after the deaths of around 90,000 people since 1983 in the Tamil Eelam struggle. This included some 24,000 LTTE guerrillas. What did the Tamils gain after all this bloodshed, he was asked. Karuna replied: "Nothing."

(IANS, 20 May 2009)

# 69

(During a visit to New Delhi post-Prabhakaran, Basil Rajapaksa, the President's brother, outlined his government's thinking on the rehabilitation of the displaced Tamils. Amid continuing international concern, this has emerged as one of the trickiest as well as thorniest issues for the Sri Lankan government.)

## Displaced Tamils to be resettled by 2009-end: Rajapaksa

SRI LANKA is confident of resettling and providing a new lease of life to the 250,000 Tamils displaced by war in the north by the year-end, according to Senior Presidential Advisor Basil Rajapaksa.

Rajapaksa, brother of President Mahinda Rajapaksa, said the government had the experience and ability to undertake the massive exercise because of what Colombo achieved after the killer tsunami. While many Tamils would be able to return to their original abode dominantly in the districts of Kilinochchi and Mullaitivu within 180 days, almost all others would get their homes back by 31 December 2009.

Asked if these deadlines were realistic, Rajapaksa said the government had already resettled a similar number in the eastern province, which the military captured from the Tamil Tigers in 2007. "We resettled about 40,000 Muslims in Mutur in a record 44 days. And in Vakarai (in Batticaloa), we settled 60,000 people in three months," Rajapaksa said in a telephonic interview to IANS, a day after meeting India's National Security Advisor M.K. Narayanan and Foreign Secretary Shivshankar Menon.

"When the people fled their homes in the east, they had no good bus (service), no good roads, no electricity, no school. When they returned, all this was there. They got the best school in the eastern province. We have the best record in the world in reconstruction and resettlement."

Sri Lanka's victory over the LTTE followed months of heavy fighting during which hundreds of thousands of Tamils fled their homes. Many retreated with the LTTE as it began pulling back in the wake of a punishing military offensive from December 2008. Eventually, only after all the civilians vacated the LTTE zone did the military crush the Tigers.

The displaced population is presently housed in large camps. Barring hardcore LTTE fighters, all others are expected to go home over the coming weeks and months. The entire region has been devastated by years of Tamil separatist war, leaving houses, agriculture land, school and government buildings and even hospitals damaged.

Rajapaksa also promised that the authorities would undertake massive reconstruction work so that the people find new roads, hospitals and schools, as well as water and power supply when they resume their lives.

Two key reasons why the resettlement would take longer time in the north compared to the east are the large number of landmines strewn across the region and the sheer size of it. Rajapaksa said:

The challenges in the north are different. There is high level of mines. The main concern is de-mining. Apart from our military, we are grateful to the Indian government for helping us with de-mining. They have agreed to send more teams. The north is also very big in land area.

He said while some NGOs were also engaged in de-mining, their quality was not as good as that of Sri Lanka's military and the Indian teams.

Rajapaksa, who is overall in-charge of the rehabilitation, said the authorities had learnt valuable lessons from the eastern province. "We will also take care of farmland and paddy fields; irrigation too. When people return to their homes, we will make sure they can start working from the very next day."

How much will all this cost?

Rajapaksa declined to hazard a guess but remarked, in apparent reference to the West, that "countries who talk a lot about Sri Lanka abroad (criticizing its rights record) don't come to help, countries who don't talk a lot do help".

(IANS, 22 May 2009)

# 70

(This is one of the pieces I wrote about Prabhakaran after his death. It focused on the man, his fetish for cleanliness and his other human traits, based largely on research I had conducted when I wrote the man's biography.)

## Swat the fly, kill the foe

FOR someone who died such a messy death, Velupillai Prabhakaran was a meticulously clean man. Cleanliness and discipline came naturally to him. This was evident to anyone who visited the offices of the LTTE in Chennai. Even in the earlier uncertain days when getting enough to eat was a problem for him and his friends, Prabhakaran would tell everyone to be crisp and clean. It didn't matter if the clothes they wore were old, he would decree, but they should be washed.

If seated on a sofa at the LTTE office, he would wipe the armrests if he spotted dust. He hated cobwebs. If he found any dirt, he would express his displeasure to his cadres: "What is this? Is this your way of maintaining cleanliness?" LTTE members were also expected to keep the toilets in the office spotlessly clean. As the LTTE grew and grew, the trait spread to all the training camps in India and Sri Lanka.

Even when Indian troops waged war against the LTTE, Prabhakaran's fetish for cleanliness did not desert him. In the thick forests of Mullaitivu district (where he would die one day), flies were a constant source of irritation. Since he did not like pesticides, the guerrilla asked his cadres to swat them. There was even a competition to see who swatted how many flies! Some killed as many as 1,000! The fly killing competition gave him immense joy. He also ordered that flowers be grown in and around the training camps.

It was this Prabhakaran that I first met in 1985.

The LTTE chief was in New Delhi in the company of other Tamil militant leaders for discussions with then Prime Minister Rajiv Gandhi. They had been put up in the small but comfortable Hotel Diplomat on the tree-lined Sardar Patel Marg. When I was introduced to Prabhakaran, he was seated on a cot and seemingly lost in thought. He looked anything but a rebel leader.

During the conversation, I asked Prabhakaran if he would take me to Jaffna in one of their speedboats that plied between Sri Lanka and Tamil Nadu. He pondered over my question and said: "Leave your details and we will get back to you." He never did. Only much later I realized how perennially suspicious the LTTE was of all outsiders.

Even as I followed the Sri Lanka story for decades, I did not get to meet Prabhakaran again until April 2002 when he addressed his first (and what turned out to be last) major press conference. That was in Kilinochchi, a northern Sri Lankan town the LTTE had made the hub of its de facto state. By then, the Prabhakaran I encountered a long time ago had grown into a legend. He was described by his adoring ideologue Anton Balasingham as the "Prime Minister and President of Tamil Eelam".

The boy who had fled his home in Jaffna way back in 1972 after a police crackdown had come a long way.

What conquered him early on was love—love at first sight.

The year was 1984, and some Jaffna University students were on a hunger strike. The increasingly assertive and intolerant LTTE decreed that the era of peaceful protests was passé. It packed off the hunger strikers to Chennai. One of them was a pretty young woman with big eyes, Mathivathani. In Chennai she was put up with Adele, the Australian wife of Balasingham. One look at her and Prabhakaran concluded she was for him. Adele would later say: "He was absolutely besotted with Mathy and she with him."

Balasingham prodded Prabhakaran to marry Mathy. In the presence of a small group of friends and family members, the two exchanged garlands at a Hindu temple not far from Chennai on 1 October 1984. The rebel tied the "thali" around her neck, putting the religious seal on the marriage. A beaming Prabhakaran wore a tie—for the first time in his life. The couple had three children: two sons and a daughter. The elder son was named after Charles Lucas Anthony, a buddy from Trincomalee who fell to security forces a long time ago.

The marriage created a sensation because Prabhakaran had only some years ago sacked a senior love-struck colleague, saying that romance was not for revolutionaries. In 1985, during a visit to the LTTE office in Madras, he noticed a girl in a nearby house waving at someone in his office and disappearing into her house. He was told that she was probably having an affair with an LTTE member. Prabhakaran did not like the idea of one of his boys falling for an Indian girl. He packed off the erring guerrilla to Sri Lanka.

Behind his shy frame and quiet nature lay a man with a penchant for unlimited violence that virtually destroyed Sri Lanka. Prabhakaran had all the traits of one capable of supreme destruction. He also had a photographic memory and would remember people he had only fleetingly met years earlier. He was paranoid about security. As he built the LTTE, he created a corps of personal bodyguards supremely loyal to him. It didn't always work that way. Karuna, the eastern regional commander whose 2004 revolt seriously weakened the LTTE, was once Prabhakaran's bodyguard. So was his younger brother Reggie. After Karuna's rebellion, Prabhakaran had Reggie murdered. Prabhakaran also killed countless other Tamils, often simply for differing with him.

Years earlier in New Delhi, Prabhakaran went one evening to the Chanakya cinema near the diplomatic enclave and saw an English movie *The Blue Lagoon* with three friends. On another occasion, the Indian government arranged a tour of Delhi for Prabhakaran and other militants—after pressure brought on them to talk to Colombo led to tensions. At the Raj Ghat, the mausoleum of Mahatma Gandhi, the LTTE boss grabbed the hands of K. Pathmanabha, leader of the EPRLF, and told him sarcastically: "Look, let us give up our violent path and take to non-violence. This is what the Indians want us to do."

Years later Prabhakaran felt no guilt when he ordered his assassins to mow down Pathmanabha and his friends at a Chennai house with AK-47 assault rifles. This too was Prabhakaran's trait.

During our 1985 meeting in Delhi, I had thrown one last question at him. "Why have you taken off your moustache," I wanted to know. Prabhakaran was clearly taken aback. He managed a quick reply: "We grow our moustaches only when we fight. We take them off when we come for talks." It may have been an off the cuff remark but Prabhakaran did not have a moustache when he signed the Norway-brokered ceasefire agreement with Colombo in 2002. And when he died, he did.

(*The Telegraph*, Calcutta, 24 May 2009)

# 71

(A post-mortem. In its death, the LTTE proved that it too was mortal. Had it realized the truth early on, Sri Lanka's Tamil community could have escaped the needless suffering it underwent for over a quarter century, simply because one man claimed he knew how to chart their destiny.)

## So, the Tamil Tigers were mortals after all...

THE dramatic collapse of the Tamil Tigers, accompanied by white flags and surrenders even as some suicide bombers kept exploding themselves, is a sad commentary on the politics of uncompromising mayhem the rebels pursued for so long in Sri Lanka.

Here was a group called the LTTE that set out to form an independent Tamil state by breaking up the north and east of Sri Lanka. They never fought any elections but prided themselves as the sole and authentic representatives of the Tamils. It appears now that this was not the only contradiction in their personality.

The steady revelations about the final moments of the LTTE leadership speak poorly of the Tigers who declared a sudden love for peace when their own lives were at risk, after contemptuously dismissing all past efforts at peace making.

When they were repeatedly called to go for negotiations, they decided to settle for nothing less than independence. Those who wanted to shake hands with the Sri Lankan state were dubbed traitors and killed. By the time a quarter century of unceasing bloodletting passed, more than 90,000 people lay dead, many thousands were injured and maimed, the Tamils were in ruins, and there was no trace of Tamil Eelam.

But the LTTE would not call a halt to the fighting, telling incredulous Westerners even in the last few weeks that another generation would pursue the Eelam campaign even if all the Tigers died fighting. As if to fulfil that vow, thousands of children mainly from poor Tamil families were forced to enlist and wage war, the like of which was unseen anywhere in the world.

Young men and women became suicide bombers—killing themselves and others till the very end. Others sailed with explosives-laden boats to ram navy ships. The LTTE even acquired planes; given the chance, it could have come up with submarines.

Yet, it was a war over which the ordinary Tamils, both in and outside the LTTE, had no control. As it kept winning one battle after another, as it kept killing one "traitor" after another, as Colombo started to bend its knees, the LTTE came to be seen, rightly, as a never-say-die group.

At his April 2002 press conference in Kilinochchi, LTTE chief Velupillai Prabhakaran even declared that he too could be dubbed a traitor and killed if he turned his back to Tamil Eelam. In ordinary words, this meant the LTTE would never surrender or show the white flag, come what may. Yet this is precisely what it did—at the first opportunity.

As the military closed in, the LTTE stunningly announced that its struggle had reached a "bitter end" and it was silencing its guns. In no time, S. Pulidevan and B. Nadesan, heads of the Peace Secretariat and the political wing in the LTTE respectively, began urging people in distant lands to intercede so that they could give themselves up.

Of course, there was nothing wrong if Pulidevan and Nadesan wanted to live. The tragedy was that the LTTE killed several Tamils like Nadesan and Pulidevan, simply because they too desired peace. If only this had not been the case, tens of thousands—Tamils, Sinhalese and Muslims—would be alive today.

But those were the times when Prabhakaran decreed, year after year, that there could be no compromise on Tamil Eelam. In hindsight, one can say that this misplaced arrogance came because the LTTE's top leaders never faced any serious danger—until recently.

No wonder, even as late as November 2008, in his annual speech, Prabhakaran mocked at President Mahinda Rajapaksa, daring him to capture LTTE-held territory in the north.

It took only six months of merciless military assault to force the LTTE to beg Western powers to save it from destruction. Tragically, even as the leaders were preparing to give up, the foot soldiers continued to fight and die, carrying out suicide attacks as late as 17 May. The next day, Prabhakaran lay dead and the LTTE was in ruins.

Even after his death, the LTTE's love for fantasy did not abate. It kept claiming that Prabhakaran was alive and well—before sheepishly admitting the truth a week later. Their awesome reputation notwithstanding, the Tamil Tigers finally proved that they too were mortals.

(IANS, 25 May 2009)

# 72

(After a quarter century of conflict, one of the bloodiest and most heartless, Sri Lanka finally crushed the LTTE in May 2009. This piece, written mainly for a foreign audience, explained who Prabhakaran was—and how he met his ugly end.)

## How the tide turned

FOR well over a quarter century, it looked as if Velupillai Prabhakaran could never be vanquished. Since its birth in 1976, his LTTE had grown from a rag-tag outfit to one of the world's deadliest insurgent groups commanding thousands of fighters. At one time, the Tamil Tigers presided over a third of Sri Lanka's land area and two-thirds of its coastline as they ran a de facto state. A Norway-brokered truce went into effect in 2002 but failed to bring lasting peace. Finally, after years of bloody uncertainty, Sri Lanka finally crushed the LTTE in May this year, delivering a knockout blow from which it will never recover.

Sri Lanka's decisive victory over the LTTE is the biggest success story in the world of anti-terrorism. It is in sharp contrast to the dragging military campaign the US leads against the Taliban and Al Qaeda in Afghanistan and Pakistan. It also outshines the collapse of the Maoist Shining Path movement in Peru. And it came about despite emerging evidence that a section of the West tried to save at least some LTTE leaders before the war ended on 18 May.

When Prabhakaran fled his home for good in 1972, few people would have thought that he would one day almost end up breaking Sri Lanka.

The LTTE he founded with a small group of friends in 1976 sought an independent Tamil state in the northeast of Sri Lanka. It alleged that the largely Buddhist Sinhalese majority in the island nation discriminated against the mainly Hindu Tamil minority.

The LTTE struggled to exist until an ambush of an army patrol in Jaffna in July 1983 killed 13 soldiers and sparked off anti-Tamil violence leaving hundreds dead and igniting Tamil insurgency.

India, Sri Lanka's northern and bigger neighbour, covertly began training Tamil militants to pressure the country to go for a negotiated settlement with moderate Tamil leaders. The strategy backfired. The moderates got eclipsed and the LTTE slowly took charge of the Tamil community—with disastrous consequences. India and Sri Lanka signed an agreement in 1987 to end Tamil separatism but it led to a war between the Tigers and Indian troops deployed in the island.

Once the Indians withdrew, the LTTE took control of Jaffna and expanded its domain, fighting and winning many battles against Sri Lanka. By then the LTTE was presiding over a de facto state with its own army, navy and police. It boasted of an 'air force'—its two-seater planes bombing Colombo towards the end of the conflict. The LTTE even owned a shipping line that ferried arms and ammunition when it was not legitimately trading in cargo. The LTTE's most lethal weapon was suicide bombing. The Tigers' VIP victims included former Indian Prime Minister Rajiv Gandhi (1991) and Sri Lankan President Ranasinghe Premadasa (1993).

For years, as the war see-sawed, it looked as if the LTTE would exist forever as a permanent nuisance even if it did not overcome the Sri Lankan state. The LTTE opened offices in several countries, mainly in the West. Its support base in the West came from the large expatriate Tamil community that had fled Sri Lanka over the years and contributed to the Tiger kitty. The LTTE extorted money from those who were not its supporters.

The 2002 international peace process gave the LTTE a certain legitimacy it never had before. But it was too good to last. The LTTE pulled out of the peace talks in 2003. A year later, it suffered a crippling split when one of its top commanders, Karuna, revolted with thousands of followers in the eastern province. As the LTTE pursued its politics of murder, Canada and the European Union outlawed it. India, the US and Britain had declared the Tigers terrorist much earlier. All these badly hit the Tigers' fund collection drives.

Once Mahinda Rajapaksa became Sri Lanka's President in November 2005, events galloped fast. In April 2006, Sri Lanka's army chief escaped an audacious assassination attempt by a LTTE woman suicide bomber who had sneaked into the army headquarters in Colombo. Gotabaya Rajapaksa, the Defence Secretary and the President's brother, survived an LTTE-sponsored assassination attempt in December of the same year. By then, a full-scale war was raging between the LTTE and a military determined to change the tide.

In 2007, the LTTE lost control of the eastern province—after many years. Its losses continued through 2008. As 2009 dawned, it lost Kilinochchi town, its political hub, and began to retreat into the interior. In their last stages the Tigers tried to hold on to hundreds of thousands of civilians to prevent the final military onslaught. But that did come in May, leaving Prabhakaran and all his top lieutenants dead in a strip of land in Mullaitivu district.

Five major factors contributed to the eventual and complete destruction of the LTTE, which itself was responsible for four of these.

The first was the 1991 assassination of Rajiv Gandhi, the former Indian Prime Minister. The LTTE killed him because it feared he would return to power and may deploy the Indian army again in Sri Lanka to take on the LTTE. The LTTE thus alienated itself from the Indian ruling class, which prevented the Tigers from using its soil and closed ranks with the Sri Lankan establishment. Gandhi's killing catapulted his widow, Sonia, into politics. She was a key pillar of India's ruling coalition when the LTTE went down.

The LTTE decision to pull out of the peace process in 2003, after the US did not invite it to a Washington conference, angered the West, which wanted to promote democratic values in the group. The unending recruitment of children into its army as well as the continued killing of its critics during the peace process also alienated the West.

The 2004 split by Karuna caused unprecedented damage to the LTTE, from which it never recovered. Karuna was no ordinary guerrilla but a trusted lieutenant of Prabhakaran who understood his (Prabhakaran's) mindset perhaps more than anyone else. He not only took away thousands of fighters but also provided invaluable intelligence about the ultra secretive LTTE to Colombo.

The Tigers' biggest blunder after Gandhi's killing was the 2005 appeal to Tamils to boycott the presidential election. In the process, Ranil Wickremesinghe, who signed the 2002 truce with Prabhakaran, was defeated narrowly (after losing Tamil votes that would have gone to him). This led to the victory of Mahinda Rajapaksa, who proved to be the LTTE's nemesis.

The final factor was the cohesiveness of the Rajapaksa regime. While the President presided over the country, one of his brothers, Gotabaya, ran the defence establishment with a singular aim: finish off the LTTE irrespective of the consequences. Another brother, Basil, handled the political front of the government, giving a cohesiveness that no previous administration had. The unison of mind also helped Sri Lanka ward off strong Western pressure when the military push against the LTTE reached a decisive stage and when some countries insisted on a ceasefire, albeit to save civilians trapped in the war zone. But the Rajapaksa brothers carried on until Prabhakaran lay dead.

(*Asian Affairs*, Britain, June 2009)

# Postscript: A new dawn

I

ALMOST one full year before the Tamil Tigers were crushed, a discerning Sri Lankan diplomat summed up, in simple prose, how, and in what circumstances, would the war in his country end. As he spoke to me from Geneva in June 2008, there was no doubt in Dayan Jayatilleka's mind that the conflict would keep raging as long as Prabhakaran was not neutralized. This, of course, went against the conventional wisdom that only negotiations would halt the bloodshed.

Said Jayatilleka:

> It will all end the way it all ended in Angola after decades of conflict when (rebel leader) Jonas Savimbi was killed by the Angolan armed forces. It will all end the way it did in Chechnya when the Russian army got Djokar Dudayev, defeated the Chechen separatist militia in fierce combined arms warfare... Angola and Chechnya are peaceful and prosperous now. It cannot end while Prabhakaran has not been demilitarized one way or another.[1]

Foresight? Crystal ball? Extraordinary intelligence? Call it what you will, that is exactly what happened in the marshy tract of Mullaitivu in May 2009 when the military gave a death blow to the LTTE, wiping out virtually its entire leadership, Prabhakaran included.

Yet, there was a time, and not long ago, when it looked as if there would be no return to peace in Sri Lanka minus Prabhakaran.[2] But the rebel chieftain slipped on the political art of compromise and accommodation so badly that Sri Lanka concluded that his elimination was necessary to unlock the knot it was in, ever since Prabhakaran vowed to settle for nothing less than an independent Tamil Eelam. What is equally extraordinary is that neither the LTTE leadership nor those in the Tamil diaspora who backed it to the hilt, realized where they were headed. Power corrupts. Totalitarian power destroys.

Notwithstanding his fingers on the pulse of Sri Lanka, diplomat Jayatilleka was politely asked to head home once Prabhakaran became history. Left with no choice, Jayatilleka went back to his first love, academics and journalism. He was convinced that he had been shown the door because of his views on how Sri Lanka's political contours should be in the times to come. His thoughts on political give-and-take and devolution of power to the minorities had put him on the wrong side of hardliners within the majority Sinhalese community who possessed a different worldview. In some ways, Jayatilleka's journey from Geneva to Colombo is a mirror on the battle of ideas now raging in Sri Lanka.

Whatever the character of the LTTE and however clichéd this might sound, Prabhakaran did not create what came to be known as the Tamil problem. He was its creation. What, however, he did was to completely overhaul the character of a Tamil ethnic struggle that wanted the community to be treated at par with the Sinhalese. Using violence as a weapon, he snuffed out the movement's democratic credentials and injected an uncompromising bloody streak that robbed it of its innocence. The LTTE soon became a hegemonic force in the Tamil community, wielding a veto over any attempt at reconciliation. This led to a prolonged war, which the Tigers thought they would never lose.

The unending violence, the LTTE's cruel streak and its adamant unwillingness to drop its Tamil Eelam idea together combined to alienate almost everyone who came into contact with the group. The LTTE had plenty of opportunities to reach a political settlement and chart a new course for the Tamils at large. They may or may not have led to the most ideal solution to the crisis in hand but would have certainly provided a widely acceptable framework to move on. But the man chose to jettison them all. Prabhakaran thus ended up giving birth to a Sri Lankan leadership in Colombo that became a mirror image of the LTTE and eventually dealt with the Tigers in the very same manner in which the LTTE dealt with its foes, real and imaginary. It too refused to compromise.

Since the Tigers prided themselves as the sole and authentic representative of the Tamil community, Tamils at large suffered due to the follies of the LTTE. Large sections in Sri Lanka's Sinhalese community came to unfortunately view the LTTE and the Tamil problem as two faces of the same coin. Many others outside of Sri Lanka also came to share this opinion, which, although seemingly sound, was inherently flawed. The natural outcome of this was that military assaults on Tamils per se were construed in Colombo as a justified, even if unfortunate, price the community had to pay for supposedly supporting the LTTE. It was a perverse vicious cycle. Ordinary Tamils who did not want the war, and no love for the LTTE, would wonder why they were being punished for crimes they never committed. The LTTE, of course, benefited from the messy situation because it could then justify its policies and very existence. How would the Tamils survive without the LTTE? So went the argument.

The reality was that the LTTE had become an impediment to a possible resolution of the Tamil conflict a long time ago. It was neither prepared to shake hands with Colombo nor would it allow anyone to make up with the Sri Lankan state. Those within the Tamil community who showed guts to think and act differently were either murdered or forced to live caged lives to escape the LTTE's highly efficient killer squads.[3]

History was repeatedly cited to show that Sri Lankan leaders (read the Sinhalese) would never offer meaningful concessions to the Tamil community. But if, and when, a Chandrika Kumaratunga was ready to make peace, war was ignited. The blame for the warfare and consequent civilian suffering was of course conveniently heaped on Colombo. When a Sri Lankan administration professed its willingness to talk, the LTTE would take credit; but it would slowly propel the negotiations to another round of conflict—and more suffering.

Regrettably, sections of the Tamil political class, who should have known better, subjugated themselves to the Tigers, further undermining the Tamil cause. "I had no choice," said one Tamil MP who was once fiercely anti-LTTE but later became its apologist. "I would have been killed otherwise." Rightly or wrongly, these Tamil politicians were under the illusion that the Tigers could guarantee their security. As later events proved, this was an illusion. Eventually, the LTTE could not even save itself.

A complex interplay of war and politics in Sri Lanka has led to a situation where national reconciliation appears a distant and difficult proposition. There now exists in Sri Lanka a government wedded to a mindset that there never was an ethnic conflict, only a terrorist problem; now that the LTTE has been crushed beyond recognition, the menace of terrorism is over, although security concerns remain. So there is no need to bring about any constitutional or administrative changes in Sri Lanka to please the minorities. The country will remain unitary in character, take it or leave it.

It is of course easy and tempting to blame Sri Lanka's current crop of leaders for such a stand. But it needs to be borne in mind that Mahinda Rajapaksa became the president only in November 2005. By then, Prabhakaran was three decades old in the ethnic conflagration. He contributed more than anyone else to widening the ethnic divide in the country, so much so that meaningful compromises by any government became politically near impossible. There was a time when it seemed that Colombo was ready to accommodate the LTTE. The group's intransigence, however, turned the tables. Towards the end, proposals suggesting far reaching constitutional changes to give due political space to the minorities (Tamils and Muslims) were shot down. The Rajapaksa regime became convinced—and so did many others—that there could never be a political settlement to the conflict because the LTTE would never reach out for one—unless it was wholly on its terms. The war had to be fought—and won.

The LTTE's biggest of all blunders was that it convinced itself, until the last moment, that Sri Lanka would never be able to win the war. By the time reality dawned on a chastened Prabhakaran, Colombo was in no mood for any further compromise, in no mood to spare the LTTE, and in mood to embrace a corps of men and women who seemed to be enthralled by violence.

The dominant thinking now in Colombo is that the Tamil community needs relief and rehabilitation, particularly in the northern and eastern provinces, nothing more; a region that saw nothing but war for over two decades needs economic development to merge it with the larger Sri Lanka. It is highly unlikely that this assessment would change in the near future. I will be happy to be proved wrong.

It is not that Sri Lankan leaders do not understand the need for the various ethnic communities to live together in harmony. It is not that they are against nation building. It is just that they have their own idea of how to weave together a multi-ethnic, multi-religious and multi-lingual Sri Lanka.

Even as he conducted a punishing war against the Tigers, Gotabaya Rajapaksa told me more than once that Sri Lankans needed to think and live like Sri Lankans, not as Tamils, Sinhalese or Muslims. But he and his President brother Mahinda Rajapaksa seem to be convinced that federalism or a federal structure of governance that the minorities pine for is not what their country needs. Federalism, to them and to many others in Sri Lanka, is a dirty word, the ideological fountainhead of Tamil separatism. The Indian model of governance may have its strengths, but Sri Lanka cannot be compared to India.

This is why there is so much opposition to the India-sponsored 13th amendment to the constitution that dented, for the first time, Sri Lanka's strong unitary character, by giving birth to provincial assemblies. This accompanied the Indian military intervention in Sri Lanka in 1987, an experiment that began with a lot of promise but which ended in disaster. Much later, as long as it fought the LTTE, the Sri Lankan leadership provided repeated assurances to the international community that it was committed to implementing all the provisions of the 13th amendment. Now that the LTTE has been decimated, there is a rethink in Colombo.

The U-turn is linked to Sri Lanka's larger understanding that the LTTE can never rise again and that outside powers have no business to hector Colombo over what needs to be done to bring about national reconciliation.

Indeed, the LTTE can never rise again. The LTTE that went down in May 2009 was not just about men, money and weapons; it had a central living organism called Velupillai Prabhakaran. The man was its biggest strength—and weakness too. To those who believed in him and his vision, he was an icon and a god; he could do no wrong. And he would lead them to Tamil Eelam one day.

It never happened like that.

Provoked into a war ignited by the LTTE, Sri Lanka neutralized Prabhakaran in the most unexpected manner. The LTTE founder leader had enveloped his outfit in Tamil nationalism, even if it was of a narrow variety, one that ultimately destroyed the soul of the Tamil community. He built the LTTE meticulously, brick by brick. It took over a quarter century to accomplish what he had accomplished. By the 1990s, the LTTE had grown into a monstrous and mammoth entity that could rival the Al Qaeda if it wanted to. The credit for this feat should go to Prabhakaran. No one can ever take his place. And minus him and his close and long-time associates, there can be no LTTE.

Those who fear that continuing ethnic discontent could lead to the rebirth of the LTTE have no idea of the realities on the ground where ordinary Tamil folks had been pining for peace even when the Tigers were immersed in war. The misery the Tamil population has suffered on account of the LTTE's uncompromising nature would ensure that they never again side, even remotely, with an inherently nihilist group. Tamil parents would never again want to see their sons and daughters lured or snatched from them to fight a war that only guaranteed death in the garb of martyrdom for a cause.

The LTTE that survives today is largely an expatriated body. Those who escaped the military onslaught and took to the jungles are neither in large numbers nor can they expect to survive for long. Those who managed to flee Sri Lanka cannot hope to return to that country. And those who now claim to lead what remains of the group enjoy neither credibility nor aura except perhaps in the circles that know them intimately.

Indeed, the more the Tamil diaspora keeps alive the shadow of the LTTE, the more difficult will life become for the mass of Tamils in Sri Lanka. The pro-LTTE diaspora's persistent aggression can only further militarize Sri Lanka—and legitimize Sinhalese hardliners. The LTTE that existed and thrived for decades can never be revived.

The Tamil side in Sri Lanka can claim its legitimate political space only if it eschews the violent and insular politics of the LTTE. A complete break from the past is necessary for those who had aligned themselves with the Tigers. And they would need to join hands with those Tamils whom they shunned earlier. In some ways, this is already beginning to happen. Ironically, part of the credit for this nascent process should go to Colombo's adamant refusal to be magnanimous in victory. Its wholesale rejection of Tamil political aspirations is bound to propel Tamils of various hues to pool their energies to campaign for what they feel is their due in a united Sri Lanka.


## II

IT should not be forgotten that military victory over the Tigers has come at a Himalayan cost. The history of bloodshed in global hotspots such as Ireland pales into insignificance compared to what Sri Lanka underwent since Tamil militancy galloped from 1983. The widely estimated death toll in the ethnic conflict stands at over 90,000 with tens of thousands wounded or maimed, on all sides of the ethnic divide. Destruction to movable and immovable assets has been colossal. For a country of just over 20 million, this is a hugely traumatic figure. Also, hundreds of thousands, mainly Tamils, have fled the country and became refugees the world over. The economy has taken a battering. So have human values and democracy—the first casualties of any dragging internal war.

The final months of the war saw unprecedented human tragedy. While many officers and soldiers of the overwhelmingly Sinhalese military showed sincere concern for ordinary Tamils, as indeed numerous individual Sinhalese have done in the past, the fact remains that Tamil civilians were punished in the name of fighting the Tigers. Unceasing artillery, MBRL (Multi Barrel Rocket Launcher) and air attacks took a massive toll, killing and maiming those who neither wanted the war nor took part in it. The "us-and-them" ideology based on narrow ethnic nationalism failed to adequately recognize that the state could not be a carbon copy of the LTTE, which of course had contempt for civilian lives, Tamil, Muslim or Sinhalese.

If the agony of the war was not enough, over 250,000 Tamil men, women and children of all ages got locked up in military-supervised camps—after escaping the clutches of the LTTE. This is a largely civilian population that had been promised liberation from the Tigers. These were Tamils who had endured the worst of the war. These were Tamils who had been pushed to starvation,[4] who saw fellow civilians bleed to death, whose only ambition was to somehow get away from it all. When they tried to do that, the LTTE mercilessly and callously shot at them. But once they left the shrinking LTTE territory, the Tamils found themselves locked up once again, this time by Colombo.

Sri Lanka no doubt has legitimate security concerns since many Tigers had escaped in civilian garb. But the continued confinement of a population in camps, making them virtual prisoners, has ceased to make sense beyond a point. In the process, their anger, until then directed dominantly towards the LTTE, has turned against Colombo.

True, de-mining of vast areas in the north and east of Sri Lanka is no easy task. But if the Tamils need to wait until de-mining gets over even substantially, many would end up spending the rest of their lives in camps!

All this is intimately related to Sri Lanka's future. Ultimately, it is only the people of Sri Lanka who can and will decide what kind of a society they want. Human rights and good governance are closely linked; one cannot exist without the other. Good governance includes democracy, including the legitimate and peaceful right to dissent. The LTTE denied both to people living under its umbrella. Sri Lanka cannot afford to emulate the LTTE any further. Now that the war is over, the state needs to embrace its people without bias, and truly so. The LTTE's pet theme was that Tamils would never be able to trust the Sinhalese and Colombo; the Sri Lankan leadership needs to prove the Tigers wrong if the country has to really have a new dawn.

## Notes

1. IANS moved the story on 1 June 2008. Jayatilleka was Sri Lanka's permanent representative to the UN and other international organizations based in Switzerland.
2. I ended my unauthorized biography of Prabhakaran (*Inside an Elusive Mind*) with these words:

   > Sri Lanka today stands at a decisive turning point where it will have to take politically mature, even if popularly unpalatable, decisions towards a practically workable solution to resolve the larger issues of ethnic divide and economic development. If it were to fail, for whatever reason, the destiny of Sri Lanka and its 20 million people would still be in the hands of one man: Velupillai Prabhakaran.

   These words were written in early 2003—although the book came out only in September that year. Until then, five key developments had not taken place: the LTTE had not walked out of the peace process; Karuna had not split; the LTTE had not assassinated Foreign Minister Lakshman Kadirgamar; Prabhakaran had not replaced KP with Castro; and, the most important of all, Prabhakaran had not ordered Tamils to boycott the presidential election, thus ensuring the defeat of a politician who had been prepared to do business with him. In retrospect, my understanding was not wrong; except that instead of making peace with him, Colombo decided to do away with Prabhakaran.
3. Many years ago I was in a car with PLOT leader Sitharthan, who would later become an MP, and one of his aides in Colombo. As we approached a bend, the aide suddenly asked the driver to turn left and take another road. When I enquired why, the aide explained that he had spotted a man standing by a parked motorcycle some 30 feet ahead. "We don't take risks," the man went on. "That man could be from the LTTE. Why take a chance?" In the euphoria surrounding the military victory, it will be easy to forget that it were Tamils who opposed the Tigers politically who waged the most bitter struggle against the LTTE—and paid a heavy price for their bravery.

4. By the time the LTTE got crushed in May 2009, starvation levels had peaked in its territory. A LTTE cadre told a relative in a European city over satellite telephone:

> When I sat down under a tree to eat, a group of children came over and stood watching me silently. There was hunger in their eyes. I consumed a bit of my lunch but could not continue. I just did not have the courage to eat in front of them. I gave away my food to them. I said to myself that I was only hungry but these kids were starving.

# About the author

A graduate of Delhi University, M R Narayan Swamy took to journalism in 1978. He began his career with the United News of India (UNI), a premier Indian news agency. After over eight years, he switched over to the French international news agency AFP where he served for more than 13 years. And after a stint in Singapore, he returned to India and joined the IANS news agency in 2001, where he is now the Executive Editor.

Narayan Swamy is the author of two previous and path-breaking books on Sri Lanka. The first, *Tigers of Lanka* (1994), details the origins and growth of Tamil militancy, including India's overt and covert involvement. The second, *Inside an Elusive Mind* (2003), is the only biography—albeit unauthorized—of the now dead LTTE chief, Velupillai Prabhakaran. Both books are considered a must read for all those trying to understand Tamil militancy in Sri Lanka.